Place and Identity
in Classic Maya Narratives

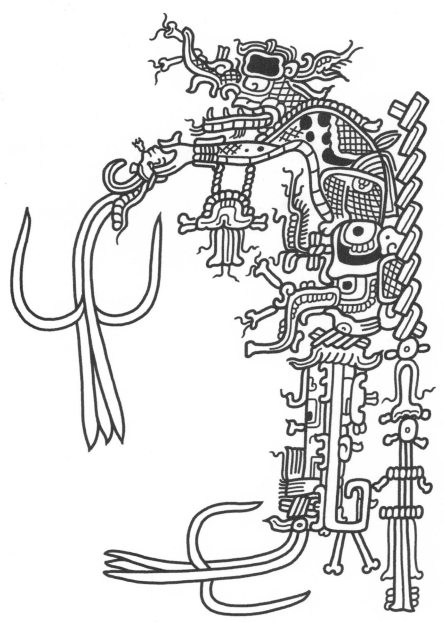

Place name in the costume of the maize god, detail of a Late Classic vessel (K4464)

STUDIES IN PRE-COLUMBIAN ART AND ARCHAEOLOGY
NUMBER THIRTY-SEVEN

Place and Identity in Classic Maya Narratives

Alexandre Tokovinine

DUMBARTON OAKS RESEARCH LIBRARY AND COLLECTION
WASHINGTON, D.C.

LIBRARY OF CONGRESS CATALOGING-IN-PUBLICATION DATA

Tokovinine, Alexandre.

Place and identity in classic Maya narratives / Alexandre Tokovinine.

pages cm. — (Studies in Pre-Columbian art and archaeology; number thirty-seven)

Includes bibliographical references.

ISBN 978-0-88402-392-0 (paperback : alk. paper)

1. Inscriptions, Mayan. 2. Names, Mayan.

3. Names, Geographical. 4. Mayas—Antiquities.

I. Title.

F1435,3.W75T65 2013

972'6—dc23

2012047845

GENERAL EDITORS: Joanne Pillsbury and Mary Pye

ART DIRECTOR: Kathleen Sparkes

DESIGN AND COMPOSITION: Melissa Tandysh

MANAGING EDITOR: Sara Taylor

COVER IMAGE: Mural 6N, Structure 1, La Sufricaya. Drawing by Heather Hurst; courtesy of the Holmul Archaeological Project.

www.doaks.org/publications

CONTENTS

ACKNOWLEDGMENTS

THIS MONOGRAPH IS LARGELY BASED ON MY DOCTORAL DISSERTATION. I am immensely grateful to everyone who helped me on this road. First and foremost, I thank William Fash. The dissertation and the subsequent monograph would have never happened without his insight, support, and encouragement. I am deeply grateful to Stephen D. Houston and Dmitri D. Beliaev for their guidance and support during my graduate and postgraduate career. My appreciation goes to Gary Urton and David Stuart, who have also greatly contributed to my academic growth.

My project of collecting place names in Classic Maya inscriptions was only possible because the directors of the Corpus of Maya Hieroglyphic Inscriptions at the Peabody Museum of Archaeology and Ethnology at Harvard University, Ian Graham and Barbara Fash, gave me the opportunity to work with the superb archives of the Corpus. I want to thank Francisco Estrada Belli, the director of the Holmul Archaeological Project, for the two productive field seasons at La Sufricaya. My thanks go to the Instituto de Antropología e Historia and to Vilma Fialko, who kindly invited me to participate in the Proyecto Arqueológico de Investigación y Rescate Naranjo. Fieldwork at La Sufricaya and Naranjo contributed greatly to my understanding of Classic Maya landscapes.

My postdoctoral research at the Corpus of Maya Hieroglyphic Inscriptions and the Dumbarton Oaks Research Library and Collection allowed me to explore new data and elaborate my research questions and theories. I am profoundly grateful to the Corpus director, Barbara Fash, and to the director of Pre-Columbian Studies at Dumbarton Oaks, Joanne Pillsbury, for the opportunity to be part of these great institutions and for supporting and encouraging my studies. I would also like to express my deep appreciation of the staff and fellows at Dumbarton Oaks, particularly Emily Jacobs, Reiko Ishihara-Brito, and Miriam Doutriaux.

I am immensely grateful to all fellow epigraphers, especially Marc Zender, Albert Davletshin, Alexandr Safronov, Simon Martin, Christophe Helmke, John Justeson, and Mathew Looper, who examined my work, shared published and unpublished materials, and discussed, challenged, and enriched my ideas and arguments. I would also like to thank Simon Martin and the anonymous reviewer for the many comments and observations that substantially contributed to the improvement of this monograph.

My research would not be possible without the support from several institutions. My fieldwork at La Sufricaya and Naranjo was funded by the Bowditch Exploration

Fund of the Peabody Museum, Harvard University. The epigraphic research was supported by grants from the Foundation for the Advancement of Mesoamerican Studies, Inc., and from the Pre-Columbian Art Research Institute, as well as by fellowships from the Graduate School of Arts and Sciences, Harvard University. I had a wonderful opportunity to complete my dissertation research at Dumbarton Oaks.

1 | INTRODUCTION

UNDERSTANDING THE WAYS IN WHICH HUMAN COMMUNITIES DEFINE themselves in relation to landscapes has been one of the crucial research questions in anthropology. The present monograph addresses this question in the context of the Classic Maya culture that thrived in the lowlands of the Yucatan peninsula and adjacent parts of Guatemala, Belize, and Western Honduras from AD 350 to 900. The Classic Maya world of numerous polities, each with its own kings and gods, left a rich artistic and written legacy permeated by shared aesthetics and meaning. This monograph explores the striking juxtaposition of similar cultural values and distinct political identities by looking at how identities were created and maintained in relation to place, uncovering what Classic Maya landscapes were like in the words of the people who created and experienced them. It also investigates the ways in which members of Classic Maya political communities placed themselves on these landscapes. In other words, it attempts to discern Classic Maya notions of place and community as well as the relationship between place and identity.

Key categories and concepts used in this study—such as "landscape," "place," and "identity"—have multiple and sometimes contradictory meanings in anthropology, sociology, humanistic geography, and art history. Therefore, it is essential to outline my understanding of these terms. For example, there does not seem to be a notion of landscape shared by most scholars in the field of anthropology. Definitions tend to be broad and all-inclusive (Anschuetz et al. 2001:160–161; Bender 1992:735; Smith 2003:5; Tilley 1994:25), probably due to the initial vagueness of the term in humanistic geography and architecture (Giddens 1986; Pred 1984; Rapoport 2002; Sauer 1963:343). One may even wonder if scholars really need landscape as a heuristic category distinct from physical environment, built environment, or any other kind of conditions or settings involving objects and people in space. One may also wonder if landscape is a category that truly sets apart the contribution of anthropology to the study of objects and people in space from that of geography. This monograph, however, adopts a more specific notion of landscape as a means to see the environment in a certain way, to represent and to modify it in accordance with such perceptions and representations. It is important to keep in mind that "landscape" was introduced into English as a technical term used by painters (Cosgrove 1985). A scene was called a "landscape" because it reminded the viewer of a painted landscape—that is, it looked like a picture. Therefore, landscape as defined in this monograph is not about kinds of objects in space but about ways of perception and representation.

If landscape is ways of seeing and representing objects in space, then the next two important categories to be defined are objects in space and objects in a landscape. Since there is no way yet to look directly into people's minds and witness the process of one category becoming another, the actual relation is between objects in a landscape as represented by someone else and either other representations or our own perceptions of those objects. For example, one can compare an object represented as a combination of the words *usiij* and *witz* ("vulture mountain") in Classic Maya written narratives (Stuart 2008) with an object shown as contour lines on a map of the archaeological site of Bonampak, a linear perspective or isometric drawing, or a photograph, assuming that the object in the reference landscape relates to the object in the narratives. The present monograph uses the term "place" for objects or features in a landscape and the term "locale" for my perception of objects or features in space, or in a reference landscape like a map or a photograph.

One of the main challenges of studying an ancient landscape is to understand the principles of its representation, often without knowing what is being represented and in what context. In that sense, Maya studies are in a privileged position because it is possible to study and compare different kinds of representations—words, images, and architecture—in order to deduce common patterns and principles.

Words seem to constitute the key form and context for representations of objects in space. Whenever a story involves space and time, it evokes operations and practices that summon up places (Tilley 1994:31–33, 59). Landscapes are (re)constructed through narratives and serve as referents for many cultural structures, including history and myth (Reese-Taylor and Koontz 2001). Not only do places acquire biographies; stories acquire part of their value if they are rooted in places. Narratives introduce temporality into landscapes and transform locales into markers of individual and group experiences (Basso 1984).

Other forms of representation, including imagery and architecture, are also part of landscape as defined above, but our ability to access these forms and to understand their meaning and context usually depends on the availability of related written and oral narratives. One needs to understand the nature of the cultural discourse, the poetics in particular space and time, in order to uncover the role of architectural programs and broader landscape in this discourse. Aesthetics as a reflection of the "inner form of collective thinking and feeling" (Shapiro 1953:287) is primarily a figure of speech and then other forms of expression. In the absence of spoken and written narratives, we would never know, for instance, that for the inhabitants of Santiago de Atitlan in Guatemala, the flowering mountain is a concept that links "vegetation, the human life cycle, kinship, modes of production, religious and political hierarchy, conceptions of time, even of celestial movement" (Carlsen and Prechtel 1991:27).

So far, we have defined landscape as perception and representation of objects in space, suggested that it consists of places as named locales, and assumed that it is contextualized in narratives and other forms of representation. The next important issue is the relationship between the landscape and the society that creates it. This study adopts an assumption that such a relationship inherently involves underlying social interests, inequalities, factional competitions, and political actions (Connerton 1989; Joyce 2000, 2001; Joyce and Hendon 2000). The political landscape, as a physical environment ordered by political forces and signs shaping one's sense of place, consists of places that maintain the imagined community and evoke "memories and emotions central to the experience of political belonging" (Smith 2003:8).

The representations of Maya society in Classic texts and iconography are not random glimpses but deliberate messages produced by the "hyper-elites" (Houston and McAnany 2003). Maya scribes and carvers were part-time specialists who belonged to the upper social classes of Maya polities—sometimes being junior members of royal families (Houston 2000; Inomata 2001; Inomata and Stiver 1998). We may assume that landscapes created in Classic Maya texts and imagery were instrumental in maintaining the political order.

The study of the relationship between a society and the landscapes it perceives and (re)produces is impossible without defining another problematic category—identity. Brubaker and Cooper (2000:6–8) argue that there are at least five common uses of "identity" in the social sciences, from particular categorical attributes (which serve as a ground of social and political action) to some kind of sameness among members of a certain group (a core aspect of individual or group selfhood), to a product of social and political action, multiple and competing discourses, and ultimately a reflection of the ever-changing and fragmented nature of the contemporary "self." Psychoanalytical studies, particularly works by Erikson (1950, 1959, 1968), should be credited with the introduction of "identity" as a category of analysis and interpretation (see Gleason 1983:914–919). Sociologists adopted the concept, but its original meaning underwent substantial changes within the frameworks of role theory (Linton 1936:113–131), the theory of reference groups (Merton 1957:225–386), where "identity" became "identification" (Foote 1951), and of symbolic interactionism (Meltzer et al. 1975), where "identity" replaced "self." As a result, there are two conflicting interpretations of identity: identity as something internal, essential, and resistant to change, and identity as a situational category of ascription, the product of the external interaction between the individual and the society. The understanding of identity in this monograph is closer to the sociological interpretation—as a process of identification by which individuals locate themselves or are located by others in relation to other individuals or in a system of certain categories. Identity is also a resulting sense of one's location or membership in certain social categories. The term "political identity" refers to one's identification or sense of membership in a political group.

The category of "community" is often used to describe the relationship between social or political groups, identities, and landscapes. This study borrows the definition of community as a socially constituted entity, a conjunction of "people, place, and premise" (Yaeger and Canuto 2000:5). Even if community members are not coresident, they should interact frequently enough to maintain their shared identity. A "natural community" where such interaction indeed takes place may be contrasted with the "constructed community" as an idea or a sense of place rather than an objective place (Canuto 2002; Canuto and Fash 2004; Isbell 2000), essentially the same concept as Anderson's "imagined community" (1991). Consequently, a study of landscapes as defined in this monograph is an investigation of "imagined communities" that aims to elucidate an emic system of categories contributing to one's sense of place, as well as practices (patterns in the written discourse) that create and maintain perceived commonalities and differences.

From the perspective of postmodern scholarship, the archaeological past is the battle-ground of conflicting reinventions of culture and identity, as well as a plural setting of multiple readings performed by scholars, states, local authorities, tourists, and indigenous communities (Castañeda 1996:113–129). The present study of Classic Maya landscapes does not pursue the immediate goal of reviewing or critiquing other landscapes created by archaeologists, ethnographers, historians, and epigraphers. Nevertheless, the findings of this project may serve as a basis for a discussion about the analytical usefulness of some categories and concepts in Classic Maya landscapes as we see them today.

This monograph is based on a survey of place names and their contexts in Classic Maya inscriptions (Tokovinine 2007a) that incorporated all references to toponyms on monu-ments, buildings, and portable objects in the Southern Maya Lowlands. In contrast to previ-ous place name studies, this survey included direct references to places and all occurrences of place names in personal names and titles. When possible, full sentences with place names were transcribed and transliterated. Nevertheless, the sample considered here suffers from certain constraints that are inherent in any study of Classic Maya texts. Nearly all texts

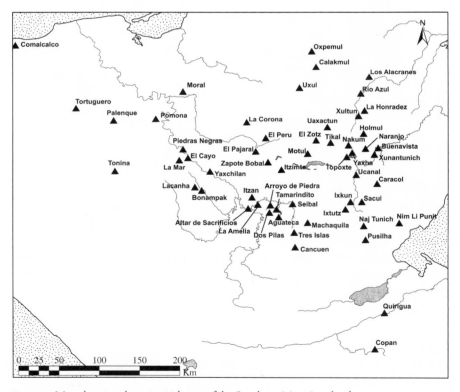

Figure 1 Map showing the principal sites of the Southern Maya Lowlands.

PLACE AND IDENTITY IN CLASSIC MAYA NARRATIVES

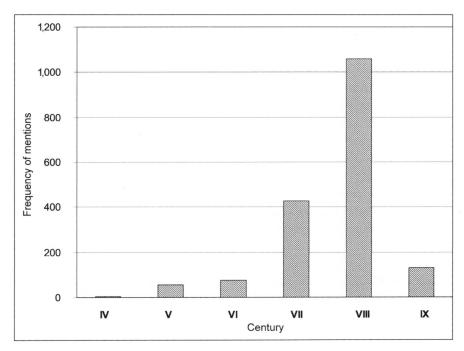

Figure 2 Frequency of place name references in Classic Maya inscriptions on monuments, buildings, and portable objects.

considered in this project are from the Southern Maya Lowlands (Figure 1) because of the abundance of cross-references to toponyms in this area and because of the Classic Maya perception of this region as a distinct geographical entity (to be discussed in Chapter 5). The bulk of the data comes from major archaeological sites with large corpora of inscriptions. Sites with fewer texts are underrepresented in the survey and do not offer enough distinct contexts to explore the significance of local place names. The sample is dominated by eighth-century inscriptions (Figure 2). Consequently, an exploration of Classic Maya landscapes is inevitably a synchronic study of the eighth-century situation with some small digressions into a diachronic analysis when relevant samples are large enough.

It is important to emphasize that representations or perceptions of the political landscape in the written discourse and imagery would be in practice related to or even substituted by other forms of experience. Classic Maya political landscapes also consisted of built and natural features to be seen, walked through, touched, smelled, and heard. The written narratives themselves would be experienced in many different ways (such as through performances) and would likely be embedded within a larger and diverse oral tradition.

An epigraphic study of place in Classic Maya political landscapes cannot be equated with a study of Classic Maya cartography. Some Classic Maya codices, monuments, murals, or even painted textiles may have featured maps and long descriptions of near and distant lands. But none of these documents have survived to this day. Instead, scholars are left with references to landscapes embedded in other genres of texts and visual representations.

This situation makes all reconstructions of larger landscape concepts highly tentative. Nevertheless, it still allows for an investigation of the role of place within the Classic Maya political discourse by examining and comparing all kinds of narratives associated with the political landscape.

My background on the subject of Classic Maya landscapes is closely related to a particular scholarly tradition that can be traced to the Harvard Chiapas Project as well as to works by Evon Vogt and his students, including Gary Gossen, John Watanabe, and David Stuart (Gossen 1972, 1974; Stuart 1997; Stuart and Houston 1994; Vogt 1964, 1965, 1969, 1981; Vogt and Stuart 2005; Watanabe 1990, 1995). This tradition is characterized by an emphasis on worldviews and landscapes as well as by an interest in understanding and explaining social structures and processes and attempting to see relations between place and identity. While I do not agree with all of the conclusions and assumptions made by this group of scholars, it is important to explicitly identify their works as a foundation of the present project.

The monograph builds upon the study of Classic Maya place names by Stuart and Houston (1994), which laid the groundwork for any future investigation of Classic Maya landscapes. Stuart and Houston should be credited with identifying toponyms and related categories in Classic Maya inscriptions and with highlighting key questions in exploring the links between the landscape and the protagonists of the narratives. In the nearly two decades that followed the original publication by Stuart and Houston, the amazing progress in the decipherment of Maya writing and the growing corpus of documented inscriptions mean that it is perhaps time to return to this topic with new data and new insights. In many ways, this monograph reflects an evolution in the scholarly understanding of the Classic Maya world.

The present discussion of places and identities in the landscapes of Classic Maya narratives is organized into four chapters. The first two chapters explore the very notion of place by looking at the toponyms themselves and by reviewing the landscape categories found in the inscriptions. This step is necessary to avoid an immediate projection of Western notions of space and place embedded in concepts such as "site," "city," and "polity" onto the Classic Maya data. The following two chapters address the question of how individuals and groups identified themselves and were identified by others in relation to places. The fifth chapter, in particular, investigates evidence of broader sociopolitical communities in the Classic Maya landscape, expressions of group identities that transcended or complemented known political boundaries. The concluding sixth chapter presents a synthesis of the research.

NAMING PLACES

A STUDY OF PLACES AND IDENTITIES IN CLASSIC MAYA INSCRIPTIONS should begin with the place names themselves. The way Classic Maya narratives named and classified the environment reveals important practices and concepts about landscape and the people in it. Of equal importance for the present study are patterns in narrative strategies or choices made in talking about places.

The contexts of most, if not all, place names in Classic Maya inscriptions and imagery may be classified as direct and indirect references. The direct references are contexts where a place name is mentioned as a location or an object of someone's actions. If the context is a sentence, then the place name is part of the predicate. For example, an event may be accompanied by a reference to its location, as in *uhtiiy lakam ha'* (Figure 3a)—"it happened [at] *Lakam Ha'*"—a common sentence in many narratives at the archaeological site of Palenque, of which all or part is associated with that toponym (Stuart and Houston 1994:30–31). A place name may also be the subject of sentences where actors are underemphasized or removed, as in *ch'ahkaj lakam ha'*—"*Lakam Ha'* was chopped (devastated)" (Figure 3b)—according to the narrative on the Palenque Hieroglyphic Stairway (Martin 2000:110). If the context is imagery, such as a scene on a carved monument, the "direct" context is a so-called toponymic register—a caption clarifying the location of the action depicted in the scene that is usually placed in the lower register of the image (see Stuart and Houston 1994:57–68). In all the cases mentioned above, there is a direct relationship between the hypothetical narrator and the place name in the story and between the place name and the event. The relationship is not mediated by the nature of the protagonist of the narrative unless the protagonist is the place itself.

Indirect references are contexts where place names are incorporated into the name phrases of the protagonists. Such contexts are not necessarily related to the nature of the narrated events, but instead depend on the protagonist's status in relation to the hypothetical narrator, the genre of the narrative, its historical setting, and even its physical context (i.e., the kind of object on which the text is inscribed). Indirect references are far less constrained in terms of complexity, as the same name phrase may contain multiple,

a   b   c

Figure 3 Direct and indirect references to place names in Classic Maya inscriptions: a) detail of a tablet (M14), Temple of the Foliated Cross, Palenque (after Robertson 1991:fig. 153); b) detail of Hieroglyphic Stairway 1 (C1), Palenque (after Robertson 1991:fig. 319); and c) detail of Block 6 (N2–L3), Hieroglyphic Stairway 1, Naranjo (after Graham 1978:109).

interrelated place names—as in "*Kanu'l* king in *Huxte' Tuun*, man of *Chi'k Nahb*" (Figure 3c) in the inscription on the Hieroglyphic Stairway at Naranjo (Tokovinine 2007b:19–21).

Classic Maya place names collected for the present study may also be divided into two broad categories—basic and derived terms. The basic terms are words or phrases describing a landscape feature that serves as an index to a place. Only the syntax and the cultural context suggest that the term is a place name. In the case of the derived term, its function as an index to a place is explicitly marked by means of a special suffix or a locative preposition. A derived term can always be identified as a place name regardless of the overall context and syntax.

About half of the place names in Classic Maya inscriptions are basic terms. Those with known etymologies tend to contain descriptive references to locales—such as mountains, rocks, lakes, rivers, and springs—and to various species of animals and plants, as in a place name "Big Rock(s)" or *Lakam Tuun* (Figure 4a). Many of these toponyms can be read phonetically, but their etymologies cannot be securely established.

The derived place names present similar challenges in terms of the etymology of the roots. Yet there is an additional challenge of understanding the derivational morphology. The two most common patterns attested in the inscriptions involve the *–Vl* / *–VVl* / *–V'l* suffix and the rather enigmatic *–nal* root. Several place names also appear to be derived with locative prepositions.

A vast majority of derived place names appear to feature the *–Vl* / *–VVl* / *–V'l* suffix. This pattern has been previously discussed by Lacadena García-Gallo and Wichmann (2005). The authors identify the *–iil* toponymic suffix in spellings like **ma-ta-wi-la** for *matwiil*, **YAX-ni-la** for *yaxniil* (Figure 4b), and **pa-ni-la** for *paniil*. Similar suffixes are attested in Ch'ol, in place names like *Joñajil*, *Jo'xil*, *Yäxlumil*, and *Joljamil* (Becerra 1985; Warkentin and Scott 1978:118–119), as well as in Itzaj (Hofling and Tesucún 1997:23). The significance of such place names is often "place where x abounds" (Lacadena García-Gallo and Wichmann 2005).

More than one hundred Classic Maya place names appear to have been derived with the help of the *–nal* morpheme. It is invariably spelled with the **NAL** "corncob" logogram, sometimes with the phonetic complement *–la*, and very rarely with the fully syllabic **na-la** combination. *K'an Witz Nal*, the ancient name associated with the archaeological site of Ucanal

PLACE AND IDENTITY IN CLASSIC MAYA NARRATIVES

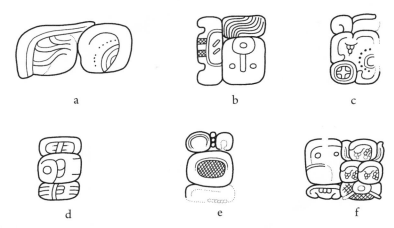

Figure 4 Place name categories in Classic Maya inscriptions: a) detail of Lintel 35 (B8), Yaxchilan (after Graham 1979:79); b) detail of Altar 4, El Cayo (after Mathews 1998:fig. 3); c) detail of Stela 32 (W5), Naranjo (after Graham 1978:86); d) detail of a panel, Temple 16, Palenque (after drawing by Peter Mathews; see also Bernal Romero 2002); e) detail of Stela 10 (B4), Naranjo (after Graham 1975:31); and f) detail of Tablet 4 (W1), Hieroglyphic Stairway 1, Seibal (after Graham 1996:59).

(Stuart and Houston 1994:20–21), is a good example (Figure 4c). The –*nal* "suffix" seems to function in the same way as the place name suffix; there are even some examples when –*nal* and –*Vl* appear to alternate in the same place name, as in T628-**MUK-WITZ-la** (RAZ, West Wall, Tomb 6, Str A-4) versus T628-**MUK-WITZ-NAL** (RAZ, West Wall, Tomb 25, Str B-56) on the tomb murals at Río Azul (Adams 1989:fig. 25b, 1999:figs. 3–17).

There are almost no examples of the –*nal* as a place name suffix in the colonial or modern Mayan languages. It is not attested in early colonial Yukatek documents (e.g., Miram and Miram 1988; Quezada and Okoshi Harada 2001; Robelo 1902). The only Chontal place name with –*nal* in the Maldonado-Paxbolon Papers is *cacmucnal* (Smailus 1975:41). Nevertheless, –*nal* substitutes for –*kab* "land" in a number of personal titles which follow the pattern "man of . . . land/*nal*" such as *ajotochkab* and *ajotochnal* for "town resident" in Yukatek.[1] The substitution with *kab* indicates that *nal* functions as a spatial classifier.

What kind of locales might the –*nal* places have been? In the Ch'olan and Yukatekan languages, the term *nal* refers to both the ear of corn and the whole maize plant, as in the classification of different races of corn (Barrera Vásquez et al. 1995:557; Bricker et al. 1998:194; Kaufman 2002:1063; Kaufman and Norman 1984:126). The **NAL** logogram in the Maya script does look like a maize ear and may be part of other complex graphemes involving corn representations, such as **TZ'AP** "to plant" (Stuart 2004c). Therefore, toponyms with *nal* may be interpreted as references to corn plants. If this hypothesis is correct, then more than a hundred places in Classic Maya inscriptions are, at least on some symbolic or classificatory level, cornfields or places of corn plants. Given the centrality of maize in the ancient and modern Maya religion and worldview, including concepts of human body and life cycle (Christenson 2006; Fitzsimmons 2009:22–24; Houston et al. 2006:45; Taube

1985), this idea does not seem to be too far-fetched: just as the Classic Maya saw themselves as "people of corn," their landscape was interspersed with corn places.

If an analogy with modern spatial categories may be of any use here, then *nal* places in the Classic Maya landscape may have also been contrasted to the wild locations devoid of humans and maize plants. Many modern Maya groups contrast the ordered human space of a town or a cornfield to the chaotic wilderness or forest (Vogt 1969:374; Watanabe 1984:71). For example, Chimaltecos (Watanabe 1984:71) distinguish between three categories—town, fields, and forest—which correspond to decreasing degrees of familiarity and security as one moves away from the town. Hanks (1990:306–308) notes a similar tripartite division for Yukatek speakers in the town of Oxkutzcab. Unlike human space, the forest lacks perimeter and internal divisions; it is unpredictable and dangerous. People walk "in" or "at" the town or a field, but "under" the forest (Hanks 1990:306). Ancient Maya imagery hints that a similar symbolic opposition of field and forest could have existed in the Classic period (Taube 2003).

The least common derivational paradigm for place names in Classic Maya inscriptions is the addition of the locative preposition *ta* as well as the locative constructions with *ti'* ("edge/mouth of") and *tahn* ("in front of"/"in the midst of"/"before"). The only place name in the corpus where the *ta* paradigm can be securely identified is **ta-u-su** *ta us* "mosquito place" (Figure 4d; PAL T 16 Pn). The *ti'* paradigm is more productive, as several place names with *ti'* are attested: *ti' pa'* (Figure 4e; NAR St 10), *ti' way* (CPN St 10, TIK St 16), *ti' chan* (PAL TS, TC, PNG Alt 1, QRG St C), *ti' ?tziil* (PMT HP 7), *ti' kab* (BPK Str 1 1:37), and *ti' yax k'uk' ha'* (YXH St 2). The locative *tahn* is usually not incorporated into place names but introduces them in narratives and occasionally in toponymic registers. Two known exceptions are a probable toponym *tahn ch'e'n* cited in Block F2 of the Tablet of the Slaves at Palenque and Block E7 of Yaxchilan Lintel 10, as well as some examples of the place name associated with the archaeological site of Seibal (Figure 4f; DPL St 15, SBL HS 1:4, St 10).

Some categories of landscape features occur with significantly higher frequency in the corpus of about 450 Classic Maya place names collected for the present study (Table 1). It does not mean that the actual physical environment consisted primarily of the highlighted features. Such patterns, however, inform us of the relationship between the environment and the practices through which it was assigned meaning—that is, they indicate which aspects of the environment were preferentially associated with the locations of human settlements, mythological events, and rituals. It is also important to remember that the relative distribution of certain terms in place names does not necessarily reflect any emic system of categories. The actual landscape features indexed by place names may not be what the names seemingly suggest. For example, river names may highlight "rocks," as in the case of the modern Lacantun River and the corresponding ancient toponym, *Lakam Tuun* ("Big Rocks").

The largest group of place names in the database involves "mountains" or "hills" (*witz*) and "rocks" (*tuun*), as in *Mo' Witz* (Figure 5a) and *Pe' Tuun* (Figure 5b). The geographical distribution of these toponyms reveals no apparent pattern with "rocks" and "mountains" throughout the region. It means that any hill or rock (common landmarks in the Southern

Table 1 Frequency of certain locale categories in place names.

PLACE NAMES		FREQUENCY
CATEGORY	DIAGNOSTIC TERMS	~450 TOTAL
mountains and rocks	*witz, tuun*	~65
watery places	*ha', nahb, witz', palaw,* T856, T578	~60
trees	*te' aa*	~30
sky	*chan*	~20
earth/land	*kab*	~14
caves	*ch'e'n, pa', way*	~7
house	*naah*	~43

Lowlands) can become highlighted, and there is a preference for hills and rocks as land-marks with which places are associated.

The second largest group consists of place names with a range of terms associated with the water, as in *Sak Ha'* (Figure 5c). These include *–a'/ha'*, *nahb*, and *witz'* as well as unde-ciphered or problematically deciphered logograms, which likely stand for words denoting certain kinds of watery objects—logograms T856, T578, and ?**PALAW**.[2] As in the case of the rocks and mountains, the spatial distribution of the water-related place names is rela-tively uniform, suggesting that bodies of water were another highly significant aspect of the natural environment that played a crucial role in the making of places.

The next most highlighted landscape feature is plant species, although the actual num-ber of such place names is higher than the listing of "trees" in Table 1. Some toponyms, however, would require a set of arguments proving that the plant species is the most plau-sible etymology. Therefore, the present study considered only the most apparent examples with the *te'* ("tree") gloss, as in *Sak Nikte'* (Figure 5d), in its assessment. As in the case of mountains and bodies of water, there is nothing particularly surprising in the abundance of place names highlighting the kinds of trees which grew or used to grow at the place or near it. Place names with animals, such as *Sak Tz'i'* (Figure 5e), are also attested but they do not constitute a large group.

The terms *chan* ("sky") and *kab* ("land, earth") are also relatively popular. *Pa' Chan* (Figure 5f) and *Jo' Kab* (Figure 5g) are examples of such place names. While terms like *sak kab* ("white earth") may be descriptive, several place names with *kab* appear to emphasize partitioning and numbering of units of land. The place names with *chan* ("sky") may also be descriptive, but the likelier interpretation is that most index a particular relationship between the place and the celestial realm.

Another large group of place names is "buildings" (*naah*). Some of them are appar-ently structures, as the terms occur in the context of dedicatory statements. Other place

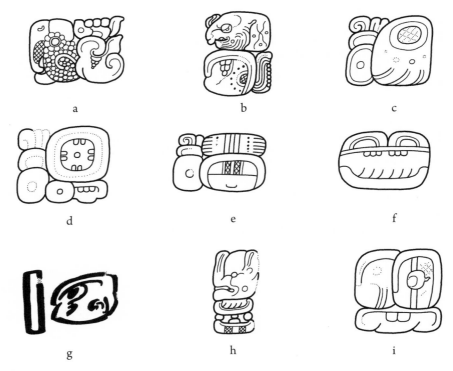

Figure 5 Landscape in Classic Maya place names: a) detail of Stela B, Copan (after Baudez 1994:fig. 5); b) detail of Stela 40 (C11), Piedras Negras (after Stuart and Houston 1994:fig. 42b); c) detail of Stela 23 (H15), Naranjo (after Graham 1975:60); d) detail of Altar 1, La Corona (after drawing by Marc Zender); e) detail of Stela 26, Piedras Negras (after drawing by John Montgomery); f) detail of Lintel 23 (N4), Yaxchilan (after Graham 1982:136); g) detail of Drawing 69 (A4), Naj Tunich (after Stone 1995:figs. 7–31); h) detail of Step 1-Tread (B3), Hieroglyphic Stairway 3, Yaxchilan (after Graham 1982:166); and i) detail of the Tablet of the Slaves (F2), Palenque (after Robertson 1991:fig. 229).

names—like *Wite' Naah*, *?Xukal/Tz'ikal Naah* (Figure 5h), *Chahk Naah*, and *Nikil Naah*—appear in contexts such as naming the origin of people and gods, the location of a battle, a defeated enemy, or a place of pilgrimage—well beyond the range of context attested for the buildings proper (dedicating, seating, visiting, performing). This pattern suggests that the built environment becomes an important feature in the practices of place-making and place-indexing. One can also interpret these examples as evidence that *naah* functions as a landscape category: certain locations are highlighted as "houses," as places where somebody dwells.

Underworld-related terms (at least the deciphered or likely deciphered ones such as *?way*, *pa'*, and *ch'e'n*) constitute a surprisingly small set of place names, like *Tahn Ch'e'n* (Figure 5i). Even if one assumes that some underworldly locations may not involve the word "cave," the conspicuous absence of caves in the Classic Maya landscape is highly significant. On one hand, the word for cave accompanies many place names and apparently functions as a spatial category (see below). On the other hand, there are almost no references to actual caves. This contradiction suggests that caves as features of the physical environment are probably not important indexing landmarks, in contrast to mountains, water, plants, and built features.

NAMING, SCALE, AND DISTANCE

The implicit assumption in the studies of place names to date is that toponyms correspond to aspects of the physical environment of different spatial scales (Stuart and Houston 1994). But there is no established method of determining the relation between any two place names which co-occur in the same narrative or in a set of related narratives and which potentially index overlapping aspects of the physical environment. Moreover, it is not clear if scale is an ontologically appropriate category for understanding Classic Maya concepts of place.

The problem of relative hierarchies of place names was introduced by Stuart and Houston (1994:7), who suggested that the place names incorporated into royal titles likely denoted larger territories under the sway of particular dynasties, whereas place names in other contexts corresponded to the locations of royal courts (Stuart and Houston 1994:19–33) and even particular structures (Stuart and Houston 1994:44, 81–89). Conversely, the more specific place names co-occurring with names for supposedly larger spatial entities were interpreted as modifiers, with an implication that the syntactic order predicted the relative rank of the place within the given landscape. Higher-order place names corresponding to larger spatial entities would follow lower-order place names indexing smaller locales.

As we will see in Chapter 4, the presence of place names in certain royal titles does not immediately qualify the corresponding locales as being of greater spatial scale than others. The order of place names in a text is also not a secure indicator of scale; it may be a rhetorical device, a reflection of their relative importance or centrality in the narrative. For example, the place names *Yehmal K'uk' (Lakam) Witz*[3] and *Lakam Ha'* are occasionally cited together in inscriptions of Palenque. Stuart and Houston (1994:30–32, 84) identified *Lakam Ha'* as the core of the archaeological site of Palenque, in particular the Otolum spring, and *Yehmal K'uk' Witz* as one of the mountains towering above the site, possibly the one known as the Mirador hill (Stuart 2006b:92–93). Two of the co-occurrences of the place names, on the door jamb from Temple 18 (Figure 6a) and on a miscellaneous panel fragment (Figure 6b), follow a pattern in which *Yehmal K'uk' Lakam Witz* appears in front of *Lakam Ha'*: " . . . it happened [on] *Yehmal K'uk' Lakam Witz*, [in] *Lakam Ha'* (*patlaj/uhti yehmal k'uk' lakam witz lakam ha'*)." Nevertheless, the narrative on the tablet from the sanctuary of the Temple of the Sun (Figure 6c) rearranges the place names for a different rhetorical impact: " . . . it happens [in] *Lakam Ha'*, [in] the sky, [in] the *ch'e'n*, [on] *Yehmal K'uk' Witz* (*patlaj lakam ha' chan ch'e'n yehmal k'uk' witz*)." It is not clear if the narratives place *Yehmal K'uk' Witz* inside *Lakam Ha'* or imply that the king's acts affected two nearby locales.

In some cases, it appears that such paired citations of place names may become a kind of higher-rank toponym that indexes the totality of two locales. These double place names

a

b   c

Figure 6 *Lakam Ha'* and *Yehmal K'uk' Lakam Witz* in Palenque inscriptions: a) detail of a jamb, Temple 18 (after Stuart 2006b:92; Stuart and Houston 1994:fig. 34); b) detail of a panel fragment (after Liendo Stuardo 1995); and c) detail of a tablet (N14–N16), Temple of the Sun (after Robertson 1991:fig. 95).

may represent actual transformations of physical locales, when two distinct communities become one. They may also reflect different reference practices and relationships between the protagonist/narrator and the place.

One set of paired place names is associated with the archaeological site of Dos Pilas. Stuart and Houston (1994:19–20, 84–88) demonstrated that the two place names frequently mentioned at Dos Pilas, *K'ihn Ha' Nal* or *K'in Nal Ha'* and T369 *Ha'al*, corresponded to the two areas of the archaeological site, the Main Plaza and the El Duende group, located at a distance of about one kilometer from each other.[4] The toponymic registers on Stelae 1 and 2 in the Main Plaza refer to T369 *Ha'al* (Figure 7a). In El Duende, the toponymic register on Stela 15 mentions *K'ihn Ha' Nal* (Figure 7b). The inscriptions on Stelae 14 and 15 in El Duende report that the "binding" of the monuments took place in *K'ihn Ha' Nal* but that the subsequent dances happened in T369 *Ha'al* (Figure 7c). Stela 11 in the Main Plaza also highlights dancing in T369 *Ha'al* (Figure 7d). The only other event in *K'ihn Ha' Nal* is a period-ending ritual of casting copal (*chok ch'aaj*) in the narrative on Stela 1, located in the Main Plaza (Figure 7e). The accession ceremony mentioned on Stela 8 in the Main Plaza "happened in the midst of the *ch'e'n* [at] T369 *Ha'al*" (Figure 7f). According to the same narrative, the burial of the Dos Pilas ruler *Itzamnaah K'awiil* also took place "in the midst of the *ch'e'n* [at] T369 *Ha'al*," and there is every reason to believe that the king was indeed buried in the temple mound behind the stela. T369 *Ha'al* is also

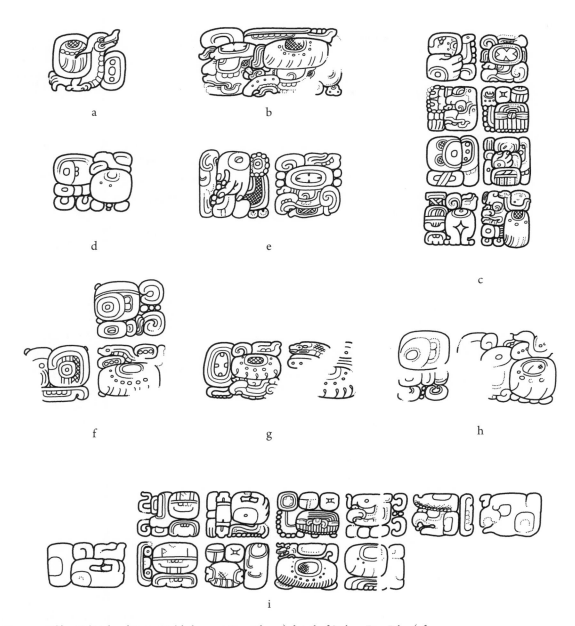

Figure 7 *K'ihn Ha' Nal* and T369 *Ha'al* places at Dos Pilas: a) detail of Stela 2, Dos Pilas (after Stuart and Houston 1994:fig. 18d); b) detail of Stela 15, Dos Pilas (after Stuart and Houston 1994:fig. 101); c) detail of Stela 15 (E3–F6), Dos Pilas (after Stuart and Houston 1994:fig. 105); d) detail of Stela 11 (E2), Dos Pilas (after Houston 1993:fig. 3-27); e) detail of Stela 1 (A4–A5), Dos Pilas (after photograph by Ian Graham); f) detail of Stela 8 (F22–G22), Dos Pilas (after Houston 1993:fig. 4-14); g) detail of Stela 8 (H6–I6), Dos Pilas (after Houston 1993:fig. 4-14); h) detail of Panel 19 (H1), Dos Pilas (after Houston 1993:fig. 4-19); and i) detail of Hieroglyphic Stairway 1, Cancuen (after photographs by the author).

the only one of two places associated with dance events, in the texts on Stelae 11, 14, and 15. Moreover, T369 *Ha'al* is the only of the two places that appears in the context of the military defeats and arrivals (from exile) of Dos Pilas rulers, according to the narratives on Dos Pilas Hieroglyphic Stairway 2. Given that the royal palace is part of the Main Plaza complex, the association of T369 *Ha'al* with accessions, public events, burials, and military fortunes of the kings makes perfect sense.

At some point in the history of the Dos Pilas written tradition, the two place names begin to appear together as a new way of designating the entire archaeological site as we would define it. The earliest reference of this kind is attested on Stela 8, which was dedicated in AD 727. The narrative on the monument states that the king "bound the stone and cast copal at *K'ihn Ha' Nal* T369 *Ha'al*" (Figure 7g). This example could still be interpreted as a mention of two sequential events. But the text on Dos Pilas Panel 19 commissioned after AD 729 explicitly comments on the scene depicted on the panel, leaving no doubt that the narrative deals with a singular event in one location: the bloodletting ceremony seen by "the Twenty-eight lords" which "happened at *K'ihn Ha' Nal* T369 *Ha'al*" (Figure 7h).

An even later inscription (after AD 767) on a stairway at Cancuen, located to the southeast of Dos Pilas, describes how the Cancuen ruler (presumably in an effort to boost his credentials and confirm his allegiances) received the royal crown before the Dos Pilas king *K'awiil Chan K'inich* at T369 *Ha'al K'ihn Ha' Nal* in AD 757 (Figure 7i) and then went to his homeland of *Haluum*.[5] The same crown was once taken by *Itzamnaah K'awiil* in T369 *Ha'al* in AD 698, according to the text on Dos Pilas Stela 8. A ceremony linked to that precious and powerful heirloom likely took place at the main royal palace at Dos Pilas. Yet the Cancuen narrative cites a double place name. This vagueness is possibly due to an outside perspective of the authors of the Cancuen inscription, who apparently did not differentiate between the two parts of the Dos Pilas and rather saw it as a single entity with two names.

The place names *Chi'k Nahb* and *Huxte' Tuun*, which, as I have argued previously (Tokovinine 2007b), correspond to the site of Calakmul and the surrounding area, form another paired set. The inscription on the Naranjo Hieroglyphic Stairway (L2–N3) clarifies the relationship between the two toponyms by stating that the Calakmul ruler is "*Kanu'l* lord in *Huxte' Tuun*, the man of *Chi'k Nahb*" (Figure 3c). *Chi'k Nahb* is associated with the site of Calakmul or part of it (Martin 1997:852, 2005). The strongest evidence comes from the captions painted on the wall of the Calakmul North Acropolis, which identify it as *chi'k nahb kot*—"*Chi'k Nahb* wall" (Carrasco Vargas and Colón González 2005:44–45). On the other hand, associations with *Huxte' Tuun* are not restricted to Calakmul. *Kanu'l* kings at Calakmul would sometimes refer to themselves as "the successors of *K'awiil* [at] *Huxte' Tuun*" or "*Huxte' Tuun kaloomte'*" (Martin 2005:7–8). In the inscriptions on Stelae 7, 12, and 14 at the nearby site of Oxpemul, local rulers are also referred to as "Oxpemul lords [at] *Huxte' Tuun*" or as "*Huxte' Tuun kaloomte'*" (Grube 2005:95–99, 2008:203–211).

In light of the aforementioned inscription on the stairway at Naranjo, it seems that *Huxte' Tuun* could be the name of a larger geographical area that incorporates Calakmul and Oxpemul. It could also be another location (or part of Calakmul) of equal importance to several dynasties in the region. As in the case of Dos Pilas toponyms, however, outside

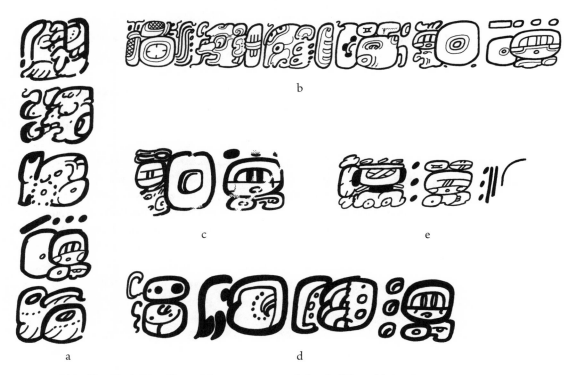

Figure 8 *Jo' Pet Hux Haab Te'* in Classic Maya inscriptions: a) detail of K1383; b) detail of K7524; c) detail of Juleki Cream sherd, Río Azul type collection (after photograph by the author); d) detail of a Late Classic vessel (after photograph in the Pre-Columbian Photographs and Fieldwork Archives, Dumbarton Oaks, LC.CB.2.499/K1256); and e) detail of a Late Classic vessel (K5022).

references apparently ignore the subtleties and cite the two place names together as one. Dos Pilas (Pn 6:B7, St 9:F4) and La Corona (Pn 1:H2, MSC 1) narratives locate distant Calakmul events "in *Chi'k Nahb*, in *Huxte' Tuun*," and even "in *Huxte' Tuun Chi'k Nahb*."

The inscriptions from the region of archaeological sites Río Azul and Los Alacranes offer another example of a place name derived from the combination of two toponyms. Río Azul lords can be identified by their exclusive title consisting of the term *nuun* and an undeciphered logogram (Figure 8a; Houston 1986:5–7, fig. 7), although two Early Classic inscriptions ascribed to Río Azul, a jade mask (see discussion below) and the Hauberg Stela, also mention the title of "*Ton* lords." The rulers of Los Alacranes are known as *Buk'a[l]* or *Buuk'* lords in the inscriptions on Los Alacranes Stelae 1 and 2 (Grube 2005:91–93, 2008:193–196). *Buuk'* or *Buk'al* lords are also mentioned on Xultun Stela 21 and two unprovenanced vases (K5241, K7524; Figure 8b). The names of the members of either dynasty may also end with the title *jo' pet hux haab te'*. The inscriptions on two unprovenanced Late Classic vessels photographed by Kerr (K1383, K2914) refer to individuals who carry the *nuun* Río Azul title followed by *jo' pet hux haab te'* (Figure 8a). Personal names in dedicatory texts on vessel fragments found at Río Azul also feature *jo' pet hux haab te'* titles (Figure 8c).[6] As for *Buuk'* or *Buk'al* lords, their link to this title is revealed in the inscription on one vessel (Figure 8b). The name of its owner in the dedicatory text includes the *Buuk'* or *Buk'al* lord title followed by *jo' pet jo' pet hux haab te'*.

Hux Haab Te' is likely a place name. It has its own *wahy* ("demon") character (Grube and Nahm 1994:706) named *K'ahk' Ohl May Chamiiy* (Figure 8d) and its own maize deity (see Chapter 5). Two individuals with the title "*Hux Haab Te'* lord" appear in the inscriptions on unprovenanced Late Classic vessels in the style similar to Xultun and Holmul vases (K2295, K5022, K7720; Figure 8e). As in the case of Xultun and La Honradez rulers, *Hux Haab Te'* individuals carry the *Huxlajuun Tzuk* title (see Chapter 5). The connection between *Hux Haab Te'* and Río Azul lords is revealed in the aforementioned inscription on the unprovenanced Early Classic jade mask (Grube and Martin 2001a:40). That text mentions the death of a certain *Sak Bahlam*, the *Ton* lord . . . *Hux Haab Te'*, and then refers to the subsequent rituals undertaken by an individual with the undeciphered Río Azul dynastic title in Block B8.[7]

It is tempting to hypothesize that *jo' pet hux haab te'* is a combination of *Hux Haab Te'* with another place name that came to designate the area comprising both locations. *Jo' Pet* or *Jo' Pet[en]* may be roughly translated as "five provinces" or "five partitions." It sounds like a place name. The aforementioned inscription on an unprovenanced Late Classic vessel mentioning a *Buk'al/Buuk'* lord *Tut K'in Chahk Jilel* (Figure 8b) seems to offer some evidence in support of this idea. *Tut K'in Chahk Jilel* carries the title *jo' pet jo' pet hux haab te'* with a curious reduplication of the *jo' pet* part. The most plausible way of dissecting this title is to assume that the first instance of *jo' pet* refers to the constituent part of a larger spatial entity: "*Jo' Pet* [of/at/in] *Jo' Pet Hux Haab Te'*."

In summary, sequences of place names in Classic Maya inscriptions inform more about their relative importance in the narratives than about spatial scale. That said, paired toponyms offer the clearest example of new, larger places emerging as a result of actual changes in corresponding locales and in perceptions of spatially related locales, particularly by those at a distance. This observation is significant because it proves that Classic Maya landscapes were not static and that transformations of places happened though time and space in terms of one's representation of distant locales.

What's in a place name? Classic Maya toponyms tend to be indexical. They do not represent physical locales directly but point to associated features such as mountains, lakes, streams, or kinds of trees. Not all things receive equal treatment. Classic Maya landscape highlights mountains, springs and rivers, and certain kinds of plants and animals. Their presence or abundance gives name to places. A large group of toponyms refers to cornfields, attesting to the centrality of corn in the Classic Maya worldview. Place names with cornfields and houses also potentially set the populated, community space apart from the uncontrolled, wild forest environment. The correspondence of places to physical locales is not constant. Double place names reveal changes in the perception of this relationship. Such changes may be due to actual transformations of the physical space (e.g., the growth of two settlements into one) or to perceptual changes through time or with increased distance from the place.

PLACE AND IDENTITY IN CLASSIC MAYA NARRATIVES

3 | CLASSIC MAYA LANDSCAPE CATEGORIES

CAVES AND LANDS:
IDENTIFYING CLASSIC MAYA LANDSCAPE CATEGORIES

PLACE NAMES IN CLASSIC MAYA INSCRIPTIONS ARE OFTEN ACCOMPA-
nied by several terms which may be defined as spatial categories or place categories and
which offer an emic view into the overarching concepts of place in ancient written narratives. While the overall function of these terms as spatial or landscape categories has been
widely accepted by epigraphers, their significance and translation(s) have remained the
subject of ongoing discussions.

The use of landscape categories is well attested in early colonial sources like the
Chontal Maldonado-Paxbolon Papers (Smailus 1975), where Mayan *kaj* ("city") and *kab*
("land" or "community") can be found alongside Spanish terms for early colonial political
landscape entities, such as *villa* and *provincia*. Besides the words for settlements and territories, the narrative features special terms denoting the relationship between territorial
and political entities such as *payolel* ("jurisdiction") as well as couplets like *kabil-kabob*,
something along the lines of "lands [and] communities," the totality of the territory, the
settlements and any other land.[8]

As in the case of many other issues pertaining to the Classic Maya landscape, the
topic of place categories was introduced by Stuart and Houston (1994) in the seminal
monograph on Classic Maya place names. These scholars noticed that the expression they
termed the "place name formula" in the inscriptions—the toponym preceded by *uhtiiy* or
uhti "it happened [at]"—was often followed by two words they dubbed the "sky-bone compound"; moreover, they noted that there was a similar "earth-bone compound" attested in
the inscriptions and in the codices that never followed the "place name formula" (Stuart
and Houston 1994:11–13). Either compound was a combination of a deciphered logogram—**CHAN** "sky" or **KAB** "earth"—with a number of undeciphered signs (T571, T598,
T599) that seemed to be allographs and that shared the same phonetic complement **–na**.
The undeciphered allographs of the "bone" sign could also appear after the "place name
formula" alone, sometimes prefixed by an ergative pronoun and followed by a personal
name. Although no decipherment was offered at the time, Stuart and Houston suggested

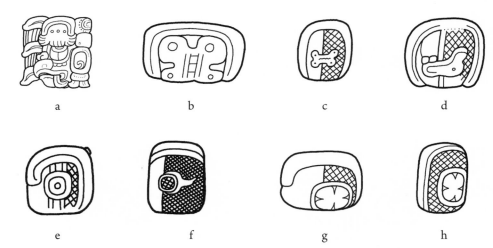

Figure 9 **CH'E'N** logogram in Classic Maya inscriptions: a) detail of Block 6 (L2), Hieroglyphic Stairway 1, Naranjo (after Graham 1978:109); b) detail of Stela 31 (F27), Tikal (after Jones and Satterthwaite 1982:fig. 52); c) detail of a tablet (M15), Temple of the Foliated Cross, Palenque (after Robertson 1991:fig. 153); d) detail of Stela I, Copan (after drawing by Barbara Fash); e) detail of Stela 8 (F22), Dos Pilas (after Houston 1993:fig. 4-14); f) detail of Altar 4, El Cayo (after Mathews 1998:fig. 3); g) detail of Lintel 3 (D6), Temple 1, Tikal (after Jones and Satterthwaite 1982:fig. 70); and h) detail of Panel 1 (B1), Cancuen (after drawing by Yuriy Polyukhovych).

that the "sky-bone compound" and the "earth-bone compound" were expressions that marked the toponyms as places of a certain kind and, in the case of the possessed "bone" sign, as places of a certain kind owned by protagonists.

Stuart subsequently proposed the **CH'E'N** (as *ch'e'n* for "cave") decipherment for the "bone" sign. The full set of arguments leading to this decipherment (Stuart n.d.) has not been widely circulated, although an abbreviated version has been published (Vogt and Stuart 2005:157–163). No phonetic substitutions like **ch'e-ne** or **ch'e-na** have so far been attested in the Classic Maya inscriptions. In fact, the sign **ch'e** remains unidentified. The only clue to the reading of the T571/T598/T599 is the phonetic complement –**na** that is occasionally replaced by –**ne** (CPN St 2:C8, St 12:A1) and –**ni** (QRG Zoomorph G:G'1) in some Late Classic inscriptions. A substitution of this kind is likely caused by the loss of vowel complexity (Houston et al. 1998; Lacadena García-Gallo and Wichmann 2004) and strongly suggests that the undeciphered sign ends in *–e'n* > *–en*, *–een* > *–en*, or even *–ee'n* > *–een* > *–en*.

In the absence of the full phonetic substitution, the argument in favor of **CH'E'N** is based on providing enough contexts where the word "cave" would be the best fit. *Ch'e'n* is the only widely attested word for "cave" that ends in *–e'n* or *–en*. Interpreting the visual origins of the sign may offer additional clues to its meaning (Figure 9). The iconographic argument centers on the prominent "darkness" cross-hatching with bones (Figure 9b–d) or disembodied eyes (Figure 9e–f), which form the constant graphic elements of the

Figure 10 **MUK** logogram, detail of Monument 159 (B3), Tonina (after Graham et al. 2006:94).

a   b

Figure 11 *Ch'e'n* references in the Jolja cave inscriptions: a) detail of Drawing 6 (after Vogt and Stuart 2005:fig. 7.9); and b) detail of Drawing 5 (after Sheseña 2007:fig. 4).

logogram (Stone and Zender 2011:132–133). The same motifs appear in the depictions of underworld locations and supernatural characters. The potential **CH'E'N** logogram also bears resemblance to the **MUK** (*muk* "burial") sign depicting a skull in the crosshatched space under steps or inside a mound (Figure 10).

According to Vogt and Stuart (2005:160, fig. 7.9), the strongest piece of evidence supporting the **CH'E'N** decipherment with respect to the textual context is provided by the two inscriptions from the Jolja cave in Chiapas, Mexico (see also Sheseña 2007). One mentions arrival to a **?CH'E'N-na** (*huli t-u-?ch'e'n*) (Figure 11a). The other refers to the completion of the four-hundred-year period [in] **?CH'E'N-na** (*tzutz pik ?ch'e'n mam . . .*) (Figure 11b). It is very likely that the two inscriptions mention the "cave" as a reference to the Jolja cave itself.

Stuart (n.d.) argues that scenes marked by representations of mountains as something that happens inside a mountain offer another good context to look for the instances of the T571/T598/T599 sign as evidence in favor of the **CH'E'N** reading. The Mundo Perdido incised vessel (Houston and Stuart 1999:II-20; Stone and Zender 2011:132) includes a textual reference to one's **?CH'E'N**, and the inscription on the so-called Saenz Throne, to be discussed further in the chapter (Mayer 1995:pl. 120), refers to one's arrival to a **?CH'E'N**.

Figure 12 Deity seating in a mountain frame, detail of a vessel, Mundo Perdido, Tikal (after photograph by Inga Calvin, K30098/MNAE 11134).

a b

Figure 13 Other "cave" glyphs: a) T510, detail of Stela 15 (B7), Dos Pilas (Houston 1993:fig. 4-15); and b) "stacked earth" sign, detail of Drawing 34 (A4), Naj Tunich (after Stone 1995:figs. 7–26).

These textual references are explicitly associated with the characters depicted within the mountains (Figure 12) and are strong cases in support of the **CH'E'N** reading.

The association between mountains and the potential sign for "caves" is implicated further by the imagery and text on the unprovenanced Early Classic vessel embellished with images of mountains and supplied with a glyphic commentary "the name of the drinking vessel is *Jo Janahb Nal ?ch'e'n*" (Stuart and Houston 1994:77–79, fig. 93). The caveat of the last example is that a number of dedicatory vessels make reference to *uyul uch'e'n* (K2914, K4387, K4572) and the term may be an emic vessel type. The interiors of Classic Maya temples as embodiments of sacred mountains are caves par excellence (Stuart 1997).

There are several problems with the **CH'E'N** decipherment for the T571/T598/T599 signs. One challenge comes from the contexts when other signs appear instead of T571/

T598/T599 as designations for caves. The pan-Mesoamerican quatrefoil motif associated with caves is well attested in Classic Maya imagery, and there is a corresponding sign T510 in the script that appears in place names (Figure 13a). Another candidate for the cave sign is a hieroglyph that looks like two **KAB** "earth" signs stacked on top of each other, the upper one featuring an indentation in the lower-left corner (Figure 13b). This sign closely resembles some of the images of caves and burials in Classic Maya iconography (Stuart 2005b:104–105, figs. 176–177). It is found as an optional part of the place name for the Naj Tunich Cave (NTN Dr 66, Dr 34). The logogram also appears in the name of the temple of GII of the Palenque triad (Stuart 2005b:104). Nevertheless, these signs should not necessarily be dismissed if the **CH'E'N** reading were correct and vice versa. The alternative cave glyphs are also complemented by –**na**, leaving open the possibility that we are dealing with a case of distinct allographs derived from representations of different kinds of caves. Allographs in the Maya writing may represent multiple manifestations of the same object or concept. The best-known example is **TZ'AK** allographs, which illustrate various pairs of complementary entities (Stuart 2003). **YAX** allographs corresponding to distinct kinds of jewels are another solid comparative case (Houston et al. 2009:fig. 2.21). Different **NEH/ne** "tails" (a jaguar tail and a coati tail) also attest to this feature of the script.

Perhaps the greatest challenge to the **CH'E'N** reading is the sheer abundance of contexts in which this sign occurs. There seems to be a general consensus among scholars supporting the reading that some of these contexts refer to caves as metaphors of some kind, perhaps related to the concept of caves as origin places of human communities and as dwellings of gods and ancestors (Martin 2004; Vogt and Stuart 2005). Does it necessarily confirm the **CH'E'N** decipherment? One rather extreme answer is to assume that there is an actual cave or spring that names every Classic Maya location. Indeed, this seems to be the implication of some arguments (Brady and Colas 2005; Vogt and Stuart 2005). The strongest evidence against this assumption is the nearly complete absence of the signs T571/T598/T599 in place names.

The occasional combination of **KAB** and ?**CH'E'N** in Classic Maya inscriptions seems to provide some support for the reading of ?**CH'E'N** and for the relation between the term *ch'e'n* and the notion of place and territory. As first indicated by Lacadena García-Gallo (2002), a direct equivalent of this couplet can be found in early colonial sources, such as the parallel passages in the books of Chilam Balam of Chumayel and Tizimin, where *kabal ch'e'en Mani* or *kabi[l] ch'e'en Mani* possibly means "the land/city of Mani."[9] Roys translated the passage as "the prophecy of Chilam Balam, the singer, of Cabal-Ch'en, Mani" (Roys 1973:167) and noted that Cabal-Ch'en was still the name of a cenote at Mani. The Late Classic text from Bonampak (SCS 1:C2–D2) features what seems an identical usage of the couplet *kab ch'e'n*: ?*kajaay tukab [tu]ch'e'n usiij witz* (" . . . he settles in the land, [in] the *ch'e'n* of Usiij Witz").

But this interpretation, which is based on the analogy between the Classic Maya inscriptions from the Southern Lowlands and the colonial texts from Northern Yucatan, should be taken with a grain of salt. The term *ch'e'en* in the landscape of Northern Yucatan denotes natural sinkholes, cenotes, which are the main sources of water in that region. Cacao groves in the collapsed sinkholes, which are an important economic resource, are also called *ch'e'en*. Colonial Yukatek land titles, such as the Códice Najul Pech and Yaxkukul surveys, attest to the significance of named *ch'e'en* sinkholes as landmarks and boundary markers (Hanks 2010:295–305). Such landscape features are noticeably less prominent in the south, however. Moreover, the terms *ch'e'en* and *kab* in narratives like the Book of Chilam Balam of Chumayel are not metaphors for a "settlement," but stand in metonymic relationship to the concept of the community (as a landscape category) as a totality of several landscape categories. This concept is aptly summarized in the following passage on the seventh page of the Book of Chilam Balam of Chumayel (in original orthography):

> *ca yumil ti Dios. lay tzol peten. Lay sihes yokol cab tulacal: la ix tzol xan: heob lae kabansah peten: u cahob: kabansah ch'een u cahob: kabansah cacab u cahob kabansah luum u cahob: tumen ma mac kuchuc uaye: Uayi u cal peten* (Miram 1988:1:55–56)

> . . . Our father who is God, it was he who ordered the (ordered, bounded) land. It was he who created the whole world, who also ordered it. As for them, it was he who named the (ordered, bounded) land, their community, named wells/cacao groves, their community, named (township) land, their community, named the (agricultural) land, their community, because no one came here, here to the edge ("neck") of the (ordered, bounded) land.

The passage clearly states that *kaaj*, as the most general category for human settlements, comprises three different kinds of "land": the one that is ordered and bounded (*peten*), the one that is presumably associated with the political landscape (*kab*), the "soil" or the agricultural land (*luum*), but also the wells and/or cacao groves (*ch'e'en*) as a distinct category. In the narrative, we find the terms *kaaj* and *luum* following place names, while the rest of the set appears as couplets. While some of the instances can be interpreted as the use of a given term in a more restricted sense (e.g., *peten* for "province"), other examples are nothing but metonymies of the overarching concept of the community as a landscape category. Therefore, a couplet like *kab ch'e'en* would still stand in a metonymic relation to *peten-ch'e'en-kab-luum* that is all *kaaj*. Other pairs of any of those terms like *kabil peten* are equally possible, as in the following passage from the Chilam Balam of Chumayel (in original orthography):

> *mul yutzcinnahob: tu yuklah <u>cabil peten</u>: Bay ti kaknab tac tu chun <u>cab</u>: U patah ix u kabaob xan yetel <u>u ch'eenil</u>* (Miram 1988:1:61)

> . . . of the mounds they constructed all over the land. From the sea to the base of the land they created names for them as well as for the wells. (Roys 1973:80)

The same place name may be associated with several terms in these colonial-period narratives. For instance, the city of Mayapan is mentioned as *luum* (CHU 75:31, 79:16) and *kaaj* (CHU 76:13, 78:12, 80:3, 103:7). A reference to its downfall evokes the term *peten* (CHU 80:3). Mayapan is also reported to comprise four *kab* (CHU 80:5–6).

Despite the importance of natural sinkholes as sources of water and places to grow cacao, the metonymic use of *ch'e'en* with place names is still rare in the books of Chilam Balam when compared to the frequency of the terms *kab*, *luum*, and *kaaj*. This pattern contradicts the situation in the Classic Maya inscriptions, where *ch'e'n* is the most frequent term. Moreover, the inscriptions frequently employ the couplet *chan ch'e'n*, literally, "sky [and] cave," that is not attested in the colonial-period sources. Stuart (n.d.; see also Vogt and Stuart 2005:160) suggests that the term indicates a totality of space of some kind, much like the word "world." Stuart (n.d.) argues that the form of representing the locations in the back racks of the dancing maize god figures in the so-called Holmul dancer scenes (see Chapter 5) as a combination of the representations of a mountain surmounted by the representation of the sky, the "sky-band," possibly reflects the concept of a place as a combination of the mountain-cave and the sky. The captions to the maize god often describe him as *tahn ch'e'n* "in front/inside the cave," seemingly supporting the hypothesis that the terms *ch'e'n* and *chan ch'e'n* denote overlapping notions of place. This interpretation leaves us with two different readings of the term *chan ch'e'n* (which are implicitly given in the latest publications, including Stuart's own translation of the inscriptions from the temples of the Cross Group at Palenque) (Stuart 2006b): "the heavens and the caves," designating the world, and "the sky, the cave" designating the place. But no argument is given to support such choices of translation.

CH'E'N AS A LANDSCAPE CATEGORY IN CLASSIC MAYA INSCRIPTIONS

If the *ch'e'n* decipherment were correct, then several important questions would remain unanswered. Why did "caves" become the main term for Classic Maya places? What kind of spatial entities does the term denote? Is it possible to discern better analogies from the colonial sources? The couplets of *chan ch'e'n* and *kab ch'e'n* also merit further analysis and explanation.

To begin with, there is a range of meanings of *ch'e'n* in Mayan languages and "cave" is only one of them. In Ch'orti' (Wisdom 1950:718), it is "opening, hole, perforation, cave, grave, ditch, well, tank, canyon, arroyo, hollow, valley, cavity." "Cave" and "hole" for *ch'e'n* are also found in Ch'ol (Aulie and Aulie 1978:53) and Chontal (Keller and Luciano 1997:101). "Graves" in Chontal are the "*ch'en* of the dead" (Keller and Luciano 1997:101). In colonial Tzeltal (Ara 1986 [1571]:265), it is "hole" and "canyon." *Ch'en* in Tzotzil (Laughlin and Haviland 1988:99, 197, 271, 294, 303, 324, 327) is "hole, burrow, cave, ravine, cliff." In Yukatek (Barrera Vásquez et al. 1995:46, 131–133), it means "hole, cistern, cave with water" as well as a collapsed sinkhole used to grow cacao. In summary, any opening in the ground can be *ch'e'n*, particularly if there is water in it. If we consider the representations of mountains discussed above, then the cleft in almost every mountain image in Classic Maya art would fit this definition of *ch'e'n*.

The few occurrences of *ch'e'n* in toponyms have been discussed in the previous chapter. We may find *ch'e'n* in toponymic registers after place names. In the narratives, the *tahn ch'e'n* expression may precede toponyms, as in "she arrives *tahn ch'e'n* [at/of] *Hux Witza'*"

Figure 14 Syntactic patterns with *ch'e'n*: a) detail of Stela 3 (B14–B15), Caracol (after Beetz and Satterthwaite 1981:12); b) detail of Block 6 (N1–L2), Hieroglyphic Stairway 1, Naranjo (after Graham 1978:109); and c) detail of Panel 1, El Cayo (after Chinchilla Mazariegos and Houston 1993:fig. 1).

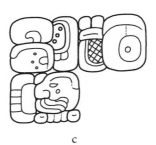

(*huli tahn ch'e'n hux witza'*) on Caracol Stela 3 (Figure 14a). *Ch'e'n* alone appears after place names, although the more common pattern is a possessed form of *ch'e'n* (frequently supplied with a locative preposition) followed by the name of the *ch'e'n* owner, human or divine. For example, the defeat of Naranjo in the narrative on the Naranjo Hieroglyphic Stairway is presented as the "downfall of *Sa'aal*, the *ch'e'n* of *K'uhxaj*," its ruler at the time of the attack (Figure 14b). *Ch'e'n* may be possessed by the toponym itself as in "he was buried in the *ch'e'n* of *Yaxniil*" (*muhkaj tuch'e'n yaxniil*) in the inscription on El Cayo Panel 1 (Figure 14c). *Ch'e'n* can also be found in compounds like *och ch'e'n* ("*ch'e'n*-entering," see below). Therefore, the term indexes places, denotes something pertaining to specific places, and highlights places owned by humans and gods.

Only about one in ten toponyms documented for the present study are referred to as *ch'e'n* in the hieroglyphic inscriptions (Table 2). Does it mean that other places do not belong to the category of *ch'e'n* locales? We need to take into account the nature of the sample. Only 530 contexts of toponyms out of 2,400 are direct, and many place names occur only a few times in the corpus. Therefore, *ch'e'n* examples become restricted to the most frequently mentioned toponyms found in inscriptions at sites with the greatest number

Table 2 *Ch'e'n* places in Classic Maya inscriptions.

PLACE NAME ASSOCIATED WITH *CH'E'N* IN DIRECT CONTEXTS	DIRECT CONTEXTS WITHOUT *CH'E'N*	TITLES OR OWNERS	INSIDE	OUTSIDE
T1018 *nal*			x	
T176	x	x	x	x
T239		x	x	
T369 *ha'al*/T369 *ha'al k'ihn ha' nal*	x	x	x	x
T5 *tuun*	x		x	
T756d-pi	x	x	x	
T856-la/*yax* T856-la *nal*	x	x	x	
. . . *tz'ikiin*	x			x
hux ahen			x	
hux k'ahk'		x		x
hux wintik	x		x	
hux witza'	x	x	x	
jo' T538 *nal*	x	x	mythological	
jo' T627 *nal*	x	x	mythological	
jo' janahb nal/*jo' janahb witz*	x	x	x	x
wak ik' [nal]				x
bolon tz'akbuul ihk' T1031 *nal*			x	
haluum	x		x	
ihk' nahb nal	x		mythological	
k'ahk' . . . a'			x	
k'ante'l		x	x	
k'ihnich pa' witz ta T856	x		x	x
ku- . . .			x	
kukuul	x	x	x	
lal		x		x
lakam ha'	x	x	x	
makanal witz	x	x		x
mi-?-NAL			x	
mutal/*yax mutal*/*k'ihn palaw nal yax mutal*	x	x	x	
naah k'an nal/*k'an nal naah*	x		x	
nikte'/*nikte' witz*	x			x
pipa'/*k'in xook witz pipa'*	x	x		x
sak T533 *lakal*	x	x	x	
sak nikte'			x	

Table 2 *continued*

PLACE NAME ASSOCIATED WITH *CH'E'N* IN DIRECT CONTEXTS	DIRECT CONTEXTS WITHOUT *CH'E'N*	TITLES OR OWNERS	INSIDE	OUTSIDE
sa'aal	x	x		x
te' nal		x	mythological	
usiij witz	x	x	x	
waka'		x	x	
wi'il				x
yaxa'/ ti' yax k'uk' ha' yaxa'	x	x	x	
yaxniil/yax ahku'l ha' yaxniil		x	x	
yax xi-T1046 *ajan*	x		mythological	
yokib/... palaw T24 *ajan nal yokib*		x		x
yootz		x		x
TOTAL 44	26	27	28	15

and variety of texts. Nevertheless, there may be a distinction between places indexed as *ch'e'n* and other locations in the narratives. The *ch'e'n* place names are often characterized by the strongest association to the site from which the inscriptions come, and are also found in emblem glyphs and titles of origin or association (to be discussed in Chapter 4). When the titles of a ruler do not evoke the local *ch'e'n*, the origins of the dynasty are elsewhere, as in the cases of the inscriptions at Palenque, Bonampak, Piedras Negras, Calakmul, Dos Pilas, Aguateca, and Cancuen. There is also a tendency to refer to the local places as *ch'e'n* as opposed to the other locations.

The presence or absence of *ch'e'n* with place names may also reflect the implicit concepts about the landscape embedded in the narrative. For instance, the place names ending in *–a'* or *–ha'* ("water") may be followed by *ch'e'n*—but *tahn ch'e'n* ("in the midst/ before the *ch'e'n*") and *tahn ha'* ("in the midst/before the water") never co-occur with the same place names, implying some kind of classification of places into *ch'e'n* ("cave") and *ha'* ("water"). The mention of "water" in a place name does not predict which of the two groups it belongs to. Nevertheless, two of the three place names introduced by *tahn ha'*— *Pa' Chan* (Figure 15a) and *Ik'a'* (Figure 15b)—are associated with large bodies of water. Motul de San Jose (*Ik'a'*) is located near the Lake Peten Itza. Yaxchilan (*Pa' Chan*) is on a partially inundated area of the peninsula formed by the loop of the Usumacinta River. The status of the third place name—*Baakal* (Figure 15c)—is unclear because it cannot be securely matched to a known physical locale. In other words, watery places may still be classified as pertaining to the land domain and the classification is not related to the presence or absence of the word "water."

Another interesting pattern is that, despite the semantic overlap between *witz* "mountain" and *ch'e'n* "cave," there are no examples of a combination [...] *witz ch'e'n*. The same

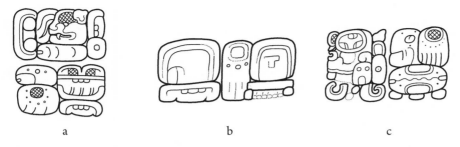

Figure 15 *Tahn ha'* expression in Classic Maya inscriptions: a) detail of Lintel 25 (I2–I3), Yaxchilan (after Graham and Von Euw 1977:56); b) detail of Stela 1 (C8–D8), Motul de San José (after photograph by Ian Graham); and c) detail of Monument 6, Tortuguero (after drawing by Ian Graham).

place name (e.g., *Jo' Janahb Nal*) may be labeled as *witz* and *ch'e'n*, but not in the same text. Mountains may have caves (e.g., *Ch'e'n Witz*), but "caves" are not "mountains," even metaphorically. A *witz* place name may have its *ch'e'n* (e.g., *tukab ch'e'n usiij witz*), but the relationship is complementary, not a substitution: where there is a "mountain," there is a "cave." The same concept is manifested in the architecture: if the building exterior represents a mountain, then the interior is indexed as a cavelike space.

The inscriptions also extend the link between caves and dwellings through relating the terms *naah* ("building") and *otoot* ("home") to *ch'e'n*. Nowhere is this link more apparent than in the inscriptions at Palenque. A number of Palenque texts refer to the temple on top of or at the foot of the Mirador hill (*Yehmal K'uk' Lakam Witz*) overlooking the palace and the temples of the Cross Group. The Dumbarton Oaks Carved Panel (PC.B.528) might even have originated the temple on top of the hill, as Stuart (2006b:92–93) recently suggested. The tablet inscriptions in the sanctuaries in the Temples of the Foliated Cross (Figure 16a) and the Sun (Figure 16b) of the Cross Group describe the same event when the gods were conjured in the *K'inich K'uk' Naah* ("Resplendent Quetzal House"), the *otoot* "home" of the king, on top of *Yehmal K'uk' Lakam Witz*, in the *ch'e'n* of the god *Hux Bolon Chahk*.[10] The text on the Dumbarton Oaks Carved Panel (Figure 16c) refers to several earlier and later rituals undertaken in the temple of *Hux Bolon Chahk*, presumably the same *K'inich K'uk' Naah* on *Yehmal K'uk' Lakam Witz* (Houston and Taube 2012).[11] The location of the rituals is referred to as the *waybil*, the "sleeping place"—a common term for temples (Stuart 1998:fig. 1)—of *Hux Bolon Chahk*, and *uwitzil uk'uhuul* "the mountain of the god of" the king. It also refers to the location as *titz*, possibly a "summit" or a "rock cliff."[12] The parallel references suggest that *ch'e'n* in this case designates a temple on a mountain, the dwelling of the local patron deity.

A somewhat similar pair of references can be found in the inscriptions at Tikal. The text on Lintel 2 from Temple 4 (Figure 17a) describes how Tikal king *Yik'in Chan K'awiil* embarks on a war against Naranjo "descending" from (*ehmey*) the place of *Sak* T533 *Lakal* as the "Seven Centipede Eagle Resplendent Lord" (Zender 2005). Tikal Stela 5 depicts the victorious king with a centipede solar disk in the back rack. The captured Naranjo ruler

Figure 16 The *ch'e'n* mountain temple of *Hux Bolon Chahk* in Palenque inscriptions: a) detail of a tablet (M6–L17), Temple of the Foliated Cross (after Robertson 1991:fig. 153); b) detail of a tablet (O8–N16), Temple of the Sun (after Robertson 1991:fig. 95); and c) detail of the Dumbarton Oaks Carved Panel (PC.B.528; after 3D scan by the author).

a

b

c

kneels before him. The text on the monument begins with the king's accession statement. "Then," according to the narrative (Figure 17b), the king "settles in *Sak* T533 *Lakal*" (*?kajaay Sak* T533 *Lakal*) that is "the home of" (*yotoot*) a local deity (see Houston 1993:101). *Yik'in Chan K'awiil* appears in the mask or headdress of this god on Stela 20 and Lintel 4 of Temple 4 at Tikal (Jones and Satterthwaite 1982:figs. 29, 74). The inscription on Stela 5 continues with stating that this "home" is also the *ch'e'n* of the "fourteen *tuun* . . . lord(s)."

The partially undeciphered reference to the "lord(s)" recalls the full name of the Tikal version of the maize god (Figure 17c) mentioned on the carved bone (TIK MT 38A) in the tomb of *Yik'in Chan K'awiil*'s father, *Jasaw Chan K'awiil*, in Temple 1 (Moholy-Nagy and Coe 2008:fig. 189a). *Jasaw Chan K'awiil*, like other Tikal lords, was likened to this maize god in life and death. Fourteen k'atuns (twenty-year periods) were completed by *Yik'in*

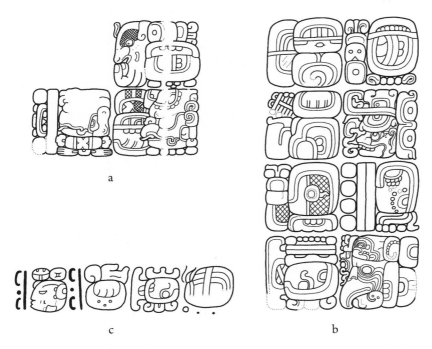

a

c

b

Figure 17 The *ch'e'n* temple *Sak* T533 *Lakal* in Tikal inscriptions: a) detail of Lintel 2 (B4–B5), Temple 4 (after Jones and Satterthwaite 1982:fig. 73); b) detail of Stela 5 (A9–B12) (after Jones and Satterthwaite 1982:fig. 7); and c) detail of a carved bone MT38 (D1–G1), Burial 116 (after Moholy-Nagy and Coe 2008:fig. 189a).

Chan K'awiil's ancestors before he acceded to kingship. Many of these ancestors were buried in the Tikal North Acropolis. This is where Stela 5 was erected, just like many other monuments that commemorated previous period endings. Therefore, *Sak* T533 *Lakal* could be the name of the North Acropolis and the *ch'e'n* in this context the tombs and ancestral shrines of the previous kings. Even if it is not the case, there is another high place that is also the "home" of a deity and the *ch'e'n* of the local maize god.

If *Sak* T533 *Lakal* was the name of the North Acropolis, then it would not be the only example of an association between burials (*mukil / muk nal*), being buried (*muhkaj*), and *ch'e'n*. The burial places can be described as "houses" *naah* (TIK Alt 5, PAL TI Tb, TZD St 1) and "mountains" *witz* (CNC Pn 1, PNG Pn 3, YAX Ln 28; Figure 18). One can also be buried in the *ch'e'n*, as in the case of the *sajal* from *Yaxniil* "buried in the *ch'e'n* of *Yaxniil*" (Figure 14c) and Dos Pilas ruler *Itzamnaah K'awiil* "buried *tahn ch'e'n* T369 *Ha'al*" (DPL St 8). At least for *Itzamnaah K'awiil*, the burial was indeed in the pyramid located within the area associated with the T369 *Ha'al* place name (see above).

The concept of *ch'e'n* as a high place is additionally illustrated by examples when *ch'e'n* alone or place names indexed as *ch'e'n* occur with "verbs of motion" (Beliaev 2006). In the text on the back of the so-called Saenz Throne, now in the collections of the Museum Amparo in Puebla (Mayer 1995:pl. 120; Zender 2005:13–14), God D's winged messenger

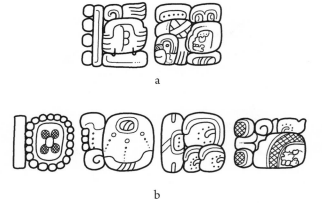

a

b

Figure 18 Burials as houses and mountains: a) detail of the West Tablet (T11–S12), Temple of the Inscriptions, Palenque (after Robertson 1983:fig. 97); and b) detail of Panel 1 (P5–P7), Cancuen (after drawing by Yuriy Polyukhovych).

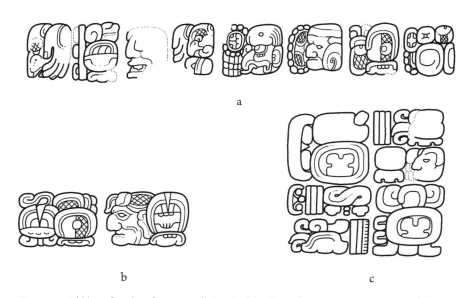

a

b   c

Figure 19 *Ch'e'n* and verbs of motion: a) detail of the Saenz/Museo Amparo Throne (after Mayer 1995:pl. 120); b) detail of Sculptured Stone 4 (D4–C5), Bonampak (after drawing by Alexander Safronov); and c) detail of Block 11, Hieroglyphic Stairway 1, Dzibanche (after Nalda 2004:44).

PLACE AND IDENTITY IN CLASSIC MAYA NARRATIVES

"descends" (*ehmey*) from the *Wak Chan Nal* ("Six sky place") only to "ascend" (*t'abaay*) to the *ch'e'n* of the "holy lord" of T856-**li** (Figure 19a). The Bonampak ruler in the narrative on Sculptured Stone 4 from the site (Figure 19b) "leaves from" (*lok'ooy*) his *ch'e'n* and "ascends" to *Pa' Chan* (Safronov 2006:94). "Ascending" is the verb of choice to describe arriving "there" in contrast to *tali* ("arrive from there"), *huli* ("arrive here"), and *bixan* ("to go"). Consequently, the action of "leaving from" a *ch'e'n* may also be called "descending from," as in the case of the aforementioned *Sak* T533 *Lakal* at Tikal or in the narrative on Stela 16 at Caracol, where *Bahlam Neen*, lord of Copan, "descends from the *ch'e'n*" (*ehmey ch'e'n*) (Grube 1990:fig. 1). One of the terms for military defeat, *jubuuy* "to fall down," is frequently applied to toponyms, apparently reflecting the same idea of place as something high but also highlighting the fact that the notion of the high place should not be taken literally.

Overall, references to warfare provide another rich source of contexts for the term *ch'e'n*. One of the more general terms is "entering the *ch'e'n*" (*ochi ch'e'n* and *och-ch'e'naj*). Some of the "*ch'e'n*-entering" events are clearly acts of warfare when other places are attacked and captives are taken (Martin 2004:106–109; Velásquez García 2004:85, 2005). References to *och ch'e'n* in the inscriptions on the hieroglyphic steps at Dzibanche (Figure 19c) are followed by mentions of captives taken by the king.[13] On Naranjo Stela 21 (Graham 1975:53), the king, in the act of "entering the *ch'e'n* in *Yootz*" (*ubaah ti och ch'e'n yootz*), is depicted standing on a captive from that place. The same paradigm holds for Palenque rulers "entering the *ch'e'n*" of Tonina lords in the text on the tablet from Palenque Temple 17 (Martin 2004:106–107). It applies to the confrontation scenes between the *Chak Xib Chahk* warriors and the young wind god with the accompanying text stating that "*Chak Xib* enters the cave," *och[i] ch'e'n Chak Xib* (Garcia Barrios 2006; Martin 2004:107; Robicsek and Hales 1981:72; Taube 2004a:74–75). A caption on a pottery fragment from Calakmul specifies that the *ch'e'n* in these confrontation scenes is *Kanu'l*, the place name in the title of Calakmul and Dzibanche rulers (Garcia Barrios 2005; Garcia Barrios and Carrasco Vargas 2006). The military triumphs of *Itzamnaah Bahlam* of Yaxchilan (YAX St 18) and Lady Six Sky from Naranjo (NAR St 24) are linked to a certain kind of *och ch'e'n* (Tokovinine and Fialko 2007:7–8, fig. 10).

Nevertheless, the contexts of *och ch'e'n* are not restricted to warfare narratives. Temples may be the intended meaning of *ch'e'n* in some "entering" events. The *ch'e'n*-entering (*och-ch'e'naj*) in a rather cryptic passage on Copan Stela P (E2–F13) takes place at Copan itself and is linked to the period-ending rituals (Figure 20a).[14] The inscription on the tablet from Palenque Temple 14 (Figure 20b) mentions entering the *ch'e'n* of a certain deity or place.[15] The act is described as the undertaking (*ehtej*) of Palenque gods. Another divine *och ch'e'n* appears in the narrative on the Tikal "Marker" in the context of *Sihyaj K'ahk'*'s arrival to Tikal in AD 378, understood by some scholars as the conquest of the city by a Teotihuacan-related warlord (Martin and Grube 2000:29–35; Stuart 2000). The aftermath of that event is described as "*Chan* lord god, western *Waxaklajuun Ubaah Kan* entered *ch'e'n*" (Figure 20c).[16] *Waxaklajuun Ubaah Kan* is also known as the Teotihuacan War Serpent deity (Taube 2000).

The other two common tropes for warfare involving *ch'e'n* are "burning" (*pul*) and "chopping" (*ch'ak*). "Burning" is the term of choice in many inscriptions on the monuments at Naranjo (eleven out of fifteen examples). It is usually the place that "gets burned"

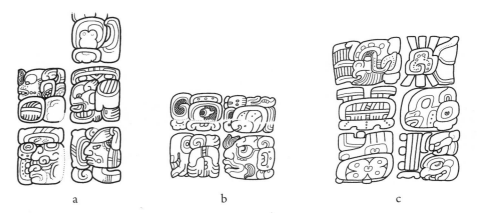

a   b   c

Figure 20 Entering the *ch'e'n*: a) detail of Stela P (F4–F6), Copan (after drawing by Barbara Fash); b) detail of a tablet, Temple 14, Palenque (after Robertson 1991:fig. 176); and c) detail of the "Marker" (C6–D8), Tikal (after 3D scan by the author).

(*puluuy*), but in two Naranjo narratives, Stelae 22 and 23, the object of burning is the *ch'e'n* of the enemy king: "the *ch'e'n* of powerless *Yaxa'* lord *Joyaj Chahk* gets burned" (Figure 21a).[17] "Chopping" is by far the more widespread term. Chopping the place name and chopping the *ch'e'n* of the enemy, as in the narrative on Tamarindito Hieroglyphic Stairway 2 (Figure 21b), are common forms of the expression. It seems unlikely that the armies embarked on burning and chopping enemy caves or that enemy lands were burned and chopped in guerilla-style attacks. It is important that the "land" (*kab*) is not mentioned as the object of these acts. Extending the meaning of *ch'e'n* as temples and dwellings to these expressions, "burning" and "chopping" may refer to the conquest of the heart of an enemy polity, much like the depictions of burning temples that symbolized conquest in the Aztec pictorial manuscripts (Marcus 1992:365, fig. 11.9). Of course, this does not mean that destructive military raids did not exist. The text on the Denver Museum panel (Biró 2005:2–8) provides an ample description of such an event (Figure 21c): "*Pe' Tuun* lord *Nik Ahk Mo'* scattered fire in the *ch'e'n* of *Sak Tz'i'* lord *K'ab Chan Te'*, *baah kab*."[18]

The final common expression of war and conquest is a verb spelled with the undeciphered "star-over-earth" or "star war" logogram (see Chinchilla Mazariegos 2006 for the latest interpretation of the glyph) followed by the name of the defeated person, the place name, or *ch'e'n*. We know from the contexts of the word that it is an intransitive verb used to describe the downfall of people and places. One of the examples is the inscription on the Naranjo Hieroglyphic Stairway (Tokovinine 2007b). The subject of the attack is *Sa'aal*, an important place at Naranjo, referred to in the inscription as the *ch'e'n* of the Naranjo king. The much later Tikal victory against Naranjo is described on Tikal Temple 4 Lintel 2 (Figure 21d) as the "downfall of the *Wak Kab Nal* [person]" (a title of Naranjo rulers) "in the *ch'e'n*" of the Naranjo patron deity, the "Black Square-Nosed Beastie" (Martin 1996b). The victories of Tonina rulers are presented on Tonina Monuments 122 and 83 as the "downfall" of *ch'e'n* or *kab ch'e'n* of the enemy kings (Figure 21e).

PLACE AND IDENTITY IN CLASSIC MAYA NARRATIVES

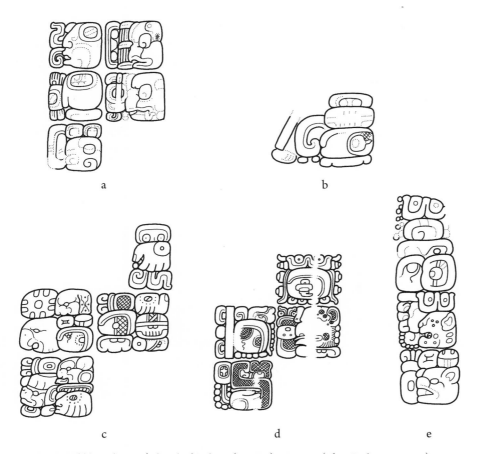

Figure 21 *Ch'e'n* and war: a) detail of Stela 23 (E9–E11), Naranjo (after Graham 1975:60); b) detail of Step 2, Hieroglyphic Stairway 2 (M1–N1), Tamarindito (after Houston 1993:fig. 4-21); c) detail of the Denver Museum panel (B5–A7; after drawing by Alexander Safronov); d) detail of Lintel 2 (B8–A10), Temple 4, Tikal (after Jones and Satterthwaite 1982:fig. 73); and e) detail of Monument 83 (D1–D4), Tonina (after Graham and Mathews 1996:113).

Is there an analogy, or a direct parallel, to the term *ch'e'n* in colonial sources? As was discussed earlier, the term *ch'e'n* in colonial Yukatek documents does not relate quite as directly to the concept of temples, burial places, and the heart of one's community evidenced in the Classic inscriptions. The Hieroglyphic Mayan *ch'e'n* can be found precisely where *kaaj* is used in colonial Yukatek and Chontal narratives like the Chilam Balam books and the Maldonado-Paxbolon Papers. One is left wondering if the prevalence of *kaaj* has something to do with the changes to the communities and the conversion to Christianity brought by the new colonial order. A recent monograph by Hanks (2010) details the dramatic impact of the new landscape and practices on the indigenous discourse. The map in the earliest section of the Xiu Papers presents a landscape of the churches, symbolizing towns and the surrounding lands bounded by crosses (Quezada and Okoshi Harada 2001:53).

Nevertheless, the books of Chilam Balam contain some interesting allusions to "caves" in the Hieroglyphic Mayan sense of the word. The aforementioned passage in Chilam Balam of Chumayel, on building countless pyramids from the edge of the sea to the bottom of the land (CHU 16), adds that the mounds and *ch'e'enil* were given names as if *ch'e'enil* designated something pertaining to the pyramids. Another revealing passage is the description of the church in Merida in Chilam Balam of Chumayel (CHU 67:22–23). The church acquires some attributes of a cave including "the mountain house" and the "darkness house" (in original orthography): " . . . *iglesia mayor u kakal na u uitzil na akab na: u uil u: Dios yumbil Dios . . .* "

The K'iche' Popol Vuh provides an important analogy to the Hieroglyphic Mayan *ch'e'n*. One of the narrative's terms for the city is *siwan tinamit* "canyon-citadel" (Christenson 2004:231, 237–242). *Siwan tinamit* is the built area that is whitewashed, plastered, and features the homes of lords and gods (Christenson 2004:237). Although the narrative contains no elaboration of the significance of *siwan*, the "canyons" appear in two distinct contexts in the Popol Vuh. First, *siwan* is one of the landscape features created in the making of the world, along with rocks and hollows, meadows and forests (Christenson 2004:16). *Siwan* can be found in the description of the wilderness (Christenson 2004:251). But there are also the "hidden canyons" in the forests and the mountains where the forefathers of the K'iche' hide their gods before dawn (Christenson 2004:183–184). The word *siwan*, therefore, acquires a new meaning as a place where the gods are kept, the shrines in the wilderness where the gods are comforted in "only bromeliads, only in hanging moss" (Christenson 2004:185). The term also evokes the place of origin, the legendary Tulan named "seven caves, seven canyons" (*wuqub pek wuqub siwan*) in the narrative (Christenson 2004:168, 170).

The significance of this analogy is not as much in the fact that caves and mountain shrines played an important role in K'iche' religion, nor in the association of shrines with caves and mountains in the wilderness, but in the pattern of extending the notion of such holy grounds to encompass the entire city, the houses of gods and lords. In this respect, the concepts of *siwan* and *ch'e'n* are remarkably similar. They overlap in terms of literal meaning, because *ch'e'n* is also "canyon." The notion of *ch'e'n* as a metaphor for sacred locations is even more inclusive than *siwan* because there is no need to couple it with another term like *tinamit*.

Applying this understanding of the term *ch'e'n* to the couplet *kab ch'e'n*, we get something like "the city (caves/temples/holy grounds) and the land/territory." Returning to the specific examples of *kab ch'e'n* in the inscriptions, it is remarkable that with one exception, all are possessed. In some cases, as the inscription on Bonampak Sculptured Stone 1 (Figure 22a), the possessor is the place name itself ("the land and the *ch'e'n* of *Usiij Witz*"), but *kab ch'e'n* is usually owned either by the king or the gods. "This is your land, your *ch'e'n*," exclaims Copan ruler *K'al Tuun Hix*, addressing his gods and ancestors on the Copan Papagayo Step (Figure 22b). The exception to this pattern is the negative statement on the Copan Hieroglyphic Stairway (Figure 22c) that somewhat proves the rule: the aftermath of the defeat is described as "no altars, no mounds, no *kab ch'e'n*" (Stuart 2005a). Therefore, if *kab ch'e'n*—the holy grounds and the land, the polity—exists, then it always belongs to somebody.

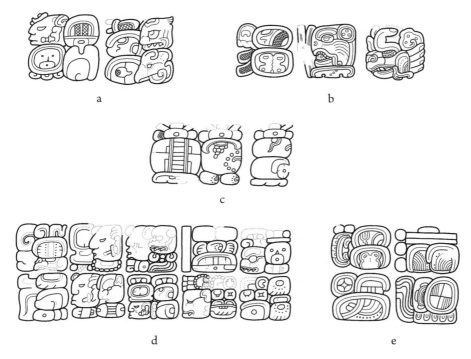

Figure 22 *Kab ch'e'n* in Classic Maya inscriptions: a) detail of Sculptured Stone 1 (C2–D2), Bonampak (after drawing by Alexander Safronov); b) detail of the Papagayo Step, Copan (after Schele 1989:fig. 3a); c) detail of Block 568, Hieroglyphic Stairway 1, Copan (after 3D scan by the author); d) detail of Lintel 56 (H1–L2), Yaxchilan (after Graham 1979:121); and e) detail of Stela 49, Copan (after Schele 1989:fig. 19a).

In this respect, the dedicatory passages on Yaxchilan Lintels 26 and 56 (Graham 1979:121; Graham and Von Euw 1977:58) provide an interesting insight into this ownership idea. The buildings where the lintels are located belong to the queens, and so each inscription begins with a reference to the dedication of a named "home" (*otoot*) of a queen. But the texts on the lintels continue by stating that "it is the *kab* of, the *ch'e'n* of" the king (Figure 22d), thus clarifying that the ownership of the buildings should be understood within a broader context of the king's authority over the city and the lands. The narrative dealing with the death of the Quirigua ruler *K'ahk' Tiliw Chan Yopaat* (QRG Zoomorph G) elaborates on this theme by providing a long (and unfortunately eroded and largely illegible) list of numbered objects and/or people who are all "the *kab*, the *ch'e'n* of T756d-**ya** lord" (Schele and Looper 1996:150). Another list of objects summarized with "my land, my *ch'e'n*" appears in the text on the carved Mundo Perdido vase, where it probably refers to items in the deity's possession (Houston and Stuart 1999:II-20) discussed above (Figure 12).

The aftermath of war can be described as the "downfall" of the *kab* and *ch'e'n* of the enemy, as in the inscription on Tonina Monument 83 (Figure 21e). Kings may "settle" in the *kab* and *ch'e'n*, as in the aforementioned Bonampak text (Figure 22a). Period-ending rituals bring order to the *kab* and *ch'e'n* of gods, as in the passage on Copan Stela 49: "the *kab*, the *ch'e'n* of the three by eleven bak'tun lord(s), I put it in order" (Figure 22e).[19] Nevertheless, most contexts dealing with some kind of interaction between the protagonists and the landscape do not use this couplet but mention only *ch'e'n*. This distinction is possibly due to the fact that most events mentioned in the inscriptions take place at, or at least directly affect, the *ch'e'n*, the holy grounds of Classic Maya polities. Just as *kab ch'e'n* is owned by kings and gods, it is the *ch'e'n*, the homes of kings and gods, which matter most in the Classic Maya political landscape.

IN HEAVENS, IN *CH'E'N*

The discussion of *kab ch'e'n* brings us to the second couplet involving *ch'e'n*—*chan ch'e'n*, literally "sky-cave." The syntactic contexts of this couplet are restricted. We find it after place names in "toponymic registers" (Stuart and Houston 1994:57–68) and after place names and verbs like "it happened" (*patlaj, uhti(iy)*), but only twice after a place name preceded by a transitive verb (CPN St 48, TAM HS 2:2; see Figure 21b).[20] *Chan ch'e'n* couplets almost never appear without a place name or a more general spatial term like "north." The relationship with the preceding place name is never clear. There are no examples of phrases like "*t-u-chan ch'e'n* TOPONYM." One may interpret nearly every occurrence of *chan ch'e'n* as independent stative sentences: "[it is in the] sky/heavens [in the] *ch'e'n*." In fact, the aforementioned Tamarindito inscription offers the only example when *chan ch'e'n* is possessed. Consequently, the meaning of the couplet is probably distinct from *kab ch'e'n* and *ch'e'n*. On the other hand, we find *chan ch'e'n* and *ch'e'n* in nonverbal predicates (like toponymic registers) and occasionally after intransitive verbs following place names with no distinct patterns in terms of syntax or meaning. For example, the toponymic registers on Yaxha Stelae 2 and 7 (Grube 2000b:figs. 197, 200a) mention *Yaxa' chan ch'e'n* and *Yaxa' ch'e'n*. The text on Tikal Stela 1 (Jones and Satterthwaite 1982:fig. 1) refers to *Yax Mutal* (one of the place names associated with the site) as *chan ch'e'n*, but the toponymic register in the scene on the same monument indexes *Yax Mutal* as *ch'e'n*. Therefore, the meanings of *ch'e'n* and *chan ch'e'n* overlap, but the range of contexts where *chan ch'e'n* can be used is more restricted.[21]

The range of themes associated with place names followed by *chan ch'e'n* is also rather narrow. The two most common contexts are period-ending rituals and the dedication of new buildings. Toponymic registers are the third most frequent context. Most of the scenes containing toponymic registers with *chan ch'e'n* depict rituals. There are also a couple of examples of accession ceremonies and *och ch'e'n* events linked to place names followed by *chan ch'e'n*. In other words, all of these contexts are rituals of some kind. The only two "arrivals" to a place name followed by *chan ch'e'n* come from the narrative on the Tikal Marker that deals with *Sihyaj K'ahk'*'s arrival (see above). This event is sometimes cast in religious terms (arrival of gods) and, therefore, the use of *chan ch'e'n* in this context may represent a deliberate choice made by the author of the text. It seems that *chan ch'e'n* as a landscape category relates to ritual landscape.

Although it is perhaps too early to propose a definite and final interpretation for *chan ch'e'n* beyond what it literally means—"the sky, the *ch'e'n*"—it is unlikely that this couplet means "world." As we will see below, the concept of the "world" is linked to the couplet *chan kab*, found alone and as part of a rare *chan kab ch'e'n* expression. The couplet *chan ch'e'n* seems to denote something else, possibly the part of the world where gods act and dwell.

There are several examples that demonstrate the link between *chan ch'e'n* and the world of the divine. The couplet appears in the 819-day cycle statements on Palenque monuments (Palace Tb, T Cross Pn) when gods reveal themselves in different cardinal directions, in *chan ch'e'n* (Figure 23a).[22] The passage on the altar associated with Stela 13 on the eastern edge of Copan (Figure 23b) states that "the food for *Huk Chapaht Tz'ikiin K'inich Ajaw* (solar deity) [in] the east, [in] *chan ch'e'n*, is prepared."[23] Evidence of food preparation (fragments of *manos* and *metates*) was recently found near the altar (William Fash, personal communication 2007).

The appeasement of gods in the narratives at Copan also involves a rare *chan kab ch'e'n* collocation that probably sheds further light on the significance of the more common *chan ch'e'n* couplet. According to the passage on Copan Stela B (Figure 23c), celestial gods and terrestrial gods were *mih-ohl* on the fifteenth k'atun anniversary in AD 731 when the monument was dedicated.[24] The inscription on Copan Altar S (Figure 23d) refers to the same event with a prophetic statement, "[it is] the *mih* of the *ohl* of *chan kab ch'e'n* of five k'atuns," where "five k'atuns" are the amount of k'atuns (twenty-year periods) remaining until the future bak'tun (four-hundred-year period) completion event in AD 830.[25]

The term *ohl* defines one's nonmaterial heart responsible for emotions (Barrera Vásquez et al. 1995:603–604) and appears in other Classic Maya narratives, such as the main text from the sanctuary of the Temple of the Inscriptions, where the king appeases the "heart(s)" (*ohl*) of his divine patrons (Lacadena García-Gallo 2009:44, fig. 47). The common translation of *mih* as "zero" does not seem to fit these contexts. Several years ago, Hull (2002) proposed that *mih* with "hearts" in Copan inscriptions could be related to the root **mij-* in Ch'orti' that may be found reduplicated in verbs like *mijmijres* "to enliven, to make more active, to make content" (Hull 2005:83) and *mijmijran* "to grow" (Pérez Martínez and Quizar 1996:142). Hull's hypothesis is strengthened by the fact that the same root is present in Tzeltal verbs *mihij* "to abound" and *mihijtes* "to increase something" (Ara 1986 [1571]:334).[26] Further support comes from the inscription on Blocks 378 and 379 of the Copan Hieroglyphic Stairway (Figure 23e), which contains the full spelling of the *mih* verb: **mi-ha-ja yo-OHL 1 pi/PIK K'UH** for *mihaj yohl juun pik k'uh*, "the heart(s) of eight thousand gods are made content."

If the inscription on Stela B praises the contentment of gods' hearts, then the passage on Altar S takes it a step further by evoking the totality of space and time. This metonymic connection between the divine and the fabric of space-time is evident in the second inscription that mentions *chan kab ch'e'n*—the narrative on Tikal Stela 31 (Figure 23f): "eight thousand celestial gods, terrestrial gods half-diminished; it happened in *Kukuul*, in the sky, in the earth, in the *ch'e'n*."[27] As pointed out by Stuart (2011a:273–274, 2011b), the context of the phrase (and of a similar statement earlier in the narrative) is a k'atun midstation—its "half-diminishing"—so the passage clearly implies that gods and sacred time are one. Just as in the case of the Copan texts, evoking this concept necessitates the use of the extended *chan kab ch'e'n* phrase. The appropriate translation of *chan kab ch'e'n* in these

a

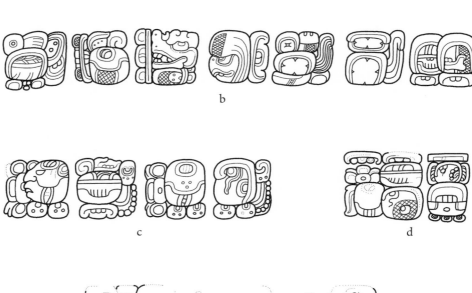

b

c   d

e

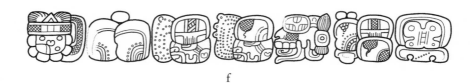

f

Figure 23 *Chan ch'e'n* in Classic Maya inscriptions: a) detail of a tablet (A14–B15), Temple of the Cross, Palenque (after Robertson 1991:fig. 9); b) detail of the altar of Stela 13, Copan (after drawing by Linda Schele); c) detail of Stela B, Copan (after photograph by the author); d) detail of Altar S (F1–G1), Copan (after photograph by the author); e) detail of Blocks 378 and 379, Hieroglyphic Stairway, Copan (after 3D scan by the author); and f) detail of Stela 31 (F24–F27), Tikal (after Jones and Satterthwaite 1982:fig. 52).

a

b

c

Figure 24 *Yax chan ch'e'n* in Yaxha imagery: a) detail of Stela 10 (after drawing by Ian Graham); b) detail of Stela 6 (after drawing by Ian Graham); and c) detail of Stela 13 (after photograph by the author).

contexts would be "the world and the *ch'e'n*," where *ch'e'n* corresponds to the holy grounds of the city, not unlike *Urbi et Orbi*.

Another significant example of *chan ch'e'n* related to period-ending events and supernatural locations comes from three monuments at Yaxha (St 6, 10, 13). The ritual circumstances surrounding the erection of the Early Classic Stelae 6 and 10 are unclear, but the Late Classic Stela 13 commemorates the *"tzih pik"* anniversaries of the third year of the k'atun. The toponymic registers on all three monuments depict a saurian creature with a wide-open mouth floating in the oceanic environment marked by anemones (Figure 24), somewhat similar to saurian creatures on top of mountains surrounded by the ocean on the Balamkú stucco frieze (Baudez 1996). The scene above the toponymic register takes place right above or within the mouth of the creature named "ix.tzutz.nik." The location of the events is labeled in the captions as . . . *te' nal yax chan ch'e'n* (" . . . tree corn [place],

a

b

Figure 25 Celestial ancestors: a) detail of Stela 45, Naranjo (after photographs by the author); and b) detail of Stela 1, Yaxchilan (after drawing by Ian Graham).

the green-blue *chan ch'e'n*"). This place name may reference the blue-green center of the world, the place of the world tree—an excellent location for the calendar-related world renewal ceremonies. Once again, the couplet *chan ch'e'n* denotes a kind of sacred space, possibly the blue-green world center.

The sky plays a prominent role in the representations of the divine and the unseen in Classic Maya imagery. Gods and ancestors are often depicted floating above the protagonists, sometimes in the space indexed by the sky band/frame. The examples include the figures of constellations, deities, and ancestors looking down from the upper registers of the scenes on the Bonampak murals, floating above the kings on Early Classic stelae (TIK St 31, NAR St 43, 45; Figure 25a), and sitting upon sky frames and surrounded by sun and moon cartouches on Late Classic monuments (YAX St 1, 3, 4, 6, 8, 10, 11; Figure 25b). The mountains and caves, as has been discussed above, are also the dwellings of gods and ancestors. The couplet *chan ch'e'n* sums up the two sacred domains and is used in the narratives to highlight the moments when those of *chan* and *ch'e'n* are directly involved in the affairs of those of *kab* and *ch'e'n* and vice versa, when the landscape of the living becomes fused with the landscape of the ancestors and gods. One may compare this metaphor of the divine and the unseen with the Popol Vuh story about the "womb of the sky, womb of the earth" *upam kaj upam ulew*, which were once visible to the four ancestors and then hidden from view by the gods, who decided that only a bit of the earth surface within one's eyesight would be enough (Christenson 2004:156–160).

KAB AS A LANDSCAPE CATEGORY IN CLASSIC MAYA INSCRIPTIONS

In contrast to *ch'e'n*, the other widespread place category in Classic Maya inscriptions—*kab*—is somewhat less enigmatic. *Kab* frequently appears in the colonial Yukatek and Chontal documents, which constitute our main analogy and source of comparative data for understanding Classic narratives. The Chilam Balam examples discussed above emphasize the general meaning of "land" or "earth" versus the more specific "territory," or even the sections of the city (see above). Calepino Maya de Motul (Ciudad Real 1995) singles out three main translations of the word *kab* as "world," "region," and "town" (CMM:59r), but different entries scattered across the dictionary provide contexts in which the three meanings are given more nuanced interpretations. Besides the "world" connotations, the semantic domain of *kab* may emphasize place.[28] It can also mean "land" in general, which can be subclassified.[29] Finally, *kab* means "land" in the sense of one's territory or community.[30] These translations of the term *kab* hold for the Acalan Chontal Maldonado-Paxbolon Papers (Smailus 1975), where the terms *kab* and *kabil* are attested alone and as a couplet (see above).

Interestingly enough, *kab* does not seem to be the word of choice to accompany place names in early Yukatek texts. When it does, it is usually part of couplets like *kab ch'e'en* (*cabal chen mani* [TIZ 19:22]) or complex terms like *kuch kabal* (*v cuch cabal Mani, Mutul, ettz.: la prouinçia o comarca de Mani, Mutul, ettz.* [CMM: 86r]). The preferred category is *kaaj*. This pattern is interesting given that the Spanish translation of the terms *kab* and *kaaj* as "town" (*pueblo*) is often identical and that the two terms occur in so many expressions with similar or overlapping meaning.

Some kinds of postcontact discourse exclude the term *kab* altogether. For instance, the earliest of the so-called Xiu Papers, *Memoria de la distribución de los montes* (Quezada and Okoshi Harada 2001:55–65), makes no reference to *kab* despite the fact that the entire document is about the distribution of lands. But this seems less peculiar after a closer look at the document: it deals with dividing the "wilderness" (*k'a'ax*) and setting the boundaries of the agricultural lands (*luum*) performed by the officials who gather in the town (*kaaj*). The term *kab* does not fit the subject matter: *Memoria de la distribución de los montes* is about lands for cultivation, not political territories. Other Yukatek texts of the same genre—"notarial documents" as defined by Hanks (2010:283–309)—including the Códice Nakuk Pech, Yaxkukul surveys, and the titles of Ebtún reveal a similar preference for *luum* at the expense of *kab*. Terms like *aj-luum-kab* ("resident who owns a house or a piece of land in the town" [CMM:22r]) also imply that *kab* is a more general category than *luum*.

The Chontal Maldonado-Paxbolon Papers make greater use of the term *kab*. This is to be expected given the document's greater emphasis on the political landscape. Yet the overall pattern of citations is similar to Yukatek texts. The named "towns" are always *kaaj*. The term *kab* is employed to denote a territory belonging to a *kaaj*, as in *uchuki kabob tachakk'am* "he took the lands of Tachackam" (Smailus 1975:32). It may also designate a territory of an ethnic group, as in *hainix uchuki ukab kiach masatekat* "as for him, he took the land of the *Cehache Mazatecat*" (Smailus 1975:30). It appears in the couplet *kabil kab* discussed above and in expressions like *upam kab*, as in *tupan kab kakchutte* "in the head of the land of *Cacchutte*" (Smailus 1975:47). Finally, the term *kab* is preferred when one's dominion over the land is emphasized, as in *umotbel ubaob kablel ajawlel baob* "gathered the lords of the lands (lit. 'lands [of] rulership heads')" (Smailus 1975:48) or as in *taliketix to takkab takkotot takkahil* "you would come first to (from?) our land, our home, our city" (Smailus 1975:55). The last passage is usually interpreted as an invitation to come to the city of *Itzamk'anak* before embarking on a campaign, but it may well be an invitation to leave from *Itzamk'anak* for the campaign.

The pattern in the usage of the term *kab* in the hieroglyphic inscriptions is very similar. Our first window into the potential meanings of *kab* is the place names themselves. Toponyms like *Sak Kab* ("white *kab*") (Figure 26a) and *Ihk' Kab* ("black *kab*") (Figure 26b) likely emphasize the meaning "earth" or even "soil" without any spatial significance. The "earth-biting house" *Kaatz Kab Naah* (Figure 26c) and "hot earth" *K'ihn(i) chil Kab* (Figure 26d) place names are likely in the same group. On the other hand, *kab* with numbers in place names *Bolon Kab* "nine lands" (Figure 26e), *Jo' Kab* "five lands" (Figure 5g), *Jo Pet Kab* "five bounded lands (provinces)" (Figure 26f), *Wak Kab Nal* "six land (corn) place" (Figure 26g), *Huk Kab* "seven lands" (Figure 26h), place names with locatives like *Ti' Kab* "edge of the land" (Figure 26i), and descriptive toponyms like *Kot Kab* "wall land" (Figure 26j) highlight the second possible translation closer to "land" and "territory."

The term *kab* never follows place names in hieroglyphic inscriptions, although some examples such as *K'ihnchil Kab* are ambiguous because they appear with and without *kab*. Another potential exception to the pattern is the passage *uhtiiy kab kaaj* "it happened in the land *kaaj*" in the text on Quirigua Stela C (Figure 26k), if one assumes that *kaaj* is a place name.[31] But the combination of *kab* and *kaaj* may be an otherwise unattested couplet analogous in meaning to *kab* and *kaaj* in the colonial-period sources. Since the context is unique, there is no way to tell which option is the best. *Kab* appears in couplets with *ch'e'n* possessed by people, gods, ancestors, and place names, suggesting that the term *kab* refers to something associated with and yet distinct from spatial entities denoted by toponyms. The best analogy would be *kab* meaning "territory" in the sense of one's political domain, as in the colonial narratives discussed above.

A few interesting examples from the Classic inscriptions seem to corroborate this hypothesis. The narrative on Naranjo Stela 22 mentions the accession of the *Sa'aal* lord *K'ahk' Tiliw Chan Chahk*. The passage is followed by the account of the military campaign against the neighbors of Naranjo, *K'ihnchil Kab*, *Tubal*, and *Bital*, presumably aimed at asserting *K'ahk' Tiliw Chan Chahk*'s authority over these places. The narrative is concluded

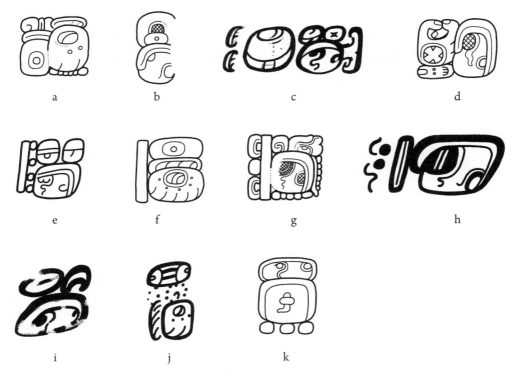

Figure 26 *Kab* in place names: a) detail of Stela 15, Nim Li Punit (after Wanyerka 2004:fig. 29); b) detail of Stela 3, Piedras Negras (after Stuart and Graham 2003:26); c) detail of a vessel (K1004); d) detail of Stela 22 (E14), Naranjo (after Graham 1975:56); e) detail of a vessel (K5454); f) detail of a cartouche (Block 3), East Court, Palace, Palenque (after Robertson 1985:fig. 333); g) detail of Lintel 2 (A9), Temple 4, Tikal (after Jones and Satterthwaite 1982: fig. 73); h) detail of a vessel (MT 16), Tikal (after Culbert 1993:fig. 42c); i) detail of Caption 37, Room 1, Structure 1, Bonampak (after drawing by John Montgomery); j) detail of Pendant 14B, Comalcalco (after drawing by Marc Zender); and k) detail of Stela C (A11), Quirigua (after Looper 2003:fig. 5.1).

with the phrase *nitz'ak kab* "[it is] my land-ordering" (Figure 27a).[32] The term *kab* "land" in this context likely designates *K'ahk' Tiliw Chan Chahk*'s political domain that is restored— literally put in order or brought back together under the control of his dynasty through the successful campaign.

The second important example comes from the inscription on Altar 3 at Altar de los Reyes in Campeche, Mexico. As pointed out by Grube (2008:181–183; Šprajc and Grube 2003), the main inscription on the sides of the altar mentions thirteen dynasties associated with different places. The caption on the top of the altar reads *k'uh[ul] kab huxlahuun [tzu]k* "holy land[s] thirteen partitions" (Figure 27b). The reference to "lands" and numbered "partitions" in the context of naming the same number of dynasties suggests that the term *k'uhul kab* "holy land[s]" designates the domains of every *k'uhul ajaw* "holy lord" mentioned on the same monument (see Chapter 5).

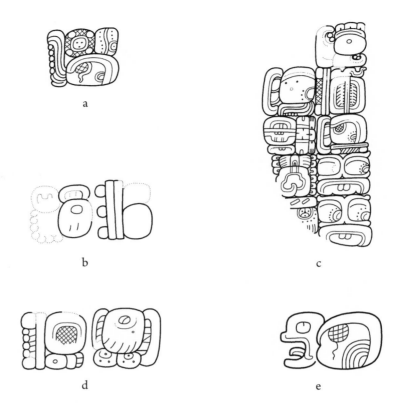

Figure 27 *Kab* as "land": a) detail of Stela 22 (E19), Naranjo (after Graham 1975:56); b) detail of Altar 3 (pA1–pB1), Altar de los Reyes (after Grube 2008:fig. 8.6); c) detail of Altar 2 (B2–B6), Naranjo (after Skidmore 2007:fig. 1); d) detail of Panel 7, Piedras Negras (after photograph in CMHI archive); and e) detail of an Early Classic mirror back (Jade Museum, Disk 6528; after drawing by Christian M. Prager).

Some examples of *kab* indicating land or territory in the context of personal names and titles are more problematic but fit the overall picture. The dedicatory text on Altar 2 at Naranjo refers to the king or to the new road as *kaba'* or *kabaj* of certain gods (Figure 27c)—something or someone pertaining to the land of the local deities.[33] The title of the *Hix Witz* lord mentioned on Piedras Negras Panel 7 is *Aj Paat Kabal Naah* "man of the back land house" (Figure 27d). It features the adjectival form *kabal*. The text on the unprovenanced mirror (Grube and Martin 2001a:II-40) mentions its owner, the *Pa' Chan* lord, whose father is *aj-kab* "man of the land" (Figure 27e).[34] The protagonist of the dedicatory inscription on the unprovenanced Late Classic vessel (Figure 26e) carries the titles of "*Bolon Kab*" lord—either referring to the place of *Bolon Kab* or praising the owner as the one who rules over "nine/many lands."

The second meaning of the term *kab*—"earth" in general—is also well documented in the Classic inscriptions. One set of contexts with this meaning is expressions like *pas kab* "earth opening," linked to tomb reentering, and *tal kab*, also known as "earth touching" and

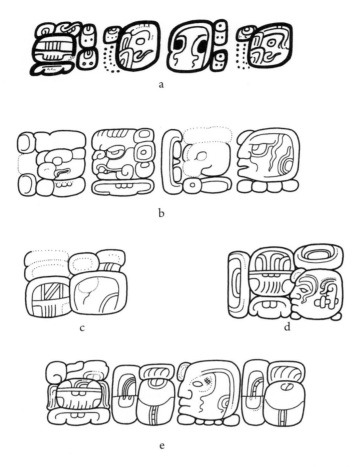

Figure 28 *Kab* and *chan* couplets as "world": a) detail of a Late Classic vessel (K7750);
b) detail of Stela J (C10–D11), Quirigua (after Looper 2003:fig. 3.29); c) detail of Stela 31
(A22), Tikal (after Jones and Satterthwaite 1982:fig. 52); d) detail of Stela A (G7–H7),
Copan (after drawing by Barbara Fash); and e) detail of the Center Tablet (B6–A8),
Temple of the Inscriptions, Palenque (after Robertson 1983:fig. 96).

likely referring to one's birth (Stuart 2005b). The most important set of examples with *kab*
as "earth" are couplets when *kab* "earth" and *chan* "sky" are paired to indicate the totality
of places, the whole world, and whatever pertains to it. One **TZ'AK** allograph illustrating different complementary pairs is a combination of **CHAN** and **KAB** symbols (Stuart
2003:fig. 1c).

We find this kind of pairing in the lists of gods where eight thousand "celestial" and
"terrestrial" gods (*chanal k'uh kabal k'uh*) (see Figures 23c, 23f, and 28a) are mentioned.
The royal titles like "the pole/pillar of the sky, the pole/pillar of the earth" (*uyookte'*
chan uyookte' kab) (see Figure 28b) and "the earth lord, the sky lord" (*chan kab ajaw*)
(see Figure 28c) likely reflect the conceptualization of the world as the earth and the sky.

The reference to the "shining/jade sky, shining/jade earth" (*?lem chan ?lem kab*) (see Figure 28d) in the context of the period-ending rituals probably highlights the all-encompassing nature of the ceremony in which the whole world is ritually renewed. "Celestial jewels and terrestrial jewels" (*chanal ikaatz kabal ikaatz*) (see Figure 28e)[35]—part of the passage that evokes abundance and good governance in k'atun prophecies at Palenque (Lacadena García-Gallo 2007:207–208, 218; Stuart 2006a:136–137, fig. 138)—are another important example. The bundles of jewels at the celestial court of God D may be labeled as *chanal ikaatz* (Boot 2008:15, fig. 11a). The *ikaatz* bundle of God L's underworld court (as in the scene on K7750) is probably its terrestrial counterpart.

The concept *chan kab* as world may also be found in colonial texts, with the K'iche' couplet *kaj ulew* in the Popol Vuh (Christenson 2004) being the closest analogy. We also find the combination of **KAB** and **CHAN** in the scaffold accession scenes (PNG St 6, 11, 25): the ruler sits on top of the celestial alligator, within the sky band frame, but the scaffold underneath is marked with **KAB** signs as if the whole construction were a re-creation of the cosmos with the king at the center.

PICTURING A PLACE

A discussion of places in Classic Maya landscapes is incomplete without addressing the issue of pictorial conventions. Researchers have already highlighted the close relationship between text and iconography in Classic Maya representations of place. Stuart and Houston (1994:57–68) discovered that place names often appeared in the lower register of scenes depicted on monuments, beneath the feet of the protagonists, and traced the convention of such toponymic registers back to the Preclassic monuments at Takalik Abaj and Izapa. Stuart (n.d.) based the "cave" decipherment on the association between captions with **CH'E'N** and representations of individuals inside mountains. Stuart and Houston (1994:57, 69, 72) noted that some conventions were more general. Icons like sky, earth, and water "bands" were identified some time ago (Schele and Miller 1986:45–47, figs. 22–28). Such conventionalized icons imply that a kind of classification of landscape features was at work.

One of these generic toponymic registers is a horizontal band with **KAB** signs (Figure 29a), as in the case of the Moral-Reforma (Balancan) Stela 4 (Stuart and Houston 1994:fig. 68). It is likely not meant to be read phonetically, as there is no associated place name or reference to *kab* in the inscription on the monument. The likely interpretation is that such a band simply indexes the location as something taking place on the surface of the earth. Another clearly nonglyphic example is the **KAB**-marked earth surface, out of which the ancestors sprout as fruit trees on the Temple of the Inscriptions sarcophagus at Palenque (Robertson 1983:65–73, figs. 174–176). Similar earth bands can be found on Calakmul Stelae 62 and 66 and Dos Pilas Stelae 14 and 15 (Houston 1993:figs. 3-24, 3-25).

The last two earth bands are particularly interesting. The earth band on Stela 14 features a hieroglyphic text intermingled with **KAB** signs that is unrelated to the location of the event, indicating once again that the earth band is part of the imagery and can be used opportunistically as an extra blank space for inscriptions. The earth band on Stela 15 (Figure 29b)

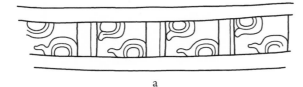

a

b

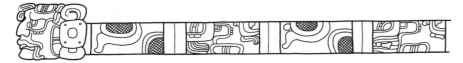

c

Figure 29 Earth bands: a) detail of Stela 4, Moral-Balancan (after Stuart and Houston 1994:fig. 68); b) detail of Stela 15, Dos Pilas (after Stuart and Houston 1994:fig. 101); and c) detail of a tablet, Temple of the Sun, Palenque (after Robertson 1991:fig. 95).

also contains a nontoponymic hieroglyphic inscription. The band also separates the upper register of the scene with the dancing lord and the lower register with the place name **K'IN-HA'-NAL**, "the hot water place" toponym mentioned previously. The iconographic classification of the location as an earthly domain apparently highlights the relational nature of the place name. Even though the toponym evokes a body of water (a spring?), the place is a firm earthly surface on which the king stands.

A possible version of the earth band also appears in the scene on the main tablet in the sanctuary of the Temple of the Sun at Palenque (Robertson 1991:fig. 95). This band is supplied with the sun god's head at each end and T24 (?**LEM**) "celt" signs interchanging with "earth" signs (Figure 29c). The intention might be to provide a spelling for the place name. The likelier explanation is that the inclusion of T24 only emphasizes the shiny, precious, and perhaps even hot nature of the earth surface. The "celt" sign may appear alone in toponymic registers, possibly indicating a shiny or precious surface of its own kind, maybe even something like a plaster floor. El Chal Stela 4 (Morales 1993:fig. 4) is a good example of a celt-only toponymic register. But it may also be a reference to a specific "jade hearth" place identified by Taube (1998:442–446, figs. 448–449), or a place where the maize god's tree sprouts out of a jade seed.

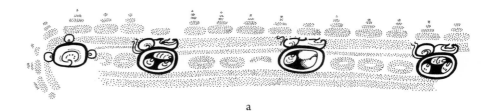

a

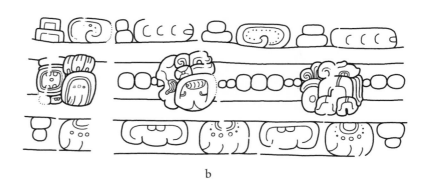

b

Figure 30 Water bands: a) detail of the "Cosmic plate" (after photograph by the author); and b) detail of a tablet, Temple 14, Palenque (after Robertson 1991:fig. 176).

Another widespread convention in the representation of places is the so-called water band. This motif was identified and discussed in some detail by Schele (1988:300–302, fig. 310.305), although the most detailed description (including its evolution through time and its possible variations) was offered by Hellmuth (1987a:88–199, figs. 162–262, 310–420, 1987b:99–159, figs. 136–199). The water band motif cannot even be reduced to a single phonetic reading. It can be linked to iconographic origins of several water-related signs including **HA', HA'AL, NAHB**, and **PALAW**, as well as syllabic **na** and **le**. As a toponymic register, the water band can appear alone or in combination with captions indicating particular watery locations. The "Cosmic plate" water band (Figure 30a) is marked as [*Ihk'*] *Nahb Nal* and is associated with two other place names (Schele and Miller 1986:310–311, pl. 122; Stuart and Houston 1994:72–74). The water band on the panel from Temple 14 at Palenque (Figure 30b) is labeled *Jo' Nikte' ?Akan Ti' K'ahk' Nahb Sak* T579 *Nal* (Schele 1988:299–308, fig. 210.294; Schele and Miller 1986:272–273, fig. VII.272; Stuart and Houston 1994:69–70). The water band in the toponymic register on the main tablet of the Temple of the Foliated Cross sanctuary (Robertson 1991:fig. 153) engulfs the mountain labeled *Yax ?Han Witz Nal* and the shell tagged as *K'an* T579 *Ha' Matwiil* (Stuart 2006b:145). The anemone–water lily version of the water band (Hellmuth 1987b:151–159, figs. 189–199) accompanies the depiction of the saurian deity and the toponymic caption ... *Te' Nal* on Yaxha Stelae 6, 10, and 13 (Figure 24, see above). Therefore, as in the case of the earth band, the motif functions as a way to assign specific place names to a broader category of watery locations.

The third general icon attested across the entire corpus of Classic Maya imagery is a sky band (Figure 25b). As in the case of the water band, the iconography of the motif is complex and not reducible to a single sign (Carlson 1982, 1988; Carlson and Landis 1985; Stuart 2005b:70–75). It represents the body of the celestial caiman or the "starry-deer-alligator," with celestial symbols on its back including the sign **CHAN** for *chan* "sky." Although there are plenty of sky bands in toponymic registers, few can be associated with named locations. One may even suggest that the place remains rather unspecified, much like the *ta ?lem chan* "in the resplendent (jade/shining) sky" reference in the inscription from the tablet in Temple XIX at Palenque (Stuart 2005b:66–67). *Wak Chan* (*Wak Chan Nal*) seems to be one of the more specific celestial places mentioned in a number of texts. The Temple of

a

b

c

Figure 31 Mountains and mountain bands: a) detail of a Late Classic vessel (K688); b) detail of Stela 1, Bonampak (after Miller 1986:fig. 19); and c) front view of the mask, Structure B, Holmul (after 3D scan by the author and Estrada Belli 2011:figs. 5.11–15.13).

the Cross at Palenque represents a version or an aspect of that location named *Wak Chan* T170 (Stuart 2006b:109–112). Nevertheless, the toponymic register in the scene on the main tablet of the sanctuary (Robertson 1991:fig. 9) shows a generic sky band that apparently functions as a classifier in relation to a specific place, and not as an index of the sky as a whole. *Wak Chan (Nal)* as a location of God D's court in the scene on a Late Classic vessel (Boot 2008) is represented with a generic sky band with a **6-CHAN** glyph.

Representations of mountains may be added to the list of bandlike spatial classifiers in the Classic Maya iconography. Although rare, they function in the same way as sky, earth, and water bands. For example, the scene depicted on one Late Classic vessel in the collections of the Museum of Fine Arts, Boston (K688), takes place, according to the inscription, on the "*Jo' Chan Naah* mountain in the north" (*uhtiiy jo' chan naah witz xaman*). The scene features a horizontal band of **WITZ** signs (Figure 31a). The mountain band apparently indexes the location as somewhere upon a mountain, whereas the inscription provides the information about a specific place. A similar mountain band is attested in the scene on Piedras Negras Stela 5 (Stuart and Graham 2003:32–33) although it may also be part of the frame format. Taube identifies a number of highly stylized mountain bands in sculpture and on pottery (Taube 2004b:fig. 13.16). A certain overlap between mountains and earth bands in the concept of the terrestrial realm is evidenced in the design of the altar of Stela M at Copan (Maudslay 1889–1902:pl. 75), which depicts an *Itzam Witz Ahiin* creature as a potential variant of the more common *Itzam Kab Ahiin* personification of the earth surface.

Some nonband images of mountains in the scenes on painted pottery also function as general landscape indexes. The mountains in scenes on ceramic vessels illustrating the motif of hero twins shooting down the Principal Bird Deity (K1226, K4546) likely indicate that the action happens somewhere in the wilderness. The same interpretation holds for the mountains in the painted scenes showing the deer god's wife carried away on the back of the deer (e.g., K1559; see Braakhuis 2001).

Many mountains depicted in toponymic registers of Classic Maya monuments represent specific locations in addition to more general concepts of place. For instance, a conflation of **USIIJ** and **WITZ** on Bonampak Stela 1 (Miller 1986:fig. 19)—the spelling of the *Usiij Witz* ("Vulture mountain") name of Bonampak (Stuart 2008)—doubles as a mountain with the emerging maize god and T24 "celt" (**?LEM**) signs (Figure 31b). A similar mountain is depicted on Tikal Temple 4 Lintel 3 (Jones and Satterthwaite 1982:fig. 74). Therefore, the calligraphic performance of a toponym's spelling seems to deliberately evoke the "Resplendent Mountain" place in association with *Usiij Witz*. It could also refer to the *Yax Han* mountain mentioned at Palenque, as Schele (1998:492–494, fig. 499) once suggested. **3-WITZ** spellings in toponymic registers of Caracol Stelae 3–6 (Beetz and Satterthwaite 1981:figs. 4–7) add emerging maize plants and solar deities to full-figure **WITZ** glyphs (see Figure 39e), as if the intention of the carvers was to invest these representations with references to some underlying ideas about the essence of a place.

The second convention of indexing place names is frames. The difference between frames and bands is not about the location itself but about the position with respect to the location—upon versus within. For instance, the water band on the outer rim of the aforementioned "Cosmic plate" functions as a water band frame, effectively indexing the scene

Figure 32 A mountain place with a cave: detail of a wall painting, Tomb 1 at Río Azul (after Adams 1999:pl. 3).

inside the plate as something that takes place in a watery environment. The same convention is apparent in the case of sky band frames on pottery vessels (Carlson 1988) or in the case of the accession scenes on Piedras Negras Stelae 6, 11, and 25 (Stuart and Graham 2003:36, 57), in which the king is depicted within the celestial frame.

The placement of a scene within a mountain or on the earth's surface introduces a new class of locations—caves. The caption to the scene inside the mountain frame depicted on one Late Classic vessel (Patterson 1992:70–73) is a straightforward *ta witz* "in the mountain." A passage on Tonina Monument 106 (Graham and Mathews 1999:135) similarly comments that the protagonist (depicted seated on the mountain) is "seated in the mountain of the fiery waterfall corn (place) mountain" (*chumlaj tuwitzil k'ahk' witz' nal witz*). As Stuart et al. have suggested (1999:64), the scenes within the mountain or earth frames represent the interiors of caves. In fact, some of these potential caves, such as one depicted on the wall of Tomb 1 at Río Azul (Adams 1999:pl. 3), are rendered as a **CH'E'N** sign in the mouth of the mountain (Figure 32).

Images of gods seated in mouthlike cave openings in mountains are common in Classic Maya art (K7750, K530, K2796; see Figure 12) and find parallels with actual statues of deities in caves (Graham 1997). These mountains are conceptualized as the dwellings of the gods and spirits, an association revealed through a combination of mountain and house features, as in the scenes on some vessels (K7750, K2796). The idea of cavelike mountain dwellings is also revealed in Classic Maya architecture, with royal palaces and temples built in the likeness of animate mountains with mouthlike entrances leading into the "caves" of the building interiors (Bassie-Sweet 1996:111–131, 215–219; Freidel et al. 1993:146–150, fig. 143:120; Schele 1998; Stuart 1997).

Figure 33 Painted landscape on Mural 6N, Structure 1, La Sufricaya (after Estrada Belli 2011:fig. 6.13).

The recently discovered facade of the Late Preclassic phase of Structure B of Group II at Holmul (Estrada Belli 2007:12–20, 2011:figs. 5.11–15.13) offers one of the earliest and the most revealing images of the *ch'e'n* mountain (Figure 31c). The masks decorating the southern side of the temple substructure depict a mountain spirit face with characteristic cleft eyebrows and a stylized mountain on its top. Unusually, the sides of the mountain face are emblazoned with bones and skulls. A Feathered Serpent, identifiable by its feathery green eyebrows, is exhaled from the mouth of the mountain, much like in the images on the San Bartolo murals (Saturno et al. 2005). Clinging to the back of the Feathered Serpent, a prototypical old god, *Mam*, emerges from the quatrefoil cave mouth of the mountain.

No other image combines in such a clear and powerful manner the idea of a mountain as a source of wind (and therefore, rain), of the place of caves, of the dead, and of the dwelling of ancestors. It is potentially significant that the later versions of Structure B served as a locale for multiple burials and likely functioned as an ancestral shrine (Merwin and Vaillant 1932:20–41).

There are almost no images of landscapes in Classic Maya art and architecture. A few significant exceptions to this pattern are confined to the Early Classic period and are related to narratives involving travels to and from the great city of Teotihuacan in Mexico. One of them is the mural in Structure 1 at La Sufricaya (Hurst 2009), which was commissioned no later than a year after *Sihyaj K'ahk'*'s arrival at Tikal in AD 378 (Estrada Belli et al. 2009). This mural (Figure 33) shows two places represented as templelike structures, connected by a road with a group of characters apparently meeting in the middle. The vertical arrangement of features on this maplike scene possibly evokes the west–east movement.[36] Similar murals adorned one of the earliest structures of the Copan royal court, although only small fragments of the original painted stucco surface have survived (Bell 2007:fig. 5.14). The choice of templelike structures as possible representations of places is significant, as it brings us to the centrality of *ch'e'n* as dwellings of gods, ancestors, and kings in Classic Maya political landscapes. No boundaries or other markings of lands or territories appear on these murals.

Place categories offer additional insights into the building blocks of the Classic Maya landscape. Available narratives largely employ two terms—*kab* ("land" or "earth") and *ch'e'n* ("cave" or "canyon")—as well as the phrases *kab ch'e'n* ("land and holy grounds/ city"), *chan ch'e'n* ("heavens and holy grounds/city"), and *chan kab ch'e'n* ("world and holy grounds/city"). The narrow range of spatial categories in Classic Maya inscriptions recalls some early colonial sources that deal exclusively with the political landscape.

The absence of terms like *luum* in relevant contexts in Classic Maya inscriptions has never been addressed by epigraphers. The most plausible explanation is that surviving ancient texts simply do not relate to agriculture or landholding. Were these issues of no concern to Classic Maya rulers? Were they reserved for other media and genres? While there is no definite answer to these questions, we need to be cautious in identifying certain themes in ancient texts and imagery based on the assumption that agriculture and related metaphors permeate these narratives.

The most frequently cited Classic Maya place names were associated with the *ch'e'n* category, suggesting that these were the names of the locales where gods and ancestors dwell in "caves" and "canyons"—the holy grounds or temples at the hearts of ancient Maya cities. Together, *kab* and *ch'e'n* constituted the totality of spaces of one's dominion. Classic Maya political landscape consisted of named *ch'e'n* and nameless *kab*, which belonged to their owners: living kings, their ancestors, and gods.

4 | PEOPLE FROM A PLACE

PEOPLE AND PLACES IN CLASSIC MAYA INSCRIPTIONS

CLASSIC MAYA NARRATIVES ARE FULL OF REFERENCES TO HISTORICAL and mythological characters identified by various titles that link them to certain places: places where they are from, places where they rule, and places of importance for their ancestors and gods. In essence, places constitute one the most widespread ways people are distinguished from one another in Classic Maya inscriptions.

Until recently, scholars largely centered on one group of titles linking people to places: the so-called emblem glyphs that combine place names with the Classic Maya word for lord, *ajaw*. The term "emblem glyph" dates to the discovery of this group of titles by Berlin (1958). Since then, the interpretation of emblem glyphs went back and forth between the hypothesis that they denoted certain royal families or dynasties and the hypothesis that they implied affiliation to or political control of certain locales (archaeological sites) by these families (Houston 1986; Marcus 1976; Mathews 1991; Mathews and Justeson 1984). It later became apparent that places names in some emblem glyphs were not the toponyms corresponding to the archaeological sites where the emblem glyph-carriers resided or to where they associated themselves by means of other titles (Houston 1993; Martin 2005; Palka 1996; Stuart and Houston 1994). It seemed as if place names in emblem glyphs represented a distinct class of spatial entities.

The dominant trend among Mayanists today is to interpret place names in emblem glyphs as polity names. One version of this hypothesis can be found in an article by Grube (2000a:553). He argues for "conceptual identity" between the Classic Maya capital city and the state, except for the exceptional cases caused by "specific historical reasons." Another version implies that place names in emblem glyphs denote polities as larger spatial entities (Martin 2005:11; Martin and Grube 2000:17–21). A less common interpretation is that emblem glyphs are names of dynasties or "royal houses" (Martin 2005:12), but it explains neither why these place names are chosen for such a purpose nor what the function of these place names in a broader political landscape could be.

There are at least three ways to investigate the significance of emblem glyphs and other titles connecting people to places in Classic Maya landscapes. One can explore spatial categories in Hieroglyphic Mayan and the notions of place based on the available written narratives and imagery, as in Chapter 3 of this monograph. Another approach is to see how place names in emblem glyphs and other titles correspond to locations in the physical landscape. Finally, it is worth considering how and in which contexts (historical circumstances and narratives) Classic Maya lords associated themselves with places in emblem glyphs and other titles.

PLACE-RELATED TITLES IN CLASSIC MAYA INSCRIPTIONS

Emblem glyphs are but one of many kinds of titles linking people to places. Emblem glyphs are often contrasted with "titles of origin" (Palka 1996; Stuart and Houston 1994). This rather misleading term denotes place names provided with an agentive prefix *aj-* (male/unmarked) and/or *ix-* (female/marked). The title of origin is, in fact, a title of association (the definition proposed in this monograph). A title of association can be derived not only from place names but from other referents. There are titles like *aj-baak* "he of captives" (somebody who took captives, a warrior), *aj-tz'ihb* "he of writing" (a scribe), or *aj-k'uhuun* "he of worship"/"he who guards" (a priest or a courtly official). Different kinds of associations between people and places may be expressed by means of a title with *aj-*: one's seat of rulership, one's place of birth, one's place of pilgrimage, one's dynastic homeland, and so on.

There is a potentially infinite range of titles that incorporate place names. Nevertheless, emblem glyphs are the most common place-related titles in Classic Maya inscriptions (Table 3). This should not come as a surprise given the political nature of available narratives. In other words, in most Classic Maya texts, if someone is related to a place, it is in the context of highlighting one's perceived lordly/royal status (emblem glyphs) or lack of it (titles of association). We can also think of titles of association as unmarked in contrast to marked associations—emblem glyphs and other titles specifying the nature of one's relation to a place. Instances of unusual place-related titles possibly reflect larger concepts of place and identity in the political landscape incorporated into broader ideological

Table 3 Place names in personal names/titles.

CONTEXT TYPE	COMMENTARY	FREQUENCY
[PLACE NAME]	DERIVATION/ASSOCIATED NOUNS OMITTED	149
[place name] *a'/ aj*	agentive formed with *–a'/–aj*	2
[place name] *ajaw*	followed by *ajaw*	1332
[place name] *winik*	followed by *winik*	26
[place name] *other*	followed by any other noun	82
aj- [place name]	agentive formed with *aj-*	165
ix [place name]	agentive formed with *ix-*	14

Figure 34 Place name—*winik* titles with maize god place names: a) detail of Block 3, Hieroglyphic Stairway 1, Tamarindito (after CMHI photograph); b) detail of a carved vessel (MT 140), Tikal (after Culbert 1993:fig. 108d); and c) detail of Stela 33 (B5–B6), Naranjo (after Graham 1978:87).

frameworks, which were common in the time and place when and where the texts in question were produced.

Combinations of place names with the word for person (*winik*) appear to be less common than titles of association. Consequently, being a person from a certain place implies some kind of special relationship. Toponyms followed by *winik* almost never appear in emblem glyphs or titles of association. Several toponyms in *winik* titles are place names associated with local maize gods (see Chapter 5): *Wak Hix Nal winik* (Figure 34a), *Wak Chan Nal winik* (Figure 34b), and *Wak Kab Nal winik* (Figure 34c).

Personal titles evoking *Wite' Naah*, a highly important place name associated with Teotihuacan imagery, fourth-century conquerors, and pilgrimages by some Early Classic kings (Fash et al. 2009; Stuart 2000), often take the form of *Wite' Naah ch'ajoom* ("*Wite' naah* he who censes") in the texts at Copan (Figure 35a), Yaxchilan (Ln 26), and Quirigua (St F, J). *Ch'ajoom* is a priestly title evoking offerings of copal during period-ending ceremonies. Its meaning is particularly obvious in the full-figure form of the **CH'AJOOM** logogram that shows a priest placing a ball of *pom* incense into a censer (Schele et al. 1984:fig. 5). Machaquila rulers associated *Wite' Naah* with ballgame skills on one of their monuments (Figure 35b). Therefore, people connected to *Wite' Naah* apparently did so in the context of their ritual credentials and possession of other kinds of special knowledge. This pattern is consistent with a pan-Mesoamerican notion of a place of pilgrimage and rulership at *Tollan*, where various founding ancestors learn arcane lore and even acquire patron deities (Christenson 2000; López Austin and López Luján 1999).

Another interesting set of titles associates members of different dynasties with the legendary place of **chi**-T316 ("Bent-cauac"/"Maguey altar"). It seems that nobody in Late Classic inscriptions claims a direct descent from its royal line. Instead, we find unmarked titles of association or **chi**-T316 *yajawte'* as on Yaxchilan Lintel 21 (Figure 35c) and Palenque Hieroglyphic Stairway 1 (Martin 2000:fig. 6).

One's position in a broader geopolitical landscape or within a specific royal family possibly determines the use of terms *ch'ok* and *kaloomte'* in some place-related titles. As I

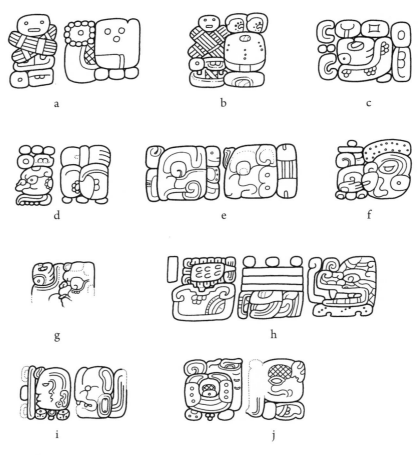

Figure 35 Rare place name incorporating titles in Classic Maya inscriptions: a) detail of the Reviewing Stand, Copan (after drawing by Linda Schele, Schele #1052); b) detail of Stela 3 (C1), Machaquila (after Graham 1967:fig. 49); c) detail of Lintel 21 (D1), Yaxchilan (after Graham and Von Euw 1977:49); d) detail of Stela 89, Calakmul (after Mayer 1989:pl. 7); e) detail of Caption 5, basement wall, West Court, Palace, Palenque (after Robertson 1985: fig. 374); f) detail of Panel 1 (D3), La Corona (after drawing by David Stuart); g) detail of Stela 22 (A6), Tikal (after photograph by the author); h) detail of the "Marker" (G6–G7), Tikal (after 3D scan by the author); i) detail of Stela 21 (A13–A14), Naranjo (after Graham 1975:53); and j) detail of Stela J (D17–C18), Quirigua (after Looper 2003:fig. 3.29).

have argued previously (Tokovinine 2007b), the place name *Huxte' Tuun* denotes a larger geographical area comprising several sites, including Calakmul and Oxpemul. There is no *Huxte' Tuun* emblem glyph. In the context of one's claims for a top role in the entire region, the title *kaloomte'* appears more appropriate than *ajaw* according to the inscriptions at Calakmul on Stela 89 (Figure 35d) and Oxpemul Stela 7. On the other hand, members of the royal family who never acceded to kingship may be called "junior [place name] lords" or "[place name] juniors," as in the case of several *ch'ok* from Santa Elena mentioned in the captions on the basement wall on the eastern side of the West Court of the Palenque palace (Figure 35e).

Gods are also sometimes associated with place names. One of the best examples is the different versions of the maize god associated with certain places (Houston et al. 1992), which will be discussed in greater detail in Chapter 5. The narrative on La Corona Panel 1 refers to a group of deities as "*Wak Mi[in] Nal* god(s)" (*wak mi[in] nal k'uh*) (Figure 35f), linking them to a toponym mentioned in the context of a number of mythical events in narratives at other sites, including Yaxchilan. *K'awiil* is often provided with a place of origin. The caveat here is that royal ancestors are also referred to as *k'awiil* of places as in the inscription on Tikal Stela 22 (Figure 35g). Some deities are clearly related to historical locations. For example, *Waxaklajuun Ubaah Kan* is called *Jo' Noh Witz Waxaklajuun Ubaah Kan* (Figure 35h) in the text on Tikal "Marker" relating the deity to the court of the *Jo' Noh Witz* ruler "Spear-Thrower Owl," who allegedly presided over the conquest of Tikal by *Sihyaj K'ahk'* in AD 378 (Stuart 2000).

Place-related titles like those with *waywal* "sorcerer," as in the inscription on Palenque Temple 17 panel, or *?yook k'in* "?foot/support of the sun" on Naranjo and Copan monuments[37] could reflect perceptions of one's position in the ritual landscape, although the contexts seem to be rather variable. Copan and Quirigua rulers' titles of "support of the sun [in/of] the house of the southern sky" (*nohol chan naah yook k'in*) (CPN St 6, QRG St A, H) or less common "pole of the southern sky" (*nohol chan ook te'*) (CPN Alt O') seem to evoke the world's quadrants. Naranjo rulers are "support of the sun [in/of] *Wak Kab Nal*" (*wak kab nal yook k'in*)—an apparent reference to a specific mythical or historical place of particular importance to the dynasty (Figure 35i). The "*Ihk' Way Nal* pole" (*ihk' way nal yook te'*) title of Quirigua rulers (Figure 35j) and a similar "pole of *Tahn Ha' Pa' Chan* (*uyook te'el tahn ha' pa' chan*) at Yaxchilan (Ln 25) seem to follow the latter pattern.

PLACES IN EMBLEM GLYPHS AND THE PHYSICAL LANDSCAPE

If a place name consistently appears in royal titles, does it mean that it is the name of a greater spatial domain, a territory of a polity? Table 4 summarizes the occurrences of place names in the emblem glyphs of the royal dynasties at sites with at least seven references to place names of any kind. The question is whether place names found in emblem glyphs denote entities of greater spatial scale than individual archaeological sites or even smaller locales. If there are toponyms for such spatial entities, then we can ask if emblem glyphs mark real or claimed political control.

In the case of Tikal, Seibal, Altar de Sacrificios, Yaxha, Ixkun, and Motul de San Jose (as well as other sites like Ucanal, which are mentioned by their neighbors but do not boast large corpora of inscriptions for various reasons, including poor preservation of monuments), there is a one-to-one correspondence between place names in emblem glyphs and place names associated with the locales or parts of what is known as archaeological sites. The correspondence can be found in the inscriptions at each site as well as in outside references. In other words, *Yaxa'* in a toponymic register on a Yaxha stela, *Yaxa'* in the titles

Table 4 Contexts of emblem glyph toponyms associated with sites with large corpora of inscriptions.

CI*	SITE NAME	EMBLEM GLYPH	CONTEXTS					
			DIRECT	IX/ AJ[X]	[X]	[X] AJAW	[X] WINIK	[X] OTHER
274	YAX	Pa' Chan	6	0	0	113	0	0
		Kaaj	2	1	0	66	0	0
167	NAR	Sa'aal	6	9	1	60	0	0
		Wak Kab Nal	0	0	6	2	5	11
158	PAL	Matwiil	12	0	1	23	0	2
		Baakal	1	0	0	45	0	1
		Tok Tahn	2	0	0	3	1	1
146	TIK	Mutal	18	3	1	88	0	0
131	PNG	Yokib	3	0	0	52	0	0
		Wayal	0	0	0	6	0	0
131	CPN	T756d	6	0	1	62	0	0
109	DPL	Mutal	0	0	0	78	0	0
97	QRG	Uun	0	0	0	20	0	0
		Ihk' T756d	0	0	0	8	0	0
		Ihk' Way Nal	1	0	0	1	0	1
69	TNA	Po'/Popo'	0	1	0	29	0	0
		pu-T609	0	0	0	1	0	1
		T533.122	0	0	0	1	0	0
		Kaaj	0	0	0	1	0	0
61	BPK	Ak'e'	0	0	0	23	0	0
		Xukal/ Tz'ikal Naah	0	1	0	24	0	0
		Usiij Witz	3	3	0	1	0	0
		T609	0	0	0	1	0	0
49	CRC	Hux Witza'	15	2	2	5	0	0
40	CNC	ya-T544.501 Ahk	0	0	0	14	0	0
35	SBL	T176	7	1	0	15	0	0
29	MQL	T174-su	1	1	0	22	0	0
27	CLK	Kanu'l	3	1	1	55	0	2
		Chi'k Nahb	7	4	0	3	0	0
		T756	1	0	0	2	0	0
25	PRU	Waka'	3	0	0	11	0	0
24	TRT	Baakal	1	0	0	15	0	0
22	TAM & ARP	T856-la	7	1	1	13	0	0
21	PUS	Uun	0	0	0	12	0	0

Table 4 *continued*

CI*	SITE NAME	EMBLEM GLYPH	CONTEXTS					
			DIRECT	IX/ AJ[X]	[X]	[X] AJAW	[X] WINIK	[X] OTHER
20	ITN	T556.686	0	0	0	5	0	0
19	ALS	T239-si	1	1	0	7	0	0
18	NMP	*Wakaam*	0	0	0	2	0	0
16	PMT	*Pakbuul*	4	0	1	11	0	0
		Pipa'	3	0	0	5	0	0
10	YXH	*Yaxa'*	5	0	0	14	0	0
7	IXK	*Julip*	1	0	0	7	0	0
7	MTL	*Ik'a'*	2	11	2	44	0	0

* CI refers to corpus size index, or the number of mentions of place names at a site.

of Yaxha rulers, and *Yaxa'* subjected to an attack mentioned on a Naranjo stela is the same *Yaxa'*, the name of what we know today as the core of the archaeological site of Yaxha. There is no evidence to suggest an alternative explanation. Or, for example, although the toponym *Ik'a'* ("windy water") sounds like an appropriate name for Lake Peten, there is no evidence showing that it refers to anything but the core of the archaeological site of Motul de San Jose located near the lake (see Tokovinine and Zender 2012).

Emblem glyphs may correspond to locales, which are actually smaller than archaeological sites. In my earlier publications (Tokovinine 2011; Tokovinine and Fialko 2007), I suggested that the place name *Sa'aal* in the emblem glyph of Naranjo rulers corresponded to just one area of what is now known as the archaeological site of Naranjo—the Eastern Acropolis where the ancestral kings were venerated. The place name *Maxam* denoted a larger area of the site, but it was less important in the political landscape of Naranjo rulers and their neighbors.

The case of Naranjo is by no means unique. The undeciphered place name in the emblem glyph of Copan rulers spelled as T756d, T756-**pu**, T756-**pi-pu**, and T756d-**pi** (Figure 36a) also seems to correspond to a section of the archaeological site of Copan and is but one of several place names associated with it. Although the earliest event at Copan in AD 159 mentioned on Stela I seems to be associated with the T756d-**pi** *ch'e'n* (Stuart 2004a:217–219), the most prominent place name in Copan inscriptions is *Hux Wintik* (Stuart and Houston 1994:23–26).[38] When the founder of the Copan dynasty *K'inich Yax K'uk' Mo'* arrived at Copan after a pilgrimage to distant *Wite' Naah* (Stuart 2004a:232–239), he "arrived (here) at *Hux Wintik*" according to the text on Copan Altar Q (Figure 36b). The text on Altar A' (later reused as a block of the Copan Hieroglyphic Stairway) mentions the rituals at the *Jom Tok* "house" (*naah*) and dedication of a monument in the "*Yax K'uk' Mo'* (corn) place" (*patlaj k'inich yax k'uk' mo' nal*) and concludes with placing the events at *Hux Wintik* ([*hux*] *wi[n]tik chan ch'e'n*; Figure 36c). The four patron gods of

Copan (Houston 2009:160) are the "guardians (*koknoom*) of *Hux Wintik*" in the inscription on the panel of Temple 11 (Schele et al. 1984) or the "guardians of *Hux Wintik* in the skies, in the *ch'e'n*" (Figure 36d) as in the text on the bench from Copan Structure 21A (Jackson 2004). Moreover, the two place names sometimes appear together, *Hux Wintik* following T756d (CPN St 10, the base of St N; Figure 36e). The passage on Stela 10 likely mentions both toponyms in the context of period-ending events because it is the main theme of the inscription. The text on the base of Stela N refers to royal accession. It is very likely that we are dealing with either nearby locales or two overlapping spatial domains.

The first clue to the relation between T756d and *Hux Wintik* comes from the narratives on the monuments in the Great Plaza at Copan. The text on Stela A goes into great detail describing the ritual opening and closing of the cruciform enclosure near the monument as part of the period-ending ceremonies (Schele and Grube 1990; Schele and Mathews 1998:160–161). The inscription mentions four supernatural place names (*Chan Te' Chan, Chan T1021 Chan, Chan Ni' Chan, Chan May Chan*); four "holy lords" (*k'uhul ajaw*) of T756d-**pi**, *Mutal, Kanu'l,* and *Baakal*; and four cardinal directions in the context of the ritual (see Figure 48a). The *Chan T1021 Chan* ("Four . . . Sky") place name also occurs on Copan Stela B located to the north of Stela A. The monument is tagged as the "image of the Macaw Mountain lord" (*ubaah mo' witz ajaw*), also known as one of the four divine guardians of *Hux Wintik*. The representation of the Macaw Mountain itself towers behind the standing figure of the deity carved on the front. The back of the stela represents a lord seated on a mountain tagged with four place names (Figure 36f). The list begins with *Mo' Witz* ("Macaw Mountain"), likely referring to the monument, and ends with *Hux Wintik*. The second place name in the list is *Chan T1021 Chan* and the third place name is *Ha' ?Tz'i' Nal* ("Water dog" [corn] place). This list is at least partially self-referential because one of the place names is the Macaw Mountain. The "Water dog" place name is also mentioned at Palenque and Quirigua. Quirigua Altar M is shaped in the likeness of this toponym, which may suggest that "Water dog" could be associated with part of the Quirigua archaeological site or that it was a mythical location of equal importance to Copan and Quirigua rulers (Looper 2003:60–62, fig. 62.67; Stuart 2004b). The number of toponyms on Stela B (four) suggests some kind of quadripartite arrangement along the cardinal directions and the absence of T756d in the list is significant.

Two other inscriptions shed additional light on the significance of the T756d place name. The text on Copan Stela 10 (Figure 36g) mentions a period-ending event "at the edge of the well, the ?shining lake place, T756d-**pi**, [in the] sky, [in the] *ch'e'n*" (*ti' ?way ?lem nahb nal* T756d-**pi** *chan ch'e'n*). This text is not self-referential with respect to the monument and its dedication. It may describe a sequence of rituals at three different locations. Nevertheless, it suggests that T756d is a concrete spot on the landscape.

The only self-referential inscription mentioning T756d place is the dedicatory text on the step at the entrance to one of the early phases of Temple 11 (Figure 36h) possibly commissioned by the eighth ruler of Copan, *Wi' Ohl K'inich*. The narrative on the bench mentions the fire entering (*och-k'ahk'*) into the "holy T756d-**pu** house" (*k'uhul* T756-**pu** *naah*), the "dwelling of" (*yotoot*) the royal ancestors (Wagner and Prager 2006). The dedicatory text of the Reviewing Stand on the southern facade of the later version of the same

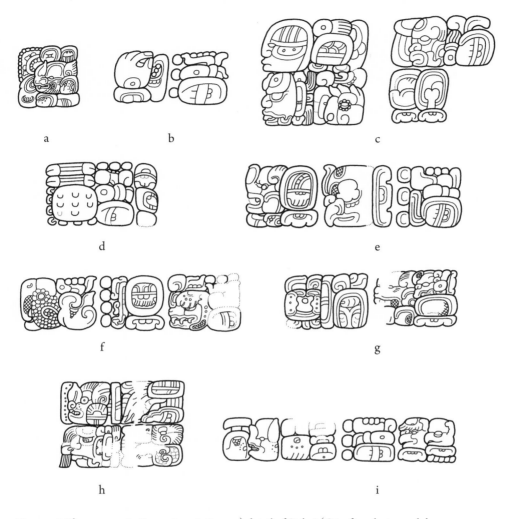

Figure 36 Place names in Copan inscriptions: a) detail of Stela I (C6; after photograph by the author); b) detail of Altar Q (C5–D5; after 3D scan by the author); c) detail of Altar A' (after drawing by Barbara Fash); d) detail of a bench, Structure 21A (M1; after Jackson 2004:9); e) detail of Stela 10 (C9–C10; after drawing by Linda Schele); f) detail of Stela B (after Baudez 1994:fig. 5); g) detail of Stela 10 (D8–D9; after drawing by Linda Schele); h) detail of a step, Temple 11 (F1–G2; after 3D scan by the author); and i) detail of the Reviewing Stand (after drawing by Linda Schele, Schele #1052).

structure (Schele 1987), while possibly mentioning the T756d *naah* in Block W, places the stair in *Hux Wintik* (Figure 36i).

The broader distribution of the *Hux Wintik* toponym indicates that it corresponds to a larger area associated with the archaeological site of Copan, whereas T756d denotes something more specific, possibly the core of the Copan Acropolis. But *Hux Wintik* is clearly less important than T756d in terms of the self-identification of Copan rulers. It seems that the Copan Acropolis—with its main palaces, dwellings of deities, and tombs of ancestors—was the locale with which Copan rulers identified themselves and were identified by their neighbors, although *Hux Wintik* was more prominent in the local geography of sacred places and divine protectors.

If we look at the other end of the spectrum and consider place names for larger-than-site spatial entities, then we would still find no evidence supporting the polity name hypothesis. For instance, as we have seen above, the toponym of *Huxte' Tuun* potentially denotes a larger geographical area that encompasses several archaeological sites associated with their own place names. But there seems to be no title of "*Huxte' Tuun* lords." Instead, different rulers from the places in *Huxte' Tuun* claim the title of *Huxte' Tuun kaloomte'* that likely reflects their aspirations for or claims to a superior political authority over all the dynasties in the region. Therefore, even when there is a measure of reality associated with such claims, there is no *Huxte' Tuun* polity, but there is a nameless political conglomerate in *Huxte' Tuun* united under a particular dynasty. Consequently, we find references to *Huxte' Tuun* as a certain location, and we find this toponym in titles reflecting claims of regional prominence. But *Huxte' Tuun* never serves as a sole indicator of one's political identity.

Even when a toponym for a region is incorporated into an emblem glyph, it still does not function as a polity name. The best case here is the place name T856-**la** attested in inscriptions at several sites in the Petexbatun region, including Dos Pilas, Aguateca, Tamarindito, Arroyo de Piedra, and Seibal (see Figure 1). The rulers of Tamarindito and Arroyo de Piedra carry the title of "T856(-**la**) lords" (ARP St 2, TAM St 4, HS 2, 3; see Figure 37a) and are also mentioned as such in the inscriptions at Seibal and Aguateca (SBL St 6, AGT St 7). The dedicatory text on a fragmentary vessel from Punta de Chimino (Burial 8, Str 7) identifies the owner as a "T856 lord" (Escobedo 1997b). The text on Stela 1 at Aguateca (Figure 37b) also states that "Eight Provinces, [person(s)] of T856" (*waxak pet aj*-T856) attended an event at Aguateca (*K'inich Pa' Witz*) "in T856-**la**" (*ti* T856-**la**).[39] The inscription on Seibal Hieroglyphic (Graham 1996:59) reports that *K'awiil Chan K'inich*, the ruler of Dos Pilas and Aguateca, the liege of Seibal lords, "casts copal," first at Seibal and then "in/at T856-**la**" (Figure 37c). But T856-**la** is not the place name for Tamarindito, Arroyo de Piedra, or Aguateca. The toponym in the toponymic register on Tamarindito Stela 3 is *Yax* T856-**la** *Nal* (Figure 37d).[40] The same toponym appears in the narrative on Tamarindito Stela 4, so it seems to be the ancient name of the locale. It is also cited in the inscription on Arroyo de Piedra Stela 6 (Figure 37e). The toponymic register on Arroyo de Piedra Stela 1, however, consists of just T856-**la**, plus a missing sign (**CHAN**?) followed by *ch'e'n* (Figure 37f). The toponym for Aguateca, *K'inich Pa' Witz* (Stuart and Houston 1994:9–12) is expanded into "*K'inich Pa' Witz* in/at T856-**la**" (*k'inich pa' witz ti/ta* T856-**la**) in the inscriptions on Aguateca Stelae 1 and 2 as well as Dos Pilas Stela 15 (Figure 37b).

In summary, T856-**la** can be used to define one's place of origin or rulership and to provide the location of certain events. It apparently comprises other locations. The sites of Arroyo de Piedra, Tamarindito, and Aguateca are all located near Lake Petexbatun. If T856-**la** is the name of the lake and the surrounding area, then it would suggest that the place names associated with the three sites were the names of specific locations near the

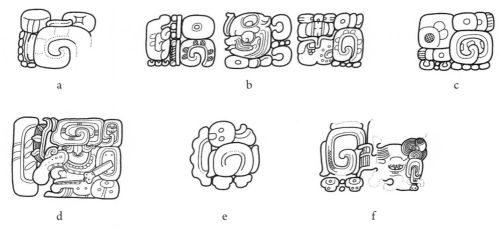

Figure 37 T856-**la** and its lords: a) detail of Stela 2 (F2), Arroyo de Piedra (after Houston and Mathews 1985:fig. 11); b) detail of Stela 1 (D8–D10), Aguateca (after Graham 1967:fig. 3); c) detail of Block 5 (Z2), Hieroglyphic Stairway 1, Seibal (after Graham 1996:59); d) detail of Stela 3, Tamarindito (after drawing by Ian Graham); e) detail of Stela 6, Arroyo de Piedra (after Escobedo 1997a:fig. 5); and f) detail of Stela 1, Arroyo de Piedra (after drawing by Ian Graham).

lake. The emblem glyph title of "T856-**la** lord" would then belong to the ruling families from the area.

In terms of the contexts of its use, the T856-**la** place name is almost a direct opposite of *Huxte' Tuun* discussed previously. Carrying an emblem glyph with T856-**la** does not indicate one's superior political authority in the T856-**la** region. In fact, for most of the Late Classic period, the area is largely controlled by the Tikal-originated *Mutal* dynasty that established itself at the sites of Dos Pilas, Aguateca, and La Amelia (Houston 1993:97–126; Martin and Grube 2000:54–67). But Dos Pilas and Aguateca rulers never incorporate the T856-**la** place name into their emblem glyphs. Only the local dynasties of Arroyo de Piedra and Tamarindito do. In fact, one of "T856-**la** lords" was a carver who signed Stela 7 at Aguateca (Graham 1967:fig. 18), hardly a supreme ruler of Petexbatun. Therefore, the "T856-**la** lord" emblem glyph does not indicate one's political control of the region and there is no such thing as a T856-**la** polity, at least not in the Late Classic historical record documented in the available inscriptions. Presumably, only members of the royal families, which likely originated in the region, take this emblem glyph to indicate their ascription to this royal diaspora.

References to the archaeological site of El Peru and its rulers present another interesting case of a toponym in the royal title that potentially indexes a larger geographical area. As suggested by Martin (2000:114–122) and recently discussed by Guenter (2007), *Waka'* is a place name for El Peru and the title "*Waka'* lord" is the emblem glyph of El Peru rulers (PRU Alt 1, St 15, 16, 19, 27, 32, 33). The dedication statement on El Peru Stela 33 (Figure 38a) refers to *Waka'* as the place where this monument was put into the ground (*utz'apaw tuun waxak ajaw waxak ihk'at . . . uhtiiy tahn ch'e'n waka'*). But the narrative on Lintel 3 in

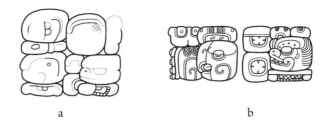

Figure 38 *Waka'* and Eastern *Waka'*: a) detail of Stela 33, El Peru (after Martin 2000:fig. 27a); and b) detail of Lintel 3 (A5–B5), Temple 4, Tikal (after Jones and Satterthwaite 1982:fig. 74).

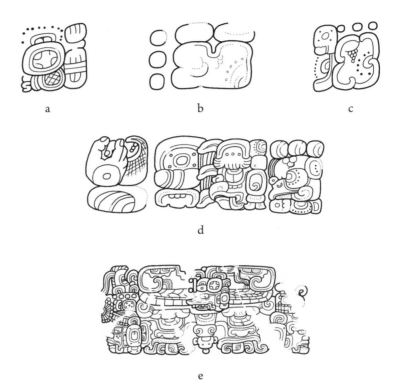

Figure 39 Titles and places of Caracol lords: a) detail of Ballcourt Marker 3 (F3; after Chase et al. 1991:fig. 3); b) detail of Stela 16 (C9; after Beetz and Satterthwaite 1981:fig. 15); c) detail of Ball Court Marker 3 (E5; after Chase et al. 1991:fig. 3); d) detail of Stela 3 (B14–B15; after Beetz and Satterthwaite 1981:12); and e) detail of Stela 6 (after Beetz and Satterthwaite 1981:fig. 8).

Temple 4 (Figure 38b) at Tikal that deals with Tikal's victory over El Peru describes the defeat of El Peru as the downfall of "*Yaxa'* East *Waka'*" (*yaxa' elk'in waka'*). This statement presents a number of challenges. El Peru texts never mention *Yaxa'* and they never refer to El Peru as "East *Waka'*." This means that the toponym *Yaxa'* does not correspond to the locale mentioned on El Peru monuments or that it does not correspond to what we know as the archaeological site of El Peru at all. Either there is another *Waka'*, or that *Waka'* denotes a geographical area that comprises several sites and can be subdivided into subregions based on cardinal directions. The main problem here is that the reference is unique and it comes from outside of the region. As pointed out by Martin (2000:114–122), there are too many options in interpreting the syntax of the phrase: "*Yaxa'* East[ern] *Waka'*"; "*Yaxa'*, East[ern] *Waka'*"; "*Yaxa'* [in the] East, *Waka'*." Moreover, *waka'* is spelled as **wa-ka-AJ/a** and not as **wa-ka-a**. Consequently, it is possible to read it as *wak(a')aj* and translate it as "*Waka'* person." This interpretation is least likely, but it may result in a translation "*Waka'* person was overthrown [at] *Yaxa'* [in the] east." The passage may refer to an attack against *Yaxa'*—the ancient name of Yaxha to the southeast of Tikal (Stuart 1985)—and El Peru. Alternatively, it could be a locale with the same name somewhere within *Waka'*. It could also be an extended version or a Tikal version of the name of El Peru. It is possible that the author of the inscription tried to avoid confusion with the other *Yaxa'* and/or with the other *Waka'*. Until more references of this kind are available, there is no way to figure out which interpretation is correct.

As mentioned above, sometimes there is no correspondence between place names in emblem glyphs and place names linked to archaeological sites. Some emblem glyphs may not incorporate place names at all. For instance, although the rulers of Caracol prefer the unusual title of *k'uhul k'antu' maak* (Figure 39a), they also carry a more typical emblem glyph of "*Hux Witza'* lords" (CRC St 13, 16; Figure 39b) or simply "those of *Hux Witza'*" (CRC Ballcourt Marker 3; Figure 39c). *K'antu'* is never cited as a place of any kind. On the other hand, the *ch'e'n* of *Hux Witza'* is mentioned in contexts such as one's arrival at Caracol (Figure 39d) and appears in toponymic registers on several Caracol monuments (CRC Alt 12, St 3, 4, 5, 6, 13, 16, 17; see Figure 39e).[41] There can be no doubt that it is the ancient name for the site. There is no evidence that it denotes a larger geographical area or a political domain of Caracol rulers. A possible reference to Caracol rulers in the list of *wahy* demons on a vessel from Motul de San Jose (K791) only mentions the title of "*Hux Witza'* lord."

Other cases are noticeably more complicated, either because the rulers in question carry multiple emblem glyphs or because there is more than one place name associated with the site, as in the case of Naranjo. The inscriptions at the site of Yaxchilan illustrate these challenges. Yaxchilan boasts the largest number of references to place names, most of which are the toponyms in the titles of its rulers. Names of Late Classic Yaxchilan lords incorporate two emblem glyphs, "holy *Pa' chan* lords" and "holy *Kaaj* lords" (Figure 40). The second emblem glyph is not mentioned in Yaxchilan inscriptions prior to the reign of *Itzamnaah Bahlam* II (Martin and Grube 2008:119). There is also another site associated with *Pa' Chan* lords—El Zotz—where an Early Classic lintel mentions a local *Pa' Chan* king, whose father carries the title of "holy *Kaaj* lord" (Houston 2008). A fragment of Terminal Classic Stela 4 recently discovered at El Zotz (Garrido López et al. 2011:fig. 4.13, 168, 337) suggests that the local dynasty of *Pa' Chan* lords resided at the site at least until AD 830 (Stephen D. Houston, personal communication 2011).

Kaaj is never mentioned in a direct context at Yaxchilan or at any other Usumacinta region site. On the other hand, *Pa' Chan* appears in texts and toponymic registers of

Figure 40 Emblem glyphs of Yaxchilan lords: detail of Stela 7 (pC5), Yaxchilan (after photograph by Ian Graham).

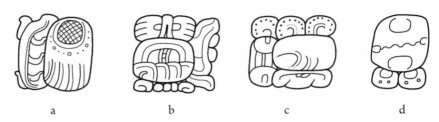

a   b   c   d

Figure 41 Places of Palenque rulers: a) **LAKAM HA'** *Lakam Ha'*, detail of a tablet (A6), Temple 17, Palenque (after Mathews 2001:fig. 1); b) **ma-ta-wi-la** *Matwiil*, detail of a tablet (D17), Temple of the Cross (after Robertson 1991:fig. 9); c) **to-ko TAHN-na** *Tok Tahn*, detail of a tablet (S2), Temple of the Cross (after Robertson 1991:fig. 9); and d) **BAAK-la** *Baakal / Baakiil,* West Tablet (T10), Temple of the Inscriptions, Palenque (after Robertson 1983:fig. 97).

Yaxchilan monuments (YAX Ln 25, St 4, 7, HS 3:3T) with and without the locative *tahn ha'* (Figure 15a). It is also cited in inscriptions of Bonampak as the sole name for the seat of Yaxchilan rulers (BPK SCS 4, 5; Figure 19b). Therefore, *Pa' Chan* should be the name for the whole archaeological site of Yaxchilan or its section.

An even greater challenge in terms of multiple emblem glyphs is presented by the corpus of Palenque. There is no one-to-one correspondence between the toponym associated with the core of the archaeological site and place names in the titles of its rulers (Figure 41). The kings of Palenque take the titles of "*Matwiil* lords" and "*Baakal* lords" (Martin and Grube 2000:155–160), but the actual place name for the area at Palenque where the main palaces and temples are located is *Lakam Ha'* (Stuart and Houston 1994:30–31; Figure 41a). Some of the earliest events in the history of the Palenque dynasty take place at *Tok Tahn*, and early kings carry the emblem glyph of "*Tok Tahn* lords" (Martin and Grube 2000:156–157).

Nevertheless, it does not mean that *Matwiil, Baakal,* or *Tok Tahn* were polity names. *Matwiil* (Figure 41b) is a mythical place name associated with the origin of the Palenque dynasty and its tutelary gods, and possibly even re-created as a setting for the Temple of the Foliated Cross at the site (Stuart 2005b:79–83, 169, 2006b:94; Stuart and Houston 1994:73–77). There is not a single reference to historical events at *Matwiil* in the inscriptions at Palenque. *Tok Tahn* (Figure 41c) is likely the Early Classic seat of the dynasty. According to the narrative on the Temple of the Cross tablet, Ruler 2 celebrated the 9.0.0.0.0 (AD 435) period ending in *Tok Tahn*. The last known event at this place dates

PLACE AND IDENTITY IN CLASSIC MAYA NARRATIVES

back to AD 496, the reign of Ruler 2's successor, while the new court location at Palenque might have been established as early as AD 490 (the first event at *Lakam Ha'* mentioned on the panel from Temple 17 at Palenque).

The *Baakal* (Figure 41d) case is complicated by the fact that the rulers of Tortuguero claim the same emblem glyph, possibly as a result of a dynastic split (Martin and Grube 2000:165). There are only two references to *Baakal* as a locale and neither comes from Palenque. The inscription on Tortuguero Monument 6 mentions—in a reference to an unknown event—that it "happens in the midst of the waters of *Baakal*." The inscription on Stela 4 from the archaeological site of Moral-Reforma refers to the accession of a local lord "before the eyes" of the Palenque ruler that "happened at *Baakal*" (Martin 2003). Neither context is strong enough to argue that there is a greater spatial entity named *Baakal*. The most plausible interpretation is that *Baakal* is either Palenque or Tortuguero, or that *Baakal* is neither Palenque nor Tortuguero but a place in proximity to both sites. The latter seems more likely because there are no direct references to *Baakal* at Palenque or Tortuguero in the context of dedications of new buildings or monuments.

To summarize this section: there is no strong evidence to support the idea that place names in emblem glyphs may denote Classic Maya polities as territorial/spatial domains. When a measure of correspondence between a place name and a physical landscape can be established, place names in emblem glyphs are nearly always the same as place names for areas of archaeological sites. When emblem glyphs do evoke names of larger geographical regions, such titles do not indicate one's control of a region in question but rather point to dynastic origins. On the other hand, real or claimed political control over a region, as in the case of *Huxte' Tuun*, is not expressed by means of incorporating place names into emblem glyphs.

EMBLEM GLYPHS AND PLACES OF ORIGINS

A discussion of toponyms in emblem glyphs would not be complete without addressing more specifically the issue of places, which are seemingly absent in the physical landscape and yet are incorporated into royal titles. These toponyms index locations in deep time, which weave the histories of particular dynasties into broader narratives about the deeds of the gods and the creation of the world.

A discrepancy between emblem glyphs and place names associated with actual centers of Classic Maya polities was highlighted in the case of the *Kanu'l* kings at the site of Calakmul, Campeche. Martin (2005) suggested that the *Kanu'l* dynasty was likely not autochthonous to Calakmul, which is known as *Chi'k Nahb* in Classic inscriptions. Sometime in the reign of *Yuknoom Ch'e'n* II (AD 636–686), the seat of the *Kanu'l* kings moved from Dzibanche in Quintana Roo to Calakmul in Campeche (Grube 2004; Martin 2005; Martin and Grube 2000:103; Velásquez García 2005). The new beginning was reflected in the zeroing down of the dynastic count, with *Yuknoom Ch'e'n* II becoming a new founder, the "first" *Kanu'l* lord (Martin 2005). The arrival of the *Kanu'l* kings to Calakmul eclipsed a local dynasty with its own "Bat" emblem glyph (Martin 2005). The "Bat" kings disappeared from public monuments for a while. Nevertheless, after Calakmul rulers suffered a series of military defeats in the eighth century AD, it was the turn of the *Kanu'l* kings to disappear from epigraphic records, while "Bat" lords reemerged as the sole rulers of Calakmul and the nearby site of Oxpemul (Martin 2005). The recent study of an unprovenanced monument likely commissioned by one of the *Hix Witz* rulers reveals that *Wamaaw Chan K'awiil* was likely the last "*Kanu'l* lord" at Calakmul (Tunesi 2007). "Bat" and *Kanu'l* dynasts shared the emblem glyph of "Calakmul kings" (*chi'k nahb ajaw*) and the title of "those of Calakmul" (*aj-chi'k nahb*), although *Kanu'l* kings had other titles (**chi**-T316 *yajawte'*, *wak chan nal winik*, and *?oox kula'*).

The important point about the *Kanu'l* dynasty is that, while the Early Classic phase of its history may be linked to the site of Dzibanche in Quintana Roo, there are no references to Dzibanche as *Kanu'l*. Long lists of successive *Kanu'l* kings on Late Classic codex-style vessels from Northern Peten/Southern Campeche point to the ancient origins of the dynasty (Martin 1997), but even these lists do not mention *Kanu'l* as an actual place.[42]

An inscription on a recently discovered stairway block at La Corona possibly mentions a Late Classic "refoundation" or "resettling" (see below) of *Kanu'l* by *Yuknoom Ch'e'n* in AD 635 (Stuart 2012). This reference is chronologically consistent with the move of the *Kanu'l* dynasty to Calakmul, but it is not clear if *Kanu'l* in this context is a reference to a relocated polity or to the perceived pre-Dzibanche location of the dynasty in Northern Peten. The narrative on the block continues with an unknown event a day after the "refoundation." If that later event took place in La Corona (the location of most events in the text), then *Kanu'l* or "new *Kanu'l*" should be located closer to La Corona in Northern Peten—and not at Calakmul as suggested by Stuart (2012). Therefore, the text potentially refers to a symbolic refoundation at a locale somewhere in the region associated with painted codex-style lists of *Kanu'l* lords.

Another direct reference to *Kanu'l* comes from a sherd (Ceramic Fragment 7; Figure 42a) recently discovered in the midden associated with Structure 20 at Calakmul (Garcia Barrios 2005; Garcia Barrios and Carrasco Vargas 2006:fig. 10). The midden contains hundreds of fragments of codex-style painted vessels representing all motifs attested on whole codex-style vases, which unfortunately tend be found in private collections across the globe. Ceramic Fragment 7 shows part of a well-known scene of a confrontation between a young wind deity knee-deep in water and a group of warriors led by *Chak Xib Chahk* (Garcia Barrios 2005, 2006). The usual commentary to this scene is that "*Chak Xib* (*Chahk*) enters the *ch'e'n*" (Figure 42b)—one of the expressions for warfare discussed above (Martin 2004). But the caption on the new Calakmul sherd is "(he) enters the *ch'e'n* [at] *Kanu'l*." *Kanu'l* turns out to be an essentially mythological, watery location associated with this narrative. Even if it is a historical place, it has mythic roots. The second set of direct references to *Kanu'l* are images and texts referring to a dancing maize deity of *Wak Chan Nal* (see Chapter 5) as he "ascends at the *ch'e'n* of *Kanu'l*" (Houston et al. 1992). Once again, the context is mythological.

The case of the *Kanu'l* dynasty is not unique. The place name of *Matwiil* mentioned at Palenque and incorporated into emblem glyphs of Palenque rulers is another example of a mythological location linked to creation narratives and dynastic origins (Martin and Grube 2000:159; Stuart 2005b:79, 2006b:94–95; Stuart and Houston 1994:73–76). *Matwiil*

a

b

Figure 42 *Kanu'l* as a deep-time place: a) Ceramic Fragment 7, Structure 20, Calakmul (after García Barrios and Carrasco Vargas 2006:fig. 10); and b) detail of a Late Classic vessel (K2096).

is referred to as "precious shell waters" and depicted likewise (Figure 43a). Therefore, just like Tulan in the Popol Vuh (Sachse and Christenson 2005), *Matwiil* is an aquatic location, maybe even an origin place within or beyond the sea. It is seemingly out of the reach of people in the present. There are at least several more place names of this kind, suggesting that there is a pattern in the way some royal dynasties place the point of their origins well into mythological space-time.

As we have seen above, the second emblem glyph of Yaxchilan rulers is "*Kaaj* lords." But there are no references to *Kaaj* as a real place in the Late Classic political landscape. Yaxchilan inscriptions make no mention of *Kaaj* in contexts other than royal titles. A clue to the significance of the *Kaaj* line comes from a monument at a secondary site of Dos Caobas that celebrates the military exploits of the Yaxchilan ruler *Itzamnaah Bahlam* (Stuart 2007c:31). As pointed out by Stuart (2007c:31), the text concludes with a double count of kings from the founders of the *Pa' chan* and *Kaaj* dynasties to *Itzamnaah Bahlam*'s father (Figure 43b), suggesting that the *Kaaj* line is much more ancient: it boasts an extra score of kings. Further clues to the nature of *Kaaj* come from other sites. The narrative on Monument 150 at Tonina (CMHI 9:84; Figure 43c) deals with the creation event on the day 4 Ajaw 8 Kumk'u (3114 BC). The protagonist is a *Kaaj* lord called the twelfth king in line.[43] That places the foundation of the *Kaaj* dynasty a few hundred years before the current creation. The inscription on Quirigua Stela C (Sharer 1990:30–31) directly mentions *Kaaj* as a location of one of the three "creation stones" on the creation day (Looper 2003:11–12). But the protagonist is not the same as on Tonina Monument 150. The text on Early Classic incised pendants from Tomb 1 in Structure 3 at Calakmul (Pincemín 1994:115–123, fig. 136; Schmidt et al. 1998:fig. 431) mentions one's arrival at *Kaaj* in a mythical narrative. Therefore, *Kaaj* is a location associated with the latest creation event and the line of *Kaaj* lords is even older.

The emblem glyph of Piedras Negras lords has a somewhat similar story to tell (Table 5). The rulers of Piedras Negras carry the title of "(holy) *Yokib* lords." But there are no direct references to *Yokib* at other sites, and the latest event at *Yokib* mentioned on Piedras Negras monuments dates back to AD 435. According to the retrospective text on Piedras Negras Altar 1 commissioned in AD 692, the creation events in 3114 BC were witnessed by a *Yokib* lord at *Jo'* T538 *Nal* (Figure 43d). This effectively pushes the origins of *Yokib* into pre-creation times. The subsequent passages on Altar 1 mention period-ending rituals conducted by *Yokib* lords in AD 297 and AD 435. Both took place at *Yokib*. These are the only known direct references to that place.

The first outside reference to *Yokib* lords on Yaxchilan Lintel 49 refers to military campaigns around AD 460 (Martin and Grube 2000:140–141). About the same time comes the first event at T5 *Tuun*, the place name associated with the site of Piedras Negras in Late Classic texts (Stuart 2004b). According to the text on Altar 1, the period ending of AD 514

Table 5 Places in the history of *Yokib* lords.

MONUMENT	EVENT LONG COUNT	DATE	EVENT
PNG Alt 1	13.0.0.0.0	3114 BC	Creation events at *Ti' Chan Yax* T176 *Nal* and *Jo'* T538 *Nal*, the latter witnessed by a *Yokib* lord
PNG Alt 1	8.13.0.0.0	AD 297	Period-ending ritual at *Yokib* performed by a *Yokib* lord
PNG Alt 1	9.0.0.0.0	AD 435	Period-ending ritual at *Yokib* performed by a *Yokib* lord
PNG Thr 1	9.0.18.16.7	AD 454	*Yokib* lord *K'inich Yat Ahk* "settles" at T5 *Tuun*
YAX Ln 49		~AD 460	*Yokib* lord *Itzam K'an Ahk* is captured by a *Pa' Chan* king
PNG Pn 12	9.3.19.12.12	AD 514	Possible accession date for Ruler C (Panel 12 was found in the fill of Structure O-13)
PNG Alt 1	9.4.0.0.0	AD 514	Period-ending ritual at *Jo' Janahb Nal Witz* performed by a *Yokib* lord (Ruler C)
PNG Pn 3	9.16.6.12.0	AD 757	Ruler 4 is buried in *Jo' Janahb Witz* (Burial 13, Structure O-13)

a

b

c   d   e

Figure 43 Deep-time places: a) detail of a tablet, Temple of the Foliated Cross, Palenque (after Robertson 1991:fig. 153); b) detail of Stela 1 (I1–J1), Dos Caobas (after Stuart 2007c:31); c) detail of Monument 150 (B3–B6), Tonina (after Graham et al. 2006:84); d) detail of Altar 1, Piedras Negras (after CMHI photograph); and e) detail of Hieroglyphic Panel 5 (D1–D4), Pomona (after Stuart 2007c:60).

was celebrated at *Jo' Janahb Nal Witz* and it is tempting to identify it as *Jo' Janahb Witz*, the name of Structure O-13 where Ruler 4 was buried in AD 757, or with the hill behind it. Interestingly enough, Panel 12, the only monument known from the reign of the king who celebrated the period ending of AD 514, was found in the fill of Structure 0-13 (Martin and Grube 2000:140, 150). The text on Panel 12 deals with the dedication of a *waybil* temple for local gods, but unfortunately does not provide the name of the structure. Therefore, sometime in late fifth to early sixth centuries AD, the history of the *Yokib* dynasty becomes grounded in places, which we find in later texts and can associate with the site of Piedras

Table 6 Places in the history of *Pipa'* and *Pakbuul* lords.

MONUMENT	EVENT LONG COUNT	DATE	EVENT
K1398	?	?	*Te' Baah Took' Baah* makes hats for gods in *K'in Xook Witz* [at] *Pipa'*
PMT HP 5	8.7.0.0.0	AD 179	Period ending is celebrated at *Pipa'*
PMT HP 3	8.13.0.0.0	AD 297	Period ending is celebrated at *Pipa'*
PMT HP 10	8.13.7.17.4	AD 305	Earth is opened at *Wak Chan Muyal Witz* by a *Pakbuul* lord
PNG St 12	~9.6.5.0.0	~AD 559	Someone arrives at *Pakbuul*
PMT HP 11	9.13.5.10.5		Earth is opened at *Chak Ich'aak Tuun Ek'* in *Pakbuul*
PNG St 12, MAR St 3	9.18.1.8.18 9.18.3.5.19	AD 792 AD 794	Piedras Negras and La Mar armies attack *Pakbuul* (the downfall and devastation of *Pakbuul*)

Negras or even its specific areas. According to Late Classic retrospective references, the place of *Yokib* appears to represent an earlier period of the dynastic history that stretches back to times of the present creation and beyond.

A somewhat similar picture emerges from looking at the inscriptions at Pomona, one of Piedras Negras's neighbors and adversaries (Table 6). Pomona rulers have two emblem glyphs—"*Pipa'* lords" and "*Pakbuul* lords." *Pakbuul* seems to be the name for the archaeological site of Pomona. An area or a building called "*Chak Ich'aak Tuun Ek'* [in] *Pakbuul*" is mentioned in the context of tomb-opening rituals. When Piedras Negras Stela 12 and La Mar Stela 3 texts describe military campaigns against Pomona, the target is *Pakbuul* and *Pakbuul* lords. Piedras Negras Stela 12 also provides a retrospective reference to the earliest known event at *Pakbuul* dated to around AD 559 (part of the distance number is missing so this date may be a few years off). On the other hand, Pomona inscriptions state that the period-ending rituals in AD 179 and AD 297 took place at *Pipa'* (Figure 43e). Needless to say, these dates are much too early for Pomona and for the region in general. Like *Yokib*, *Pipa'* seems to be a location in deep time—but a deep time that extends into the Early Classic period.

A potentially significant reference to *Pipa'* comes from an unprovenanced polychrome vase (Kerr n.d.:K1398), which, according to its dedicatory inscription, was made for the *Sa'aal* lord *K'ahk' Tiliw Chan Chahk* at Naranjo. The text and imagery on the body of the vessel recall a tale about how a rabbit stole a magic hat from God L (Beliaev and Davletshin 2007). The hieroglyphic captions and commentaries on the vase mention that the character making magic hats for gods lived in a certain "Sun Shark Mountain" in *Pipa'*. If this is the same *Pipa'*, then we have found another mythological place name associated with a royal dynasty.

For the dynasties of Tonina, Bonampak, *Sak Tz'i'*, Itzimte, Cancuen, El Palma, Quirigua, Itzan, and others, there are no secure direct references to place names incorporated into emblem glyphs. But this does not mean that such place names denote only polities or that places indexed by these toponyms never existed, even in legend. For example, as pointed out by Simon Martin (personal communication 2011), a glyph block on a stucco fragment from Temple XVII at Palenque (Morales 2002:photo 19) mentions a "person of *Po'*" (**a-po-o** *a[j]-po'*)—somebody associated with the place name in the emblem glyph of Tonina rulers. It is very likely that the stucco text dealt with the same topic of war against Tonina lords as the stone panel from the temple because the surviving fragments include the same date and similar words. The cases discussed above strongly suggest that tracing one's line to an ancient place is a well-attested strategy of Classic Maya rulers. It is also important that we have examples of dynasties that moved across landscapes, as in the case of *Kanu'l* lords at Calakmul or *Mutal* lords at Dos Pilas. The implication is that one's emblem glyph is a statement about location in the political landscape in a broader sense: not restricted to the physical environment, but rather related to one's identity, origins, and relation to other dynasties.

The significance and function of emblem glyphs is nowhere more apparent as in the titles ascribed to ancestors, particularly dynastic founders, in later narratives. For example, *K'inich Yax K'uk' Mo'*, the founder of the Copan dynasty, likely spent his childhood years in the Peten, but Copan inscriptions and some texts at Quirigua (its kings traced their line to *Yax K'uk' Mo'*) assert that he traveled to a distant place of *Wite' Naah* mentioned at other Maya sites and associated with Teotihuacan imagery (Fash et al. 2009). He took the lightning god *K'awiil* at *Wite' Naah* and only then went on to Copan carrying *K'awiil* with him (Fash and Fash 2000; Stuart 2000, 2004a, 2005a). Therefore, we may expect that *K'inich Yax K'uk' Mo'* would identify himself, or that he would be identified by his descendants and successors, with his origins at one of the royals courts where he grew up, with the place where he went to acquire the tokens of rulership, and with the place where he established a new royal line.

This is precisely the range of emblem glyphs in the names of *Yax K'uk' Mo'*. Two inscriptions (CPN St 63, J) refer to *Yax K'uk' Mo'* as "*Hux Witz[a']* lord" (Figure 44a) and "*[Hux] Witza' ch'ajoom*" (Figure 44b), apparently identifying the founder as a member of the Caracol dynasty (Stuart 2007a). The founder is also given the titles of "man of *Wite' Na[ah]*" (CPN Alt B'; Figure 44c), "*Wite' Naah ch'ajoom*" (CPN HS 1, Reviewing Stand, T11 Northwest Pn, QRG St F, J; Figure 44d), and "*Wite' Na[ah]* lord" (CPN St 12; Figure 44e). Finally, Copan and Quirigua inscriptions refer to *Yax K'uk' Mo'* by his Copan emblem glyph, "holy T756d lord" (CPN Alt B', St 11, St 12, QRG Zoomorph P; Figure 44e).

There is no evidence that the Copan founder was ever a king at Caracol, although the sixth-century Caracol Stela 16 does testify to a continuing relationship between the two dynasties by mentioning some actions of the seventh Copan ruler, *Bahlam Neen* (Grube 1990; Martin and Grube 2000:87). It is also unlikely that *Yax K'uk' Mo'* was a king of *Wite' Naah* because his credentials are only cited at Copan and Quirigua and his story seems to be more about pilgrimage than rulership at *Wite' Naah*. Consequently, the triple emblem glyph of the founder only reflects how the Copan dynasty perceived its origins and its place among other dynasties.

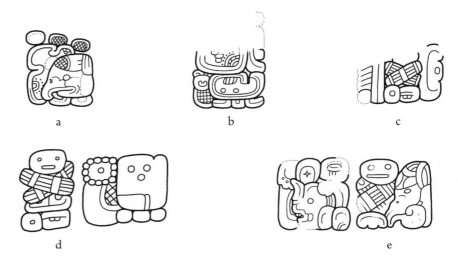

Figure 44 *Yax K'uk' Mo*'s titles in Copan inscriptions: a) detail of Stela J (after photograph by the author); b) detail of Stela 63 (pC15; after 3D scan by the author); c) detail of Altar B' (E1; after drawing by Barbara Fash); d) detail of the Reviewing Stand (E'1–F'1; after drawing by Linda Schele, Schele #1052); and e) detail of Stela 12 (D11–C12; after Stuart 2004a:fig. 4.13).

Another excellent case is that of the titles ascribed to a Calakmul dynastic founder in the dedicatory inscription on an unprovenanced Late Classic vessel in the Museum zu Allerheiligen Schaffhausen, Switzerland. According to the analysis of the imagery and inscriptions on this vase by Prager (2004), the body of the vessel features the portraits of the *Kanu'l* lord *Yuknoom Ch'e'n* the Great of Calakmul and his wife. The dedicatory text on the lid of the vase refers to another character whom Prager (2004:36–38) identifies as a dynastic founder of *Kanu'l*. But this name is not present on the lists of *Kanu'l* lords on codex-style vases (Martin 1997). Instead, it resembles the posthumous name of *Yuknoom Ch'e'n* (*K'awiil* preceded by an undeciphered logogram also found in the names of Caracol rulers) on Calakmul Stela 52, as well as other inscriptions in which this great king is mentioned as the first of the *Kanu'l* lords, presumably out of those who established themselves at Calakmul (Martin 2005:7–8, fig. 4). Therefore, the vase was dedicated to a deceased ancestor, *Yuknoom Ch'e'n*, identified by his accession name next to his portrait on the body of the vase and by his posthumous name on the lid. *Yuknoom Ch'e'n* was not the first king of the *Kanu'l* dynasty, but either he or his predecessor, *Yuknoom* "Head" (unless, as Martin [2005] suggested, *Yuknoom* "Head" was *Yuknoom Ch'e'n*'s pre-accession name), established a new *Kanu'l* court at Calakmul. He was subsequently credited with being the first of that *Kanu'l* line in the region of *Huxte' Tuun* (Martin 2005; Tokovinine 2007b:19–21) and with reestablishing *Kanu'l* proper either at Calakmul or at a yet unidentified location in Northern Peten (Stuart 2012; see above).

A string of titles attributed to *K'awiil/Yuknoom Ch'e'n* (Figure 45)[44] begins with the term *mam* ("ancestor") followed by the epithet "*Wak Chan Witziil* [person], man of **chi**-T316, man of *Wite' Naah*" (Prager 2004:fig. 12). The place name *Wak Chan Witziil* is likely

Figure 45 Calakmul founder titles on the Schaffhausen vessel (after Prager 2004:fig. 12).

the same *Wak Chan Nal* from the mythological narrative linking *Kanu'l* kings with a certain maize deity (Houston et al. 1992). The **chi**-T316 place name (also known as "Chi-Bent Cauac" and "Chi-Witz") is an important deep-time location in the history of the dynasties at Copan, Tikal, Pusilha, Yaxchilan, and Calakmul (Grube 2004:127–131; Grube and Martin 2001b:9–11; Stuart 2004a:216–220). The latest known event at **chi**-T316 dates back to AD 159. The text on the Palenque Hieroglyphic Stairway also links the **chi**-T316 place to a late sixth-century *Kanu'l* lord (Grube 2004:fig. 14a). *Wite' Naah* is also a highly important location (see above). Claims to a *Wite' Naah* connection of the *Kanu'l* lords are also revealed in a Late Classic narrative at La Corona, where Calakmul ruler *Yuknoom Yich'aak K'ahk'* takes the guise of a Teotihuacan War Serpent deity, *Waxaklajuun Ubaah Kan* (Stuart 2012). The last known historical event at *Wite' Naah* is the visit undertaken by the Piedras Negras ruler *Yat Ahk* in AD 510, when he received a helmet from an *ochk'in kaloomte'* (Anaya Hernández et al. 2002; Martin and Grube 2000:141; Skidmore 2002). By the time *Yuknoom Ch'e'n* acceded to kingship in AD 636 (Martin 2005:7), *Wite' Naah* was a place in the past, like other locations mentioned in his titles.

Therefore, just as in the case of Copan rulers, the titles of the Calakmul dynastic founder place him in the political landscape by evoking highly important locations associated with *Kanu'l* lords, beginning with a place in the time of gods and ending with a place of great importance in the Early Classic politics. *Yuknoom Ch'e'n* could not be from these places because they are so far apart in space and time, but some of his ancestors might have been.

ARRIVING AND SETTLING

If several Classic Maya royal dynasties position themselves as nonlocal, then the important question is: How is this reflected in the narratives that link them to their current places of residence? In the case of Copan discussed above, the foundation is presented as the "arrival" of its first king, *K'inich Yax K'uk' Mo'*, accompanied by *K'awiil* that he took at *Wite' Naah* (Stuart 2004a). According to Stuart (2004b), the narratives involving the "foundation" glyph on Throne 1 at Piedras Negras (Figure 46a) and the panel from the sanctuary of Temple 17 at Palenque (Figure 46b) also refer to the establishment of T5 *Tuun* and *Lakam Ha'*, respectively, as new seats of nonlocal rulers. A passage on a block of a La Corona stairway mentions another sigficant foundation event: a possible remaking of *Kanu'l* in AD 635, when the *Kanu'l* dynasty moved from Dzibanche to Calakmul (Stuart 2012).

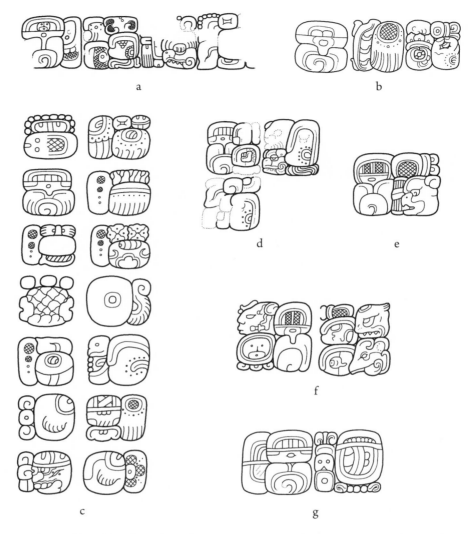

Figure 46 "Foundation" events in Classic Maya narratives: a) detail of Throne 1 (pB1–pE1), Piedras Negras (after photographs by the author); b) detail of a tablet, Temple 17 (B5–A6), Palenque (after Mathews 2001:fig. 1); c) detail of Panel 1 (G2–H7), Cancuen (after drawing by Yuriy Polyukhovych); d) detail of Panel 4 (G1–G2), Piedras Negras (after 3D scan by the author); e) detail of Sculptured Stone 4 (D8), Bonampak; f) detail of Sculptured Stone 1 (C2–D2), Bonampak; and g) detail of Stela 5 (A9–B9), Tikal (after Jones and Satterthwaite 1982:fig. 7).

Until recently, the "foundation" logogram remained undeciphered, although the second occurrence of the sign on Piedras Negras Throne 1 featured a possible final phonetic complement, **–ja**. Dmitri D. Beliaev and Albert Davletshin (personal communication 2012) recently suggested reading the logogram as **KAJ** and translating it as "to settle."[45] The verb *kaj*, "to settle, to reside," is attested in modern and colonial Yukatek (Barrera Vásquez et al. 1995:281; Bricker et al. 1998:120). Davletshin (personal communication 2011) suggests that the cognate transitive verb in proto-Western Mayan is *kaj* "to put on top of," whereas the proto-Ch'olan intransitive *kaj* "to begin" could be a different gloss.

If the "foundation verb" is *kaj* and its mediopassive form in the Classic Maya narratives *kajaay* means "to reside" or "to settle," then its contexts shed further light on the relationship between people and places. The text on the unprovenanced panel that likely came from Cancuen (commonly designated as Cancuen Panel 1) offers an example that is closest in meaning to the narratives at Piedras Negras and Palenque discussed above (Guenter 2002; Kistler 2004). The story apparently begins in *Chi'k Nahb* (Calakmul) and ends in *Haluum* (Cancuen)—a place of pools, islands, and springs. A pilgrimage to the "*Makan* Mountain" is inserted between the accession in the presence of Calakmul lords and gods and the (re)foundation of the royal court at Cancuen. In the inscription's own words (Figure 46c), "*K'iib Ajaw* came [here]; he settled in the grass, in the *tz'eek*, in the pool, three turtle island, in the heart of the turtle, polished sky water, *Haluum*."[46] The inscription on Piedras Negras Panel 4 (Figure 46d) potentially reports the foundation of La Mar by the Piedras Negras ruler *Yo'nal Ahk*.[47]

Other "foundation" events are more ambiguous. The protagonist of the narrative on Bonampak Sculptured Stone 4 "leaves his *ch'e'n*" at Bonampak, "ascends" to Yaxchilan, and "settles in his *ch'e'n*" (Figure 46e) only after the defeat of a rival lord (Beliaev and Safronov 2004). This is clearly not the foundation of Bonampak as a place because it appears in relation to earlier events in the same narrative. An even later "settling" in "the land, the *ch'e'n* of *Usiij Witz*" (Bonampak) is mentioned in the text on Sculptured Stone 1 (Figure 46f). The aforementioned *Kanu'l* foundation in AD 635 is also hardly the establishment of the original *Kanu'l*. The inscription on Tikal Stela 5 discussed previously (Figure 46g) reports the king's "settling" at a temple after his accession to lordship. This is the place that he "descended from" when he went to war against Naranjo, as we have discussed in the previous chapter.

Therefore, the available examples seem to suggest that the intended meaning of the "foundation verb" is more akin to one's arrival than to foundation, but probably with the sense of a new beginning or of establishing oneself, be it in the context of a new royal court, a restored royal court, or even a victorious royal court. The emphasis is clearly on the ruler's person—not on the place.

COMPETING DYNASTIES AND ROYAL DIASPORAS

The proposed interpretation of emblem glyphs as titles connecting certain royal families to places of their political origins brings us back to the main problem with previous ideas about the meaning and function of these titles—the occurrence of multiple contemporaneous individuals with identical emblem glyphs. The historical context and political implications of coexisting lords may vary. Their mere presence indicates nothing but claims of shared origins.

The most publicized case of coexisting rulers with the same emblem glyph is the spread of the *Mutal* dynasty in Petexbatun (Houston 1993:97–126; Johnston 1985; Martin and Grube 2000:54–67). First, *Mutal* lords establish themselves at Dos Pilas and Aguateca; then, an apparently subordinate *Mutal* line appears at the smaller site of La Amelia. Other dynasties identify rulers of Dos Pilas and Aguateca as *Mutal* lords. But the only reference to a Dos Pilas king (*Itzamnaah K'awiil*) in the inscriptions—on a carved bone from Burial 116 at Tikal (TIK MT 28; Moholy-Nagy and Coe 2008:fig. 196c)—mentions "a man of Dos Pilas"—*aj*-T369 *Ha'[al]*, suggesting that Tikal lords did not accept the *Mutal* credentials of their Petexbatun counterparts and relatives. Petexbatun *Mutal* rulers never refer to their own political domain(s) as *Mutal*.

Another well-known example is the *Baakal* dynasty at Palenque, Tortuguero, and Comalcalco. The ruler of Tortuguero, *Bahlam Ajaw*, carries the same emblem glyph of "holy *Baakal* lord" as his contemporary *K'inich Janahb Pakal* at Palenque, also the "holy *Baakal* lord" (Gronemeyer 2006:165; Grube et al. 2002; Martin and Grube 2000). The Tortuguero dynasty subsequently conquers Comalcalco, and from the mid-seventh century Comalcalco is ruled by *Baakal* lords (Zender 2001). The split between Palenque and the Tortuguero dynasty may date back to the sixth century, and there does not seem to be much friendship between the two royal lines: *Bahlam Ajaw* campaigns against lords of *Huxte' K'uh* allied with Palenque rulers.

Examples like *Mutal* and *Baakal* may suggest that multiple lords with the same emblem glyph represent a kind of unusual situation resulting from a dynastic conflict and causing subsequent friction between royal courts claiming the same ascendancy over the same spot in the political landscape. But this is not necessarily the case. The T856-**la** royal line, discussed previously in the context of emblem glyphs and scale of spatial entities indexed by place names, is an example of a dynasty that established itself at several sites with no apparent signs of internal conflicts or strain. Although the historical record for T856-**la** lords is very fragmentary, we know that they commissioned monuments at Arroyo de Piedra and Tamarindito throughout the Classic period. The parentage statement in the inscription on Stela 2 at Arroyo de Piedra suggests that the as yet unidentified place of *Chak Ha'*—possibly located near the Chac Rio stream a few kilometers from Arroyo de Piedra—was also at some time ruled by a member of the same dynasty. It mentions a certain "*Mo' Bahlam*, T856-**la** lord, man of *Chak Ha'*" (Palka 1996:221; Stuart and Houston 1994:37–38, fig. 43). Although *Chak Ha'* rulers are referred to as a distinct dynasty in other inscriptions, the emphasis on their affiliation with the T856-**la** royal line at Arroyo de Piedra makes sense given that the mother of an Early Classic Arroyo de Piedra ruler, who commissioned Stela 1 in 9.9.0.0.0, was from *Chak Ha'*. The mother of the Late Classic T856-**la** lord of Tamarindito, mentioned on local Hieroglyphic Stairway 3, was also from *Chak Ha'* (Houston 1993:fig. 4-17).

An even more interesting case of a diaspora-like spread of members of the same dynasty is the line of *Xukal/Tz'ikal Naah* lords, which came to be associated with at least five places (Table 7; Figure 47). The origins of the dynasty may be at the site of Lacanha, where we find an Early Classic monument commissioned by a local ruler in AD 593 (LAC St 7). A Late Classic panel in the Dumbarton Oaks Collection (PC.B.145), which allegedly came from the vicinity of Lacanha, is dedicated by *sajal Aj Sak Teles*, who calls himself "man of *Xukal Naah*," indicating that Lacanha was likely associated with this place name

Table 7   Places in the history of *Xukal/Tz'ikal Naah* lords.

MONUMENT	EVENT LONG COUNT	EXPLICIT ASSOCIATIONS OF *XUKAL/TZ'IKAL NAAH* LORDS WITH PLACE NAMES				
		SAK LAKAL	*BUBUL HA'*	*XUKAL/ TZ'IKAL NAAH*	*USIIJ WITZ*	"KNOT. HAIR"
BPK MSC 4	9.8.6.13.17				*Yajaw Chan Muwaan*	
BPK MSC 5	9.10.9.9.14	*Aj Jukuub*				
BPK MSC 5	9.10.15.1.8				*Winikhaab Took'*	
BPK MSC 5	9.10.15.7.4					
PNG Pn 2	9.11.6.2.1	*Aj Chak Jol*	*Yich'aak Paat*			
YAX Ln 44	9.12.17.12.0	*Sak Ichiiy Pat*				
BPK MSC 1	9.13.0.0.0				*Aj ?Nak'eey*	
Chicago Alt	9.14.10.15.0		*Ahkul Paat*			
LAC Pn 1	9.15.11.17.3			*Aj Sak Teles*		"Trophy. head"
LAC Pn 1	9.15.15.0.0					*Bahlam*
BPK Ln 3	9.15.17.2.13					
BPK St 2	9.17.18.15.18				*Yajaw Chan Muwaan*	
BPK Str 1	~9.17.16.X.X					unknown

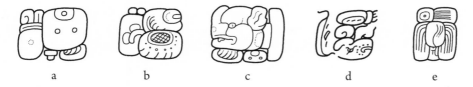

a   b   c   d   e

Figure 47 Places in the history of *Xukal Naah* lords: a) **SAK-la-ka-la** *Sak Lakal*; b) **bu-bu-lu-HA'** *Bubul Ha'*; c) **xu/tz'i-ka-la NAAH** *Xukal/Tz'ikal Naah* (PNG Pn 2; after 3D scan by the author); d) **u-si-wi-WITZ** *Usiij Witz* (BPK Str 1, Room 1:22; after drawing by John Montgomery); and e) "knot.hair" (LAC Pn 1:D5; after drawing by David Stuart).

(Palka 1996:217, fig. 216). By the end of the fifth century, Lacanha rulers established themselves at Bonampak: its Sculptured Stone 4 mentions a ceremony undertaken by a *Xukal Naah* lord at *Usiij Witz*, the place name for Bonampak (Stuart 2008), in AD 600. The text on Stela 1 at Ojo de Agua describes earth-opening rituals in AD 588 undertaken by a *Xukal Naah* lord who acceded to kingship in AD 573. There is no place name in the text, although the name of that person resembles those of later *Xukal Naah* lords from *Bubul Ha'* (Beliaev and Safronov 2004). Therefore, by the end of the sixth century, there are at least three locales with *Xukal Naah* dynasts.

The Late Classic period sees an even greater amount of *Xukal Naah* lords associated with different locations. A Bonampak monument (SCS 5) details the exploits of *Xukal Naah* lord *Winikhaab Took'* at *Usiij Witz* in AD 647. The later summoning of *Yokib* vassals in AD 658, depicted on Piedras Negras Panel 2, features four *Xukal Naah* dynasts: two without references to place names, one of *Sak Lakal*, and one of *Bubul Ha'*. Another *Xukal Naah* lord of *Bubul Ha'* dedicates the "Chicago altar" in AD 722 (Mayer 1995:pl. 92). *Sak Lakal* people are mentioned in the context of conflicts with Yaxchilan rulers in AD 642 and AD 689. A panel from Bonampak refers to a period ending celebrated at *Usiij Witz* in AD 692.

By the mid-eighth century, a new line associated with a "knot.hair" site joins the *Xukal Naah* diaspora. The Dumbarton Oaks Carved Panel mentions a *Xukal Naah* lord of "knot. hair," named "Trophy.head" *Bahlam*, as an overlord of *Sak Teles* of *Xukal Naah*. The same individual is mentioned on two panels from Nuevo Jalisco or El Cedro, the site that was possibly associated with the "knot.hair" toponym (O'Neil and Tokovinine 2012:65–67). Retrospective narratives on monuments commissioned by *Sak Teles*'s son at Bonampak refer to *Sak Teles* as *Xukal Naah* lord of *Usiij Witz* who confronted "Trophy.head" *Bahlam* of the "knot.hair" site. The conflicting narratives and the apparent confrontation within the same royal line reflect the complex political situation of the period; *Xukal Naah* lords were part of a bigger conflict between the dynasties of *Pa' Chan*, *Yokib*, *Sak Tz'i'*, and their proxies (Beliaev and Safronov 2004). In the next generation of *Xukal Naah* rulers, lords of *Usiij Witz* and the "knot.hair" site are relatives, allies, and clients of Yaxchilan kings and act together against *Sak Tz'i'* lords (Houston 2012; Martin and Grube 2000:135–137; Palka 1996:219).

There is a glimpse of another dynastic diaspora in the corpus of painted ceramic vessels from the so-called Ik' school (Reents-Budet 1994; Tokovinine and Zender 2012). Most of these vases mention or depict "*Ik'[a']* lords." The place name *Ik'a'* is securely identified as the site of Motul de San Jose, where it is mentioned in direct contexts and where carvers sign monuments as "men of *Ik'a'*" (Stuart and Houston 1994:27–28; Tokovinine and Zender 2012:31–35).

The first sign of the emerging diaspora comes from scenes on vases associated with *Yajawte' K'inich* and his successor *K'inich Lamaw Ek'* (Tokovinine and Zender 2012:44–46). The latter appears as a *baah tz'am* official as early as AD 757, according to the scene on an unprovenanced vessel (K1463). By AD 768, *K'inich Lamaw Ek'* is effectively a coruler with a full emblem glyph (K3054); although *Yajawte' K'inich* retains the exclusive use of the *kaloomte'* title, he remains some kind of a high king. The inscription on a vase in the

Museum of Fine Arts, Boston (K1728), indicates that by AD 779 *K'inich Lamaw Ek'* had attained the titles of "holy *Ik'a'* lord" and *kaloomte'*, thus becoming the high king himself.

It remains unknown if *K'inich Lamaw Ek'* had any junior corulers, but his likely successor, *Yeh Te' K'inich* II, is shown in the company of at least two lords with full emblem glyphs of "holy *Ik'a' lords*" in the dance scenes painted on vases (Tokovinine and Zender 2012:48–49, 59). One of the lords is *?Yopaat Bahlam* (K534); the other's name remains undeciphered (K1399). A courtly *ajk'uhuun* official named *Juun Tuun Chak* is present at both events, indicating that we are dealing with snapshots of life at the same royal court. Consequently, it looks as if the number of junior corulers, possibly placed at secondary sites, increased from one to two between the reigns of *Yajawte' K'inich* and *Yeh Te' K'inich* II.

The existence of competing dynasties sharing an emblem glyph alongside what looks like diasporas of royal families of the same origin raises the issue of the strategies and reasoning behind one's claims to a certain emblem glyph. Sharing an emblem glyph is not necessarily an attribute of different political regimes fighting for the same spot on the map. Members of the same royal diaspora may equally stress their shared origins and act as a kind of political confederacy where some members may play more prominent roles than others.

When it comes to the ways in which the Classic Maya identify themselves with places, the important point to keep in mind is that choices of place and kinds of association will depend on identity and context, including the narrative and its relationship to the protagonist. The dominant identity in Classic Maya landscape is one's membership in the category of *ajaw*—lords or rulers—or the lack thereof. This may be expected when the theme of the political landscape dominates available narratives. Lordly titles associated with places—emblem glyphs—are the most common contexts of toponyms. Yet emblem glyphs were one of many kinds of titles by which people in Classic Maya inscriptions identified themselves or their ancestors with different places. The choice of a particular title over others depended on the context of the reference. Emblem glyphs are all about one's status as lord, as a ruler. Therefore, there seems to be a twofold function: to identify one's status as a ruler of a certain place, and to identify someone with places that make him or her worthy of lordly rank. Some royal families consistently associate themselves with different places in order to highlight the underlying narratives and identities, which not only set them apart from, but sometimes united them with, other dynasties.

A place name of choice for an emblem glyph does necessarily index the largest spatial entity attested in the inscriptions at a given site. There is no distinct modern spatial category corresponding to emblem glyphs, but there are certain places that become more important than others in denoting one's political identity and in defining members of a particular ruling dynasty vis-à-vis other dynasties. An emblem glyph place name is often related to the deep-time history of a royal family that may or may not be associated with its current location. One's affiliation to a place or origin point may pass through descent. This observation does not imply that such a place cannot be re-created in permanent architecture or in temporal installations on certain occasions, visited through pilgrimages, or evoked in any other way. In addition, there may be multiple place names of this kind, particularly in the case of dynastic founders.

As a category of ascription to a royal line and its place of origin, rather than its place on the actual landscape, emblem glyphs can be shared by different royal families. Such shared dynastic identities likely result from intermarriages or dynastic splits. The important implication is that there may be different motives behind claims of a common place of origin. A competition for the same role in the geopolitical landscape is but one of the possible scenarios. Some diasporas of rulers with shared emblem glyphs apparently relied on the notion of common origins as a kind of political capital.

SEARCHING FOR GROUP IDENTITIES

EPIGRAPHERS HAVE LARGELY OVERLOOKED THE TOPIC OF GROUP IDEN-
tities at different levels in the Classic Maya political landscape, although it is a popular
research question for archaeologists (Canuto and Fash 2004). The problem with the lack
of community-oriented research in epigraphy may have something to do with existing paradigms, which may be defined as practical and ritualistic. The practical approach is based
on the assumption that the Maya political landscape consisted of opportunistic realpolitik
practitioners (Martin and Grube 2000). The ritualistic approach sees the very same people
as devout religious practitioners acting in accordance with certain immutable and endur-
ing principles (Rice 2004). But hieroglyphic inscriptions reveal ideas about difference and
commonality that transcend context-specific networks of alliances and hegemonies and
that are not cast in terms of religious duties. Yet there is no evidence that centers of political
power shifted in accordance with a certain pan-Maya ritual schedule.

The topic of Classic Maya group identities or geopolitical communities was introduced by Berlin (1958) along with the discovery of emblem glyphs. Berlin noticed that the
inscription on Copan Stela A (Figure 48a) contained references to four emblem glyphs
associated with the four cardinal directions and four other terms accompanied by the number four (Berlin 1958:118). Berlin's careful observation was that this text would be crucial
for understanding Maya political organization, but he did not elaborate further.

Barthel (1968) followed upon Berlin's insights and argued more affirmatively in favor
of emblem glyphs as place names and references to multiple emblem glyphs as representations of a larger geopolitical order. By that time, additional lists of emblem glyphs, always
four in number, were discovered in the inscriptions on carved bones (MT 42A–B; Figure
48b–c) from Burial 116 at Tikal (Moholy-Nagy and Coe 2008:figs. 194c–d) and on Seibal
Stela 10 (Graham 1996:31–32; Figure 48d). Therefore, Barthel was confident that the lists
provided a glimpse of an overarching "cosmo-sociological system" (Barthel 1968). In the
case of Copan Stela A, Barthel proposed that it referred to four places associated with the
cardinal points—Copan, Tikal, a location he could not identify (*Kanu'l*), and Palenque. It
did not matter that the sequences of directional terms and emblem glyphs did not match.

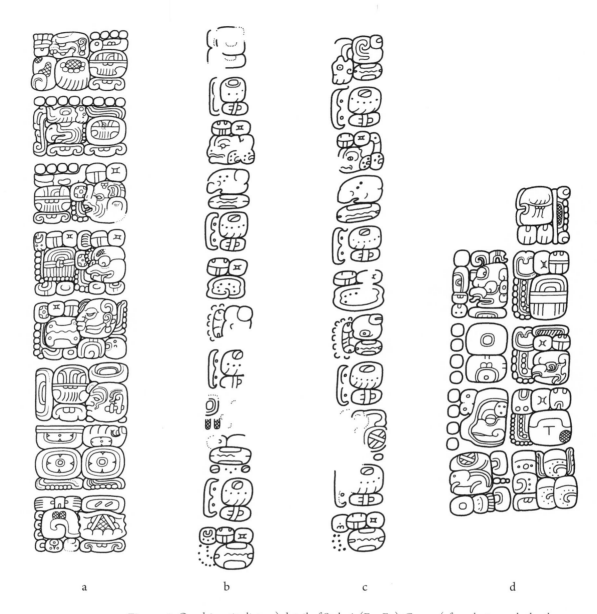

Figure 48 Quadripartite lists: a) detail of Stela A (E2–F9), Copan (after photographs by the author); b) detail of an incised bone (MT 42A), Burial 116, Tikal (after Moholy-Nagy and Coe 2008:fig. 194c); c) detail of an incised bone (MT 42B), Burial 116, Tikal (after Moholy-Nagy and Coe 2008:fig. 194d); and d) detail of Stela 10 (A6–B11), Seibal (after Graham 1996:32).

Barthel decided that the list of emblems would begin with Copan as a place in the south and then proceed counterclockwise to Tikal in the east, the unidentified place in the north, and Palenque in the west.

The Copan text was then compared to the inscriptions on Tikal bones, where Copan and Palenque emblem glyphs were also in the initial and final positions, respectively. The second place was occupied by an emblem glyph with the sign T579, which remains undeciphered. In the third place on both Miscellaneaous Texts 42A and 42B, Barthel found an eroded emblem glyph that he proposed to identify with Tikal because one of the two spellings began with T151 (he was probably confused by the presence of *nuun* in the names of some Tikal rulers). Finally, the text on the Seibal monument contained Tikal and *Kanu'l* emblem glyphs in the same positions as on Copan Stela A, while the first and the last positions were occupied by Seibal and Motul de San Jose emblem glyphs.

The differences between the earliest list at Tikal, the later list on Copan Stela A, and the latest list at Seibal, in Barthel's opinion, reflected changes in the geopolitical order: from its formation, to its maximum extent, and to a reduction when Seibal became the southernmost place instead of Copan (Barthel 1968:189–191). Moreover, according to Barthel (1968:192–193), those quadripartite schemes were likely related to the quadripartite organization of Maya polities in later accounts like the Book of Chilam Balam of Chumayel. A passage from Chumayel of particular importance to Barthel is the one that describes the foundation of Chichen Itza by four groups coming from four distinct places at different cardinal directions (CHU 77–78). As Barthel saw it, Chichen Itza found itself in the center of the Maya world divided by four equivalents of emblem glyphs. Barthel was likely influenced by Coe's article (1965) published a few years earlier. Coe proposed that quadripartite division was likely the main model for sociopolitical and religious organization of Classic Maya communities of different scale, basing these conclusions on the analysis of a variety of ethnohistoric sources with a particular emphasis on the New Year rituals as described by Landa (Tozzer 1941:135–150).

Barthel's ideas were elaborated further by Marcus (1973, 1976). While Barthel was not sure to what extent the lists of four emblem glyphs represented an actual geopolitical order or representations, or conceptualizations of that system, Marcus proposed that the lists mentioned four capitals of the Maya world and that differences between the lists accounted for shifts in political power between the cities. Probably being mindful of Barthel's problems with assigning cardinal directions, Marcus suggested that the actual location of sites associated with emblem glyphs in "our system of mapping" did not matter (Marcus 1973:913). At the same time, Marcus argued that archaeological data supported her interpretation of epigraphic sources: at any given time, there were four equidistant top-level sites in the Southern Lowlands surrounded by networks of equidistant secondary and tertiary centers, down to even smaller sites and dispersed hamlets, all integrated by means of marriages between the ruling lineages. Therefore, the question of whether there was a certain perception of an ideal geopolitical order shared by some Classic Maya elites effectively became a question of finding this order in the archaeological and historical records.

Advances in Maya epigraphy and archaeology eventually called the great capitals model into question. As Mathews pointed out (1988:352–367), while archaeological data seemed to reveal a fragmented landscape of city-states, the decipherment of emblem glyphs suggested that the Classic Maya were divided into small independent polities. Each polity had its own dynasty of lords who were called *ajaw*, a title applied to supreme rulers in early colonial sources. Mathews argued that the coexistence of rulers with the same emblem glyphs at different sites indicated that place names in emblem glyphs were also, and sometimes exclusively, polity names. According to Mathews, references to alliances, marriages, and hierarchical relations between polities were rare, while warfare without outright conquest was apparently common (Mathews 1988:368–386). There was no room for a "cosmo-sociological system" in this geopolitical order. Although Mathews never stated it explicitly, it appeared from his writings that, from a strictly historical viewpoint, a larger geopolitical order did not exist.

As more historical data became available through advances in the decipherment of Maya writing and the publication of new inscriptions, the fragmented landscape view underwent a major correction. As Martin and Grube proposed in their seminal article (Martin and Grube 1995) and outlined in much greater detail in the first monograph on the interwoven histories of major Classic Maya dynasties (Martin and Grube 2000), most Classic Maya polities were part of larger networks of alliances and hegemonies in which some polities consistently played more significant and dominant roles. The authors singled out the sites of Tikal and Calakmul as the seats of the most powerful and influential dynasties, superstates of sorts waging constant proxy wars. Tikal seems to have held the upper hand in the Early Classic period, while Calakmul surged to regional dominance in the Late Classic period. The collapse of these great hegemonies in the mid-eighth century AD could then be interpreted as one of the main reasons for the mounting conflicts, balkanization, and the eventual disintegration of Classic Maya polities in the ninth century AD.

An important feature of the new model for the Classic Maya geopolitical landscape (besides some obvious parallels with the Cold War world order) was that the actions and roles taken by political actors were considered to be pragmatic, opportunistic, and devoid of any ideological substance. Smith (2003:134) praised Mayanists for this pragmatic approach that prioritized practical, historically rooted interpolity relations, which accounted for the down-to-earth, experiential dimension of the political landscape. But the approach also implied that there were no other roles, no political identities other than those dependent upon the realpolitik of the moment. From this perspective, it was only through extensive hegemonic networks created by the Tikal and Calakmul courts that Maya elites could experience a sense of community at a geopolitical level. There is even an implication that extensive palatial complexes at Tikal and Calakmul were created largely to house hosts of voluntary and less than voluntary guests in order to assure their loyalty (and the loyalties of their families and subjects) and to foster a sense of shared political and cultural belonging (Martin 2001).

Nevertheless, the vision of the Classic Maya political landscape proposed by Martin and Grube fails to explain why, despite ever-changing alliances, hegemonies, conflicts, and feuds lasting for generations, Classic Maya elites maintained a sense of shared cultural identity. Maya nobles were using the same writing system and speaking the same language (even when it was different from local vernaculars), celebrating the same rituals related to the passage of time, venerating similar deities, sharing mythology, dancing many of the same dances, and acceding to many of the same offices. While epigraphers benefited most from these broad similarities and parallels across the Classic Maya world in terms of deciphering inscriptions, the emphasis in recent epigraphic studies has been on difference, not commonality, and on individual sites and dynasties, rather than on broader political groups. It is highly symptomatic of the current state of affairs in Maya studies that when epigraphers do come back to the issue of how the Classic Maya represented their geopolitical communities, as in the case of the recent article by Wagner (2006), the discussion essentially never goes beyond what Barthel has already said about Copan Stela A or what Coe asserted about Maya communities in ethnohistoric sources.

This state of affairs in existing approaches to Classic Maya political landscapes makes it necessary to review the entire corpus of inscriptions with some explicitly formulated research questions in mind. The first question is whether we can find terms denoting or indexing membership in broader communities. If such terms exist, then we can proceed with identifying the most frequent contexts in which such terms are used and examining whether these contexts tell us something about how broader political communities—or a sense of membership in such communities—were maintained. The next research question would be to relate these references to other pieces of evidence suggesting mutual awareness, interactions between dynasties, and roles of group identities in a larger political landscape. We can also search for historical and mythological narratives underlying the notions of group identities.

ON QUADRIPARTITE SCHEMES

The parallels between quadripartite lists and arrangements of Classic Maya kings and quincuncial Postclassic and early colonial political landscapes were the first to be discovered and to captivate minds of scholars. Therefore, a discussion of the geopolitical landscape should begin by looking at some colonial references to quadripartite organization and some possible parallels in Classic Maya inscriptions.

One of the important colonial representations of the quadripartite arrangement is the passage in the Book of Chilam Balam of Chumayel that deals with the foundation of Chichen Itza. It presents the political landscape of Yucatan as a quincuncial world order, with Chichen Itza in the center of four "divisions" (*tzuk*; see a discussion of this term below). The narrative also makes clear that *tzuk* are groups of people and not geographical areas. The foundation is described as the "coming" of these "divisions" from the four places of origin associated with the different cardinal directions. The divisions are named in counterclockwise order: East-North-West-South.

> . . . 4 Ahau was the k'atun when they sought and discovered Chichen Itza. There it was that miraculous things were performed for them by their lords. Four divisions they were, when the four divisions of the nation, as they were called, went forth. From Kincolahpeten in the east one division went forth. From Nacocob in the north one division came forth. But one division came forth from Holtun Zuyua in

the west. One division came forth from Four-peaked Mountain, Nine Mountains is the name of the land (Roys 1973:139).

Only one of the four place names mentioned in this list can be tentatively identified: "Nine Mountains" could be Salinas de los Nueve Cerros on the Chixoy River at the southern periphery of the Maya Lowlands (Roys 1973:64). Interestingly, the inscription on Stela I at Copan, the southernmost Classic Maya polity, does mention "Nine Mountains" (*Bolonte' Witz*). If the identification of the "Nine Mountains" toponym is correct, then the other three might also be related to the peripheries of the Postclassic Maya world with Chichen Itza at its center.

The division of lands into four *tzuk*, with their proper lords subordinated to the center, is also mentioned in relation to the political organization of the Mayapan (Roys 1973:51, 139, 142) and Chontal Tamactun Acalan polities (Smailus 1975:47–48). Some scholars interpret this pattern as a Postclassic innovation, part of the Zuyuá ideology striving to reproduce the cosmic order on the ground, to bring cities and the subjugated lands in accordance with the primordial Tollan (Ciudad Ruiz and Lacadena García-Gallo 2001; López Austin and López Luján 1999:61–63). Nevertheless, if we look back to Classic Maya texts, we will find some references to this principle of geopolitical organization—not in the ways the geopolitical landscape was actually organized, but in the ways it was represented.

There are two kinds of Classic Maya references which can be attributed to this group. The first kind is when some individuals associate themselves or are associated by others with certain cardinal directions. These associations can be relative/relational (e.g., "lord to the east [of somebody else]"). They can also be absolute/categorical with an implication that the entire ecumene is divided into the four quadrants and the center. We may also wonder whether all Classic Maya courts shared the same concept of ecumene (particularly its extent) and whether this concept changed through time. The second kind of association is attested in the lists of four lords associated with distinct places, which may or may not correspond to the quadripartite organization. If the lords responsible for the text are not on the list, then the important question will be whether they see themselves outside or at the center of the geopolitical landscape.

A recently discovered text on a hieroglyphic step at Sabana Piletas in Campeche, Mexico, provides an excellent illustration of a relational association between individuals and cardinal directions (Grube et al. 2011:255–256). A passage of this lengthy inscription (A33–42; Figure 49a) mentions that "the land was destroyed where the southern lords [are], where the eastern lords [are], where the northern lords [are], where the western lords [are]."[48] There can be no doubt that Sabana Piletas is the center from which the military campaigns were unleashed upon its neighbors. Consequently, these designations are relational and make sense only from the viewpoint of this royal court.

The passage from the Center Tablet in the Temple of the Inscriptions at Palenque (G7–G9; Figure 49b) refers to the defeat of the "eastern and western lords" and likely provides another example of associations with cardinal directions in a relational framework (i.e., east and west of Palenque). But Lacadena García-Gallo (2007:211) suggests that, given the genre of the text that is reminiscent of k'atun prophecies, the downfall of "eastern and

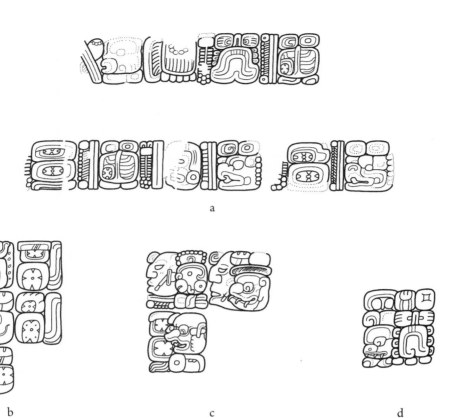

Figure 49 Relative cardinal direction titles in Classic Maya inscriptions: a) detail of Hieroglyphic Stairway 1 (A33–A42), Sabana Piletas (after Grube et al. 2011:pl. 2); b) detail of the Center Tablet (G7–G9), Temple of the Inscriptions, Palenque (after Robertson 1983:fig. 96); c) detail of Stela 10, Yaxchilan (after drawing by Ian Graham); and d) detail of Stela 1 (G9), Dos Caobas (after Stuart 2007c:30).

western lords" may function as a couplet meaning "all lords." If Lacadena is right, then "eastern lords" and "western lords" in this context are fixed categories of ascription and, therefore, are not related to the locations of these dynasts with respect to Palenque rulers.

Another example of relational associations between individuals and cardinal directions are the titles of foreign princesses in Late Classic inscriptions commissioned by the lords of Yaxchilan. Lady *Uhul Chan ?Lem* from the line of *Kanu'l* lords of Calakmul is attributed with the title of "eastern *kaloomte'*" (YAX St 10:pI2, St 34:pD6, DCB St 2:N2; Figure 49c). Lady *Wak Tuun* from the royal court of *Ik'a'* at Motul de San Jose is provided with the same title (YAX Ln 38:C4). Neither Calakmul nor Motul rulers ever claim to be "eastern *kaloomte'*" themselves. Therefore, Yaxchilan texts present a kind of local classification, where "eastern" probably means east of Yaxchilan. This is corroborated further by one of the titles of the Yaxchilan ruler *Itzamnaah Bahlam*—"the captor/guardian of the southern lord(s)" (*ucha'n nohol ajaw*) on Dos Caobas Stela 1 (Block G9; Figure 49d). No one around Yaxchilan ever calls himself a southern lord. Consequently, the likely significance of the title is that *Itzamnaah Bahlam* captured someone to the south of Yaxchilan. In fact, one of *Itzamnaah Bahlam*'s most celebrated victories was the capture of the *Xukal Naah* lord *Aj-Popol Chay*, who likely resided in Lacanha or another seat of the *Xukal Naah* dynasty (see previous chapter) to the south of Yaxchilan (Martin and Grube 2000:124).

When individuals associate themselves (or are associated in the inscriptions that they commission) with certain cardinal directions (Figure 50), such associations tend to be categorical, but there may be various reasons behind them. Late Classic rulers of Tikal, Yaxchilan, Machaquila, Ucanal, and Pusilha claim the title of "western *kaloomte*'" to stress real or imagined historical associations with Teotihuacan lords from the west and some aspirations for regional supremacy (Stuart 2000). Copan inscriptions reserve the title of "western *kaloomte*'" for the founder of the Copan dynasty, who did make a pilgrimage to the west and acquired the tokens of rulership (Stuart 2004a, 2005a). The inscription on Copan Stela 6 (C7) also uses this title when referring to *Waxaklajuun Ubaah Kan*, the Teotihuacan War Serpent deity. Therefore, being "western" in this context refers to the origins of one's claim of superior political authority tied to the *kaloomte*' title.

On the other hand, Late Classic Copan rulers, as well as their vassals and subsequent rivals from Quirigua, take the title of "southern *kaloomte*'" and the poorly understood "*?yook k'in/ook te'* of the southern sky house" (CPN Alt T, I':pN1, O', St 6:D5, QRG St H, J:43–44). This may indicate that Late Classic dynasts of Copan and Quirigua assigned themselves to the southern sector of the Maya world. Late Classic Yaxchilan rulers also called themselves "southern *?yook k'in*" (YAX HS 3:4T:A3). Consequently, either "south" included the area from Yaxchilan to Copan or we are dealing with different notions of the Maya world at these royal courts.

The titles of the Copan, Quirigua, and Yaxchilan rulers are not the only examples of royal families consistently associated with specific cardinal directions. Belize lords seem to be placed in the east of the world. The inscription on Stela 9 at Lamanai dedicated in AD 625 (Closs 1988) provides the local ruler with the title "eastern *kaloomte*'." Another eastern individual, *Til Man K'inich*, who takes the emblem glyph of "holy T579 lord," is the protagonist of the dedicatory inscription on an unprovenanced Early Classic figurine (Emmerich 1984:pl. 41). T579 lords are also mentioned at Altun Ha (Pendergast 1982:fig. 55), Naj Tunich Cave (Stone 1995:figs. 7–9), and Nim Li Punit (Wanyerka 2004:42–52). Therefore, it could be another Belize royal dynasty.

It is impossible to tease any reference to one's ascription to the western section of the Classic Maya world as a whole from references to the west as a place of origin or pilgrimage (see above). It may be significant that no one takes the title of "western *?yook k'in*." As for the north, it seems that no Maya dynasty of the Southern Lowlands ascribes itself or is ascribed by others to that cardinal direction. This pattern is clearly distinct from titles of rulers in Northern Yucatan. For example, lord *Jutuuw Kan Ek'* of a yet unidentified polity, who is mentioned in Ek Balam inscriptions, possibly as an overlord of local rulers, is called "northern *kaloomte*'" in the text of Mural A or Mural of the 96 glyphs (Lacadena García-Gallo 2003). Therefore, Northern Yucatan appears to be the northern quadrant of the Classic Maya landscape. Yet northern dynasties are of little or no concern for dynasts

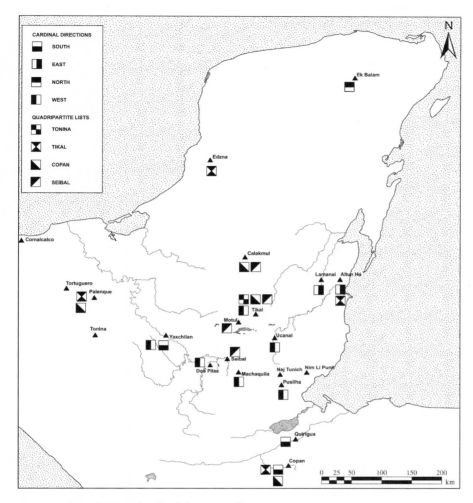

Figure 50 Distribution of cardinal direction titles.

in the Southern Lowlands to the extent that nearly all "northern" locations mentioned in southern inscriptions are mythical places.

In summary, when we consider the locations of royal families associating themselves with cardinal directions on the map and exclude all references to the "west," the places associated with these families correspond to the northern, eastern, and southern margins of the Classic Maya world as we would define it. This observation does not necessarily imply that our understanding of the Classic Maya world is the same as the ancient perception of it, but it does suggest that there was such a notion and that the Maya world as seen through the eyes of its rulers and their courts was divided—in terms of representations and classification—along the cardinal directions.

As we have established that certain royal families consistently associated themselves with certain cardinal directions, the next important data set to consider is quadripartite lists or references to groups of four rulers evoked in different kinds of narratives and contexts as representations of the geopolitical order based on the quadripartite scheme. Not all of these lists can even qualify as representations of the geopolitical landscape. In the case of Seibal and Copan inscriptions, the narratives describe actual period-ending rituals involving four lords at four cardinal directions. Neither Seibal nor Copan lords are in the center of the cosmogram. We may only speculate that these specific ritual arrangements were related to the representations of the geopolitical order.

The first true quadripartite list appears in an inscription on an Early Classic altar at Tonina (Mn 160; see Graham et al. 2006:101) that was commissioned in AD 514 (Mathews 2001). A section of the text (Figure 51) mentions the deaths of four lords who passed away a few years before the demise of a local ruler. The purpose of this narrative seems to be to provide a broader political and ritual context for his death. The choice of four rulers from four different places is hardly accidental. The list begins with a *Kanu'l* lord (D29), probably from Dzibanche. The name and titles of the second remain undeciphered (D31). The third dead ruler seems to be a *Mutal* lord of Tikal (D33). The emblem glyph of the fourth deceased king is unclear (D35).

Two inscriptions on the Tikal carved bones mentioned above provide another example of quadripartite lists. These texts resemble lists of *wahy* characters (Grube and

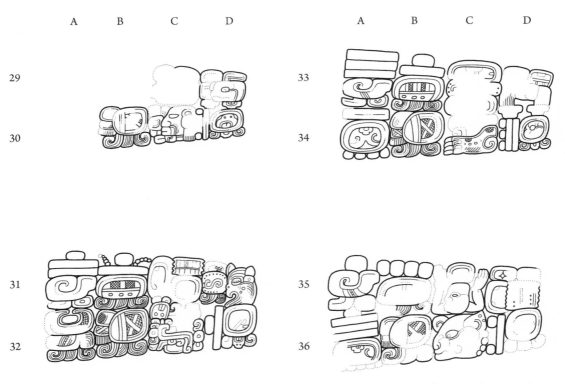

Figure 51 Early Classic quadripartite list, detail of Monument 160 (A29–D36), Tonina (after Graham et al. 2006:101).

Nahm 1994; Houston and Stuart 1989), following a pattern of associating certain kinds of objects or entities with various royal families. In this case, each royal family is associated with a distinct kind of "bone" (*baak*), which may be interpreted literally to be the same as the carved bones in the offering or as a reference to captives who are also called *baak*. If we assume that the order in which these families are mentioned is the same as in the inscription at Sabana Piletas discussed above (south lords, east lords, north lords, and west lords), then we find the royal family associated with Copan placed in the south, Altun Ha dynasty in the east, Edzna lords in the north, and Palenque/Tortuguero rulers in the west.[49] *Mutal* lords of Tikal are noticeably absent in this quadripartite arrangement. The implication of their absence could be that Tikal rulers saw themselves at the center of this quadripartite world order. This is the closest the Classic Maya texts ever get to the comparable quadripartite representations of the geopolitical order in early colonial narratives.

Nevertheless, it is hard to extend the interpretation of these Classic Maya quadripartite schemes beyond the acknowledgment that they exist. For example, Tikal lists come from the tomb of *Jasaw Chan K'awiil* in Temple 1 and were probably carved sometime around AD 734 when he died (Martin and Grube 2000). The four dynasties mentioned in the list were clearly not the only geopolitical powers at that time. Yaxchilan, Dos Pilas, and Naranjo rulers played major roles in their respective regions. Therefore, Tikal lists represent the geopolitical order in accordance with what Tikal rulers wanted to see. The intention of the author of the inscription might be to name the four principal allies or vassals of Tikal rulers, but there is no evidence in support of or against this hypothesis. The list provides no hint that Copan, Palenque, Altun Ha, or Edzna lords identified themselves with a distinct geopolitical group.

The likelier interpretation of the list would be that it evoked the four royal families placed at the boundaries of the Classic Maya world as it was represented at Tikal. This interpretation would at least find support in the fact that Copan and Altun Ha lords associate themselves with the south and the east and are seemingly located at the southern and the eastern edges of the Classic Maya world as we see it today.

The presence of these ideas also implies that there were notions of the others—foreigners, in other words, people beyond the confines of the Classic Maya landscape. The term for foreigners, *tz'ul*,[50] is attested in Classic Maya inscriptions, although only three examples are known so far. One appears on the aforementioned incised bones in Burial 116 at Tikal (Figure 52a) and possibly refers to foreign insignia or captives (*tz'ul baak* "foreign bone") in possession of Copan rulers. The other example comes from the name of the captive in the inscription on a stingray spine from Comalcalco (Figure 52b). It is significant that, given Comalcalco's location, its rulers might indeed have waged wars against some non-Maya groups. The third occurrence of the *tz'ul* term on a recently published monument fragment is particularly significant (Figure 52c). Its inscription mentions the arrival of a "foreign *kaloomte'*" (*tz'ul kaloomte'*) in AD 758, followed by an attack against an unknown location four days later (Luin and Matteo 2010; Stuart 2010). Therefore, the term *tz'ul* seems to be reserved for people and things beyond the confines of the Classic Maya world.

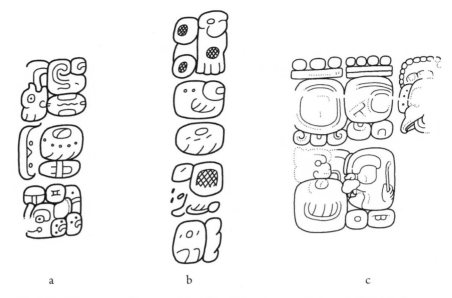

a   b   c

Figure 52 References to "foreigners" (*tz'ul*) in Classic Maya inscriptions: a) detail of an incised bone (MT 42B:1–3), Burial 116, Tikal (after Moholy-Nagy and Coe 2008:figs. 194d, 205g); b) detail of a carved stingray spine, Comalcalco (after Zender 2004:fig. 78a); and c) detail of an unprovenanced monument fragment, possibly from Southern Peten, Guatemala (after Luin and Matteo 2010:figs. 1–2).

ON SEVEN DIVISIONS AND THIRTEEN DIVISIONS

The titles *Huk Tzuk* and *Huxlajuun Tzuk* are our best candidates for terms indexing membership in geopolitical groups within the Classic Maya world. Over a decade ago, Beliaev (2000) suggested a new interpretation of these terms in an article that remained a rare, if not sole, attempt to step away from the emblem glyph–oriented visions of Classic Maya political landscapes. Individuals from different places and dynasties have consistent associations with either *Huk Tzuk* or *Huxlajuun Tzuk*. When plotted on a map, the distribution of individuals associated with these titles seems to be confined to two distinct regions: the Eastern Peten and lakes for *Huk Tzuk*, and the Central and Northeastern Peten for *Huxlajuun Tzuk* (Beliaev 2000:map 1).

The terms *huk tzuk* and *huxlajuun tzuk*—"Seven Divisions" and "Thirteen Divisions"—are never used in direct references to spatial entities of any kind and seem to apply only to individuals and groups of people. In early colonial Ch'olti' (Morán 1695), Chontal (Smailus 1975:132), and Yukatek (Barrera Vásquez et al. 1995:865–867) texts and vocabularies, the word *tzuk* means "part" or "division" of something. It is also used as a numerical classifier for counting constituent parts or divisions. The underlying implication is that there is always something whole that is divided into *tzuk*. When someone says "one *tzuk*," it can mean "first part" (of something) or "another one" (of the same kind, from the same set). This term and the words derived from it can be used to designate all kinds of fractions,

PLACE AND IDENTITY IN CLASSIC MAYA NARRATIVES

including territorial divisions and military units. Therefore, the term *huk tzuk* points to an entity divided into seven parts and the term *huxlajuun tzuk* indicates that there is another entity divided into thirteen parts. If somebody calls himself or herself "*huk tzuk*," we can translate it as "Seven Divisions [person]" or as "[a person from one of] Seven Divisions."

The initial interpretation of these terms was "provinces," and it was believed that they referred to the internal organization of Classic Maya polities (Schele and Mathews 1998:23). Colonial sources like the Maldonado-Paxbolon Papers (Smailus 1975:49) and the Books of Chilam Balam (e.g. CHU 78:1–2, 80:4–5) used the term *tzuk* to designate parts of polities. But Beliaev (2000) managed to demonstrate that Seven Divisions and Thirteen Divisions were used to distinguish people from different polities within broader geopolitical domains (Figure 53a). As mentioned above, the distribution of the two titles corresponds to two distinct geographical areas (Beliaev 2000:65–67).

While all references to Seven Divisions are from the Late Classic period, there is one hint that this group was already in place during the Early Classic period. The inscription on Stela 5 at La Sufricaya (Figure 54a)—a palace complex near the archaeological site of Holmul (Estrada Belli et al. 2009)—mentions the seating of "seven lord(s)" (*chumlaj huk ajaw*) in AD 422 (Grube 2003:695–698). Given that the region is part of the area associated with Seven Divisions in the Late Classic period, it is reasonable to assume that "seven lords" are the heads of the divisions.

Some people of Seven Divisions are differentiated into "western" and "eastern." There is an apparent correspondence with their geographical location. Naranjo lords can be referred to as "[people from] Seven Divisions" in inscriptions at Caracol (Figure 54b) and in texts painted on the vessels from the Naranjo area (K1398). A set of texts at Tikal, including the inscription on Altar 8 (Figure 54c), mention the capture of a certain *Chak Tok Wayaab*—a title of the rulers of Holmul and La Sufricaya to the north of Naranjo (Martin 2000:111–113; Tokovinine 2006)—and refer to the captive as a "*Huk Tzuk* (person)" (Beliaev 2000:74–75).

Two Naranjo queens, a lady from *Tuubal* (Figure 54d)—an unidentified location in the lakes region somewhere between the sites of Motul de San Jose, Tikal, and Naranjo (Beliaev 2000:64–65; Zender 2005:13–14)—and a lady from *Yaxa'* (Figure 54e)—the ancient name of the Yaxha Lake and the corresponding archeological site (Stuart 1985)— carry the titles of "western Seven Divisions" (*ochk'in huk tzuk*). A scribal signature on a vase painted for a Río Azul lord refers to the painter as "western Seven Divisions" and as a "person from *Ik'a'*" (Figure 54f). *Ik'a'* is a place name associated with Motul de San Jose on Lake Peten Itza (Tokovinine and Zender 2012:31–35). All three locations—*Yaxa'*, *Tuubal*, and *Ik'a'*—are to the west on the Holmul–Naranjo axis. Topoxte, located on Yaxha Lake, may also be added to the list because the inscription on a carved bone in Burial 49 (Hermes Cifuentes 2000) identifies the owner as a "western Seven Divisions" (Figure 54g).

The dedicatory inscription on yet another painted vase (Figure 54h) refers to its owner as a "*Kokom* lord from *Sak Nikte'*, eastern Seven Divisions" (Beliaev 2000:64). Other *Kokom* lords are mentioned on fragments of painted vessels uncovered in the palace dumps at the archaeological site of Buenavista del Cayo (Houston et al. 1992). Buenavista del Cayo is located some fifteen kilometers to the east of Naranjo and used to be one of

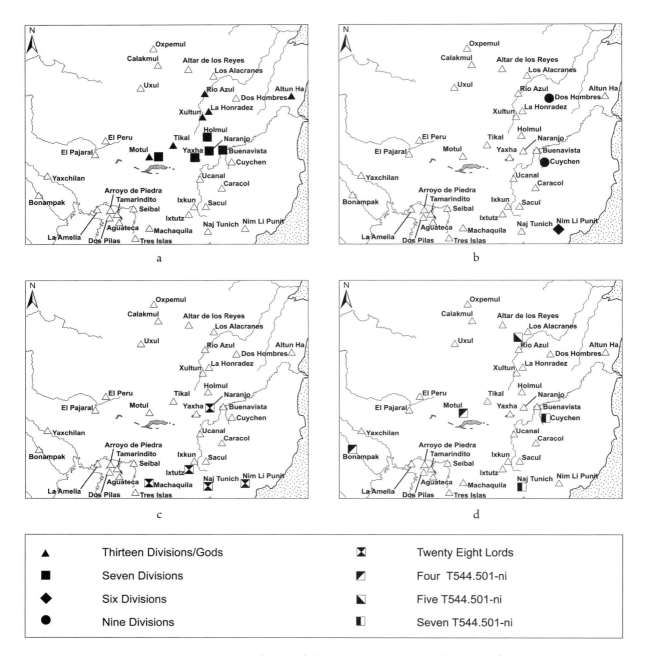

Figure 53 Distribution of Classic Maya geopolitical collectivities: a) Seven and Thirteen Divisions; b) Nine and Six Divisions; c) T544.501-ni groups; and d) Twenty-eight lords.

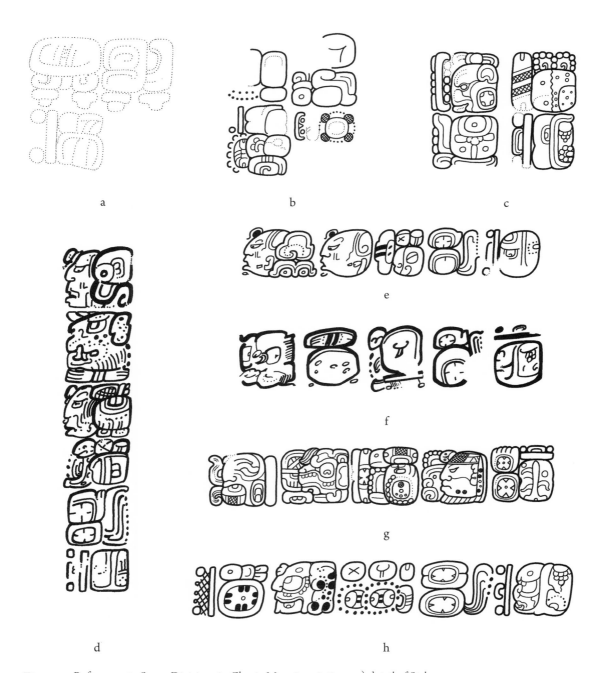

a

b

c

d

e

f

g

h

Figure 54 References to Seven Divisions in Classic Maya inscriptions: a) detail of Stela 5 (pB4–5), La Sufricaya (after 3D scan by the author); b) detail of Stela 22 (G11–H12), Caracol (after Grube 1994:fig. 9.3); c) detail of Altar 8 (A1–B2), Tikal (after Jones and Satterthwaite 1982:fig. 30); d) detail of the inscription on a Late Classic vase (K7750); e) detail of the inscription on a Late Classic vase (K635); f) detail of the inscription on a Late Classic vase (K2295); g) detail of a carved bone (A2–A6), Burial 49, Topoxte (after Teufel 2000:fig. 107); and h) detail of the inscription on a Late Classic vase (K2730).

the lesser political centers under the aegis of Naranjo rulers. If Buenavista del Cayo is *Sak Nikte'*, the residence of *Kokom* lords, then eastern Seven Divisions are another example of correspondence between the title and the actual location of people on the landscape as we see it today.

Another important aspect of the *Huk Tzuk* title is that self-identified people of Seven Divisions occur mostly in inscriptions on portable objects like painted vessels and carved bones (Beliaev 2004:fig. 4a; Hermes Cifuentes 2000:fig. 107). Known references to *Huk Tzuk* people on monuments correspond to contexts in which they do not belong to the same royal court as those who commissioned the texts (e.g., lords from other places, captives, nonlocal parents). An inscription on a polychrome vase may state that it belongs to the ruler of Naranjo *K'ahk' Tiliw Chan Chahk* of Seven Divisions (K1398), but none of the many carved monumental inscriptions at Naranjo would refer to that same king by the *Huk Tzuk* title. On the other hand, parentage statements in the inscriptions at Naranjo would refer to foreign queens as "western Seven Divisions [people]," just as the inscriptions at Caracol and Tikal would refer to people from Naranjo and Holmul as "Seven Divisions [people]" (Beliaev 2000).[51]

Based on the pattern outlined above, Beliaev (2000) suggested that the *Huk Tzuk* titles refer to a geopolitical group of royal families, or even an ethnic identity that would be evoked only in certain contexts—especially when one's political enemies or strangers are classified as "the other," subverting or denying more specific political identities. A Naranjo lord stripped of all titles is a "[a person from one of] Seven Divisions," just like other people from Seven Divisions. The subversion of this aspect of the royal identity in the monumental record was possibly an intentional trope aimed at elevating the king above other *Huk Tzuk*. No internal hierarchy between *Huk Tzuk* people is implied.

The second geopolitical entity similarly divided into *tzuk* is Thirteen Divisions, *Huxlajuun Tzuk* (Figure 53a). The three earliest references to *Huxlajuun Tzuk* people come from the inscriptions at Dos Pilas commissioned by its first ruler, *Bajlaj Chan K'awiil*. A passage on Step 3 of Hieroglyphic Stairway 4 (Figure 55a) deals with this Dos Pilas king's defeat at the hands of Tikal lord *Nuun Ujol Chahk* in AD 672, and refers to *Bajlaj Chan K'awiil*'s archenemy as *Mutal* T1006a-**li** *Huxlajuun Tzuk* ("*Mutal* . . . Thirteen Divisions [person]"). A retribution delivered to *Nuun Ujol Chahk* in AD 679 is described on the third step of the western section of Dos Pilas Hieroglyphic Stairway 2 as the downfall of *Nuun Ujol Chahk*'s weapons/armies, followed by piling skulls and pooling blood (Guenter 2003:27). Skulls and blood belong to *Huxlajuun Tzuk* and Tikal people identified by an eroded title combined with the *Mutal* place name for Tikal (Figure 55b).[52] Although the hieroglyphic block after *Mutal* is badly damaged, it probably contained the same enigmatic T1006a-**li** title. Dos Pilas Stela 9 depicts *Bajlaj Chan K'awiil* dancing in AD 682 on top of a captive who might have been one of the lords defeated earlier in AD 679. A caption identifies the captive as *Nuun Bahlam*, lord of *Wak* T510 *Nal* and a person from Thirteen Divisions (Figure 55c).

Beliaev (2000:66, 77) noticed that while *Bajlaj Chan K'awiil* is nearly always mentioned as "holy *Mutal* lord" in Dos Pilas inscriptions, *Nuun Ujol Chahk* and other Tikal characters are referred to as "*Mutal* lords," *Mutal* T1006a-**li**, and *Huxlajuun Tzuk*. Since *Nuun Ujol*

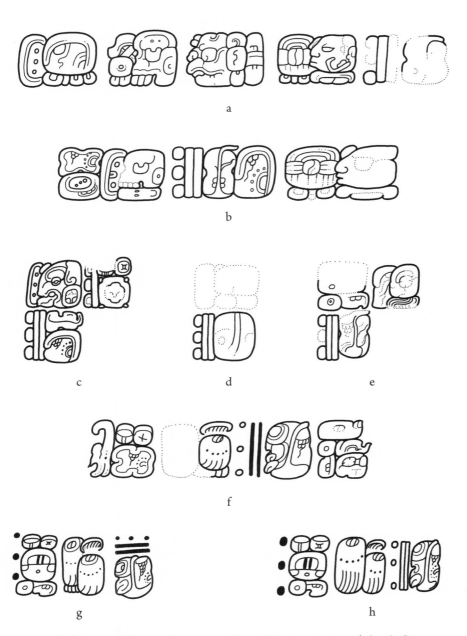

Figure 55 References to Thirteen Divisions in Classic Maya inscriptions: a) detail of Step 3 (D1–F1), Hieroglyphic Stairway 4, Dos Pilas (after Houston 1993:fig. 4-11); b) detail of Step 3 (C2–E1), western section, Hieroglyphic Stairway 2, Dos Pilas (after drawing by Ian Graham); c) detail of Stela 9 (C1–C2), Dos Pilas (after photograph by the author); d) detail of Stela 4 (B2–B3), La Honradez (after Von Euw and Graham 1984:106); e) detail of Stela 5 (C3–C4), Xultun (after Von Euw 1978:24); f) detail of the inscription on a Late Classic vessel (K8015); g) detail of the inscription on a Late Classic vessel (K2295); and h) detail of the inscription on a Late Classic vessel (K7720).

Chahk and *Bajlaj Chan K'awiil* were brothers or half brothers (Guenter 2003:3), the difference in titles likely reflected *Bajlaj Chan K'awiil's* claim to be a legitimate king of Tikal instead of *Nuun Ujol Chahk*. The use of the title *Huxlajuun Tzuk* was then part of the rhetoric aimed at presenting *Nuun Ujol Chahk* as a political "other" and a person of lesser and potentially more generic status. In this context, it is probably significant that the captive depicted on Stela 9 is not even associated with the *Mutal* dynasty or with *Mutal* as a place. The text identifies him as a member of a different royal line, but also as a *Huxlajuun Tzuk*, suggesting that the latter is a broader category comprising members of various royal families.

Tikal and *Wak* T510 *Nal* lords were not the only royal families associated with Thirteen Divisions (Figure 53a). The names of protagonists depicted on La Honradez Stelae 1 and 4 (Figure 55d) and Xultun Stela 5 (Figure 55e) also feature *Huxlajuun Tzuk* titles. An unprovenanced vase mentions a Xultun lord identified by the "*Baax Witz* lord" emblem glyph[53] and the *k'ab te' yook k'in* title (Houston 1986). His name phrase also includes *Huxlajuun Tzuk* (Figure 55f). The inscriptions on vessels commissioned by lords of *Hux Haab Te'* (Figure 55g–h) and associated with Río Azul indicate that they were *Huxlajuun Tzuk*. The distribution of *Huxlajuun Tzuk* individuals suggests that their zone extends northwest of Tikal into the Río Azul/Río Hondo basin (Figure 53a).

Perhaps the most important context of *Huxlajuun Tzuk* is the inscription on Naranjo Stela 30 (Graham 1978:79–80). It details a series of rituals undertaken in AD 714 by the Naranjo ruler holy *Sa'aal* lord *K'ahk' Tiliw Chan Chahk*, marking the third year of a k'atun, an important station in the twenty-year cycle. The front of the monument depicts *K'ahk' Tiliw Chan Chahk* with a staff. He is dressed as a fire god ("Jaguar God of the Underworld") and is standing on top of a captive. The inscription next to the figure of the king states that he is in the act of a "night headband-binding" (*ti ak'ab k'alhu'n*) in the guise of the deity. The only military event mentioned in the main text on the back of the monument is the conquest of *Sak Ha'* a few months earlier, so the captive was likely taken during that campaign.

The focus of the main text is on period-ending rituals. First, it reports that the king offered copal before two deities. Unfortunately, their names are no longer readable. The next event is a dance in T700 *Nal*, a term that is associated with dancing at various sites and either denotes a type of location designated for dancing or stands for a particular dance (Figure 56a). According to the inscription, the king is accompanied by people of *Huk Tzuk*, *Huxlajuun Tzuk*, and *Jo'* T544.501-**ni**.[54] If the interpretation of the titles *Huk Tzuk* and *Huxlajuun Tzuk* is correct, then the text claims that lords from nearly the entire Central and Eastern Peten participated in the event. The term *Jo'* T544.501-**ni** will be discussed below, but it appears to designate a group of lords from the Eastern Peten. It is the only mention of *Huxlajuun Tzuk* at Naranjo.

We need to look at the historical context of this massive performance in order to understand why all those lords would attend a dance event at Naranjo. In AD 714, Naranjo rulers were at the peak of their political influence. From the early AD 690s on, they initiated a series of successful military campaigns, first as vassals of powerful Calakmul rulers and then as independent actors after Calakmul's defeat by Tikal in AD 695 (Beliaev 2000:70–74; Houston 1983; Martin and Grube 2000:76–77). It seems that Naranjo lords acted quickly to fill the political void left by Calakmul's downfall and to become the main power in the

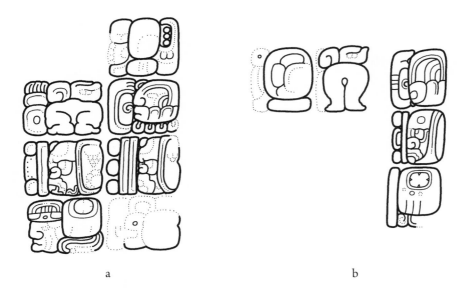

Figure 56 Public events in Naranjo inscriptions: a) detail of Stela 30 (D12–D15; after Graham 1978:80); and b) detail of Stela 13 (B1–D7; after Graham 1975:37).

Eastern Peten and lakes region. The conquest of *Yaxa'* (Yaxha Lake) and *Tuubal* put them in control of the eastern lakes region, extending their dominion to within one day's trip of Tikal and to the vicinity of the *Ik'a'* rulers of Motul de San Jose. The conquests of *Yootz* (an unknown location presumably north of Naranjo) and *K'an Witz Nal* (the site of Ucanal) presumably extended the hegemony farther north and south. According to Naranjo Stela 2, *K'ahk' Tiliw Chan Chahk* oversaw the accession of new *Yootz* and *K'an Witz Nal* lords in AD 712 (Martin and Grube 2008:77). Although we do not know the actual location of *Sak Ha'*, the fact that it is mentioned at Dos Pilas and Seibal suggests that its conquest was another important step in expanding Naranjo's hegemony farther west and south. All *Huk Tzuk* and probably some *Huxlajuun Tzuk* lords found themselves under the sway of *Sa'aal* kings. The inscription on an unprovenanced vessel (K8622), indistinguishable from the exquisite pottery painted for *K'ahk' Tiliw Chan Chahk* (K927, K1398), identifies its owner as a "Thirteen Divisions [person]." The vase might be a gift to a new vassal (Tokovinine 2006:361–362).

Therefore, in terms of historical circumstances, possible motivations of political actors, and the rhetoric chosen for the inscription on Stela 30, the presence of *Huk Tzuk*, *Huxlajuun Tzuk*, and *Jo'* T544.501-**ni** lords at a dance at Naranjo reflected its new geopolitical role as a regional power. As we know, that role was not to last. Naranjo was vanquished by Tikal in AD 744–748 (Martin 1996b; Martin and Grube 2000:78–79). But by the end of the reign of *K'ahk' Ukalaw Chan Chahk*, *K'ahk' Tiliw Chan Chahk*'s son, Tikal lords were no longer that powerful and Naranjo returned to some geopolitical prominence (Martin and Grube 2000:80–81). This resurgence is marked with another major period-ending ceremony dedicated to the middle of a k'atun in AD 780. The inscription on Naranjo Stela 13

(Figure 56b) reports that there was dancing with foreign lords once again, although the list now consists of only *Huk Tzuk* and *Jo'* T544.501-**ni**, complemented by divine witnesses typically mentioned at period-ending events—*Bolon Chan Yook k'in* and *Waklajuun Yook k'in*. The absence of *Huxlajuun Tzuk* reflects Naranjo's reduced sphere of influence.

A further insight into the meaning of *Huxlajuun Tzuk* is provided by the inscription on Altar 3 at Altar de los Reyes in Campeche, Mexico, briefly mentioned in the preceding chapter (Grube 2008:180–182; Šprajc and Grube 2003). The top of the altar (Figure 27b) features a caption that states "divine land(s) Thirteen Divisions" (*k'uh[ul] kab huxlajuun [tzuk]*). Although the last hieroglyphic block is eroded, the size of the signs is different from the nearby **ka-KAB** or **ka-ba** spelling, so its reading could be **tzu-ku**. The sides of the altar feature an inscription that likely begins with a statement like "it is their [x] thrones" and then continues by naming thirteen emblem glyph titles, although part of the text is missing (Figure 57). The list of preserved emblem glyphs includes "holy *Mutal* lord," "holy *Chatahn* person," "holy *Baakal* lord, holy *Kanu'l* lord," "holy *Ik'a'* lord," "holy T1008.552," and "holy T579 lord."

Once the altar was discovered, it became apparent that it represented a certain concept of geopolitical organization (Grube 2008:180–182; Šprajc and Grube 2003). But the precise nature of the concept remained somewhat unclear. If associating references to *Huxlajuun Tzuk* in other texts with *Huxlajuun [Tzuk]* on the altar is correct, then the concept relates directly to "Thirteen Divisions" as a set of thirteen dynasties as well as as to "holy lands" or "divine lands." The inscription on Altar 3 then expands the list of known *Huxlajuun Tzuk* dynasties and the geographical area of *Huxlajuun Tzuk*. *Baakal* lords resided at Palenque, Tortuguero, and Comalcalco. *Ik'a'* lords are associated with Motul de San Jose, and possibly other sites. The court of *Kanu'l* kings was at Calakmul and Dzibanche. The T1008.552 title is attested in the names of Edzna rulers (EDZ St 18, 21, 22, HS 1). Holy *chatahn* people lived in Calakmul and Nakbe. Lords of T579 made pilgrimages to the cave of Naj Tunich (NTN Dr 65) and attended events at Nim Li Punit (NMP St 2), but the location of their court remains unknown. The protagonist of the inscription on a jade plaque found in Tomb B-4/6 at Altun Ha (Pendergast 1982:fig. 55) seems to carry the title of "holy T579-**ni** lord," so this dynasty could be located in Belize, at Altun Ha or farther south, closer to Naj Tunich and Nim Li Punit.

None of these dynasties are explicitly associated with *Huxlajuun Tzuk* in other texts. But the case of Tikal lords mentioned in Dos Pilas inscriptions suggests that *Huxlajuun Tzuk* is not a common title and its use constitutes a kind of rhetorical device. In addition, *Ik'a'* lords carry the title *Huxlajuun K'uh* or "Thirteen Gods" in a number of texts on vessels (Figure 58a) and Flores Stela 1 (Figure 58b). This title may carry the same or similar significance as *Huxlajuun Tzuk*. It also appears in the inscription on earflares from Tomb A-1/1 at Altun Ha (Mathews 1979). The owner of the object is said to be the mother of a lord who carries the titles of *baah tuun/ba'k* and *Huxlajuun K'uh* (Figure 58c). Given that another object from Altun Ha features an emblem glyph attested in the list of Altar de los Reyes Altar 3, the appearance of *Huxlajuun K'uh* may be more than just a coincidence. The caveat here is that both portable objects at Altun Ha could be gifts from elsewhere.

Houston, Stuart, and Taube (2006:89–97) propose to interpret the inscription on Altar de los Reyes Altar 3 in the context of widespread association between representations

Figure 57 King list: detail of Altar 3, Altar de los Reyes (after Grube 2008:fig. 8.6).

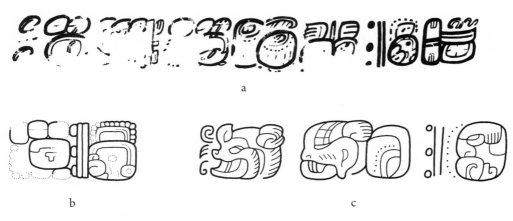

a

b   c

Figure 58 "Thirteen Gods" title in Classic Maya inscriptions: a) detail of the inscription on a Late Classic vessel (K1452); b) detail of Stela 1 (A4–B4), Flores (after field drawing by Stephen D. Houston and photographs by the author); and c) detail of the inscription on earflares (D–F), Tomb A-1/1, Altun Ha (after Mathews 1979:79).

of rulers and *Ajaw* day names of k'atuns. For instance, the portraits of a *Kanu'l* lord and his wife on the Schaffhausen vessel mentioned in the previous chapter double as *Ajaw* day k'atun names; this association is confirmed by the captions to the portraits (Houston et al. 2006:89–91, fig. 82.30). A list of thirteen holy lords on the side of a circular altar then looks like a k'atun wheel, a key space-time concept for Postclassic Maya known from early colonial sources and evidenced in precontact objects like Mayapan turtle sculptures encircled with thirteen *Ajaw* signs (Taube 1988:fig. 2a). Taube recognized these representations of the cycle of thirteen named k'atuns, and he argued that images of the turtle and early colonial depictions of the k'atun wheel symbolize the circular earth surface divided into thirteen parts, in accordance with the notion that each k'atun has its place of rulership and a divine patron. In doing so, he acknowledges that his thinking follows along the lines of an earlier work by Roys (1954). Roys identified Avedaño de Loyola's seventeenth-century account of Itza shortly before the conquest (Means 1917:141–144) and the Book of Chilam Balam of Chumayel (Roys 1973) as key sources of information about the concept. In Loyola's words,

> . . . These ages are thirteen in number; each has its separate idol and its priest with a separate prophecy of its events. These thirteen ages are divided into thirteen parts which divide this kingdom of Yucatán and each age with its idol, priest and prophecy rules in one of these thirteen parts of the land according as they have divided it (Means 1917:141).

The Book of Chilam Balam of Chumayel presents a similar picture of thirteen k'atuns, each associated with a place of rulership and certain auguries (Roys 1973:fig. 28). One passage deals specifically with the creation of this spatial and temporal order:

> . . . 4 Ahau was the name of the k'atun when occurred the birth of Pauahs, when the rulers descended. Thirteen k'atuns they reigned; thus they were named while they ruled. 4 Ahau was the name of the k'atun when they descended; the great descent and the little descent they were called. Thirteen k'atuns they reined. So they were called. While they were settled, thirteen were their settlements (Roys 1973:139).[55]

It is tempting to trace this notion of thirteen k'atuns associated with thirteen seats of power back to the Classic period. Lacadena García-Gallo (2007) recently argued that the genres of k'atun chronicles and prophecies can be identified in some Late Classic inscriptions. It would be wrong to interpret this concept of Thirteen Divisions literally as a historical account or a religious rule of shifting power every twenty years. There are no historical data to support that. Rather we have a landscape divided in space and time between thirteen royal dynasties and possibly between thirteen deities, with an implication that one polity may claim a supreme status that would not likely last. It is significant that the two "number thirteen" titles in Classic inscriptions are "Thirteen Divisions" and "Thirteen Gods," possibly making allusions to lands and gods of k'atuns.

In Chumayel, the quincunx and the k'atun wheel order do not seem to be mutually exclusive because the k'atun wheel is also subdivided according to cardinal directions. When it comes to Classic-period inscriptions, one can observe that the dynasties in the quadripartite lists are the same as those found in the k'atun wheel list on the Altar de los Reyes monument. The only exceptions are the emblem glyphs of the Copan and Seibal lords, but they might be in the missing section of the Altar de los Reyes inscription.

The issue of inclusion and exclusion becomes particularly important if we consider the fact that, with the possible exception of *Ik'a'* lords, membership in *Huxlajuun Tzuk* and *Huk Tzuk* does not seem to overlap. People from Seven Divisions are excluded from k'atun wheel lists, quadripartite lists discussed above, and even from *wahy* demon lists (see Grube and Nahm 1994). Another group of lords absent from these lists are Usumacinta royal families, with the exception of *Baakal* lords.

It is possible that Seven Divisions represents a distinct and possibly competing model of the geopolitical order. Most of the references to *Huk Tzuk* are associated with the Naranjo dynasty and its sphere of influence at the peak of its expansion and during the later resurgence. That said, as Beliaev (2000) pointed out, the notion of Seven Divisions can be linked to a concept with deep roots in Mesoamerica, manifested in Nahua *Chicomoztoc* ("Seven Caves"), K'iche' *Wukub Pek, Wukub Siwan* ("Seven Caves, Seven Canyons"), Cakchiquel *Wuk Amaq* ("Seven Nations"), or Zuñi divisions. The underlying ideas are different from Thirteen Divisions—it is not about thirteen kings and gods who descended to govern in space-time, but about a shared point of origin and the organization of entire social groups.

The seven-part world order can also be found in the books of Chilam Balam. While the Chumayel account of the foundation of the colonial landscape describes the church in the heart of Merida as a k'atun wheel cosmogram, the new world order itself is outlined as a seven-part structure (Roys 1973:fig. 27): the bottom, the top, the middle and far left, the middle and far right, and the center (Merida). One may wonder if the actual structure implied here is the pan-Mesoamerican division of space into east, north, west, south, zenith, nadir, and center.

> . . . 13 Etz'nab was the day when the land was established. 13 Cheneb was when they measured off by paces the cathedral, the dark house of instruction, the cathedral in heaven. Thus it was also measured off by paces here on earth. Thirteen k'atuns was the total count, that is, thirteen feet in heaven. Four feet, and from there nine feet, the total count of its extent in heaven. Then it is again measured off by feet from the face of the earth. Four feet separate it from the face of the earth. Mani is the base of the land. Campeche is the tip of the wing of the land. Calkini is the base of the wing of the land. Itzmal is the middle of the wing of the land. Zaci is the tip of the wing of the land. Conkal is the head of the land (Roys 1973:125–126).

As in the case of Thirteen Divisions, these parallels from colonial sources should by no means be interpreted as direct analogies. But they do suggest the presence of similar organizing principles and concepts, which may have been derived from the Classic Maya landscape.

Thirteen Divisions and Seven Divisions are not the only collectivities labeled by number and the term *tzuk* (Figure 53b). Stela 2 at Nim Li Punit (Figure 59a) mentions a nonlocal lord whose full name is *Yich'ak K'uh Wak Tzuk*—"*Yich'ak K'uh*, Six Divisions [person]." But it is not clear if "Six Divisions" in this context refers to a group identity or is just part of one's personal name.

Two examples of the *Bolon Tzuk* ("Nine Divisions") title in Central and Northern Belize represent a more compelling case. One title is attested in the name mentioned in the dedicatory inscription on a plate fragment (Figure 59b) found at Dos Hombres (Robichaux

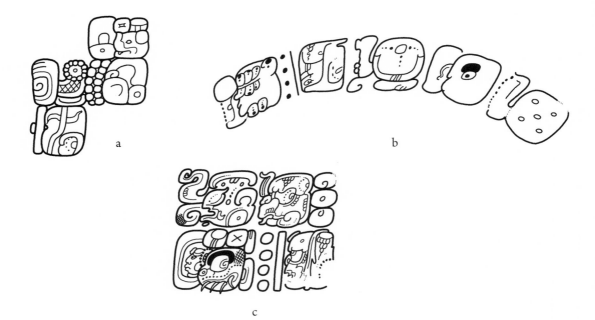

Figure 59 Six and Nine Divisions in Classic Maya inscriptions: a) detail of Stela 2 (J2–I4), Nim Li Punit (after Wanyerka 2004:fig. 17); b) detail of the inscription on a plate (B–F), Dos Hombres (after Robichaux and Houk 2005:fig. 4); and c) detail of the inscription on a vase (P6–Q7), Cuychen Cave (after Helmke n.d.:fig. 10).

and Houk 2005). This example is not particularly clear because the title is followed by a possible toponym or part of the personal name, contrary to the pattern observed with *Huk Tzuk* and *Huxlajuun Tzuk* titles, which always appear at the end of name phrases. The second occurrence of *Bolon Tzuk* comes from the text on a fragmentary vessel found in the Cuychen Cave (Helmke n.d.), and is more convincing because it follows a previously unknown emblem glyph title at the end of the protagonist's father's name (Figure 59c). Therefore, it is plausible that these two examples reveal the presence of another geopolitical collectivity of "Nine Divisions." The scarce epigraphic record of this region offers no further insights into this group.

T544.501-NI GROUPS

A reader of Naranjo inscriptions mentioning the visiting groups of lords discussed above might have noticed that *Huxlajuun Tzuk* and *Huk Tzuk* are not the only collectivities in these narratives. A third group is indexed by the enigmatic *Jo'* T544.501-**ni** title. The context strongly indicates that we are dealing with another geopolitical community defined with an undeciphered term and the number five. References to *Jo'* T544.501-**ni** are scattered throughout Late Classic inscriptions (Figure 53c). A *lakam* official featured in the dedicatory text and caption to a scene on an unprovenanced vase from the Río Azul area

(Figure 60a) is the *tat* (father?) of a Río Azul lord and also carries the *Jo'* T544.501-**ni** title. On another unprovenanced vase (Figure 60b), the mother of a Río Azul ruler is also identified as *Jo'* T544.501-**ni**. Therefore, it is possible to suggest that the term indexes a group of lords in the area of Río Azul. Although there are no examples of Río Azul lords claiming the titles of *Huxlajuun Tzuk* and *Jo'* T544.501-**ni**, it seems that this particular royal dynasty was either identified with both geopolitical groups, changed its identity (although we do not have enough chronological controls to assert that), or was effectively split between the two groups.

Although most references to *Jo'* T544.501-**ni** cluster in the Río Azul area, at least one inscription places people with this title in the western region of the Southern Maya Lowlands (Simon Martin, personal communication 2011). The name of the protagonist of a narrative from a looted Late Classic panel or stela ("Lausanne Stela"), found in the collection of the de Young Museum in San Francisco, includes *a[j]-Jo'* T544.501-**ni**—"he of Five T544.501-**ni**" (Figure 60c). He is also called a *sajal* of *Sak Tz'i'* lord *K'ab Chan Te'* (Biró 2005:27–30). Even though the precise location of the seat of *Sak Tz'i'* lords is unknown, it places the origins of the monument somewhere between the sites of Tonina, Palenque, Piedras Negras, Yaxchilan, and Bonampak (Anaya Hernández et al. 2003).

Just as *tzuk* titles, T544.501-**ni** with numbers seem to constitute a paradigm for multiple group identities. A nonroyal person from *Ik'a'* carries a *Chan* T544.501-**ni** ("Four T544.501-**ni**") title in the inscription on Stela 4 (Figure 60d) at Motul de San Jose. The Bonampak ruler *Yajaw Chan Muwaan* is also associated with this group in the caption for murals in Structure 1 (Room 2, Dr 15; Figure 60e). Both references come from local inscriptions and can be interpreted as a form of self-identification.

The third set of titles with T544.501-**ni** is known from three examples. A lord from an unknown site associated with the *Baax Tuun* place name (Prager et al. 2010) carries the title of *Huk* T544.501-**ni** or "Seven T544.501-**ni**" in Drawing 82 in the Naj Tunich Cave (Figure 60f). The title also occurs in the name of a captive trodden by the victorious king on Aguateca Stela 19 (Figure 60g). The third example of this title is found in the name of the mother of the protagonist of the text on the Cuychen vase mentioned previously (Figure 60h). That seemingly places *Huk* T544.501-**ni** individuals somewhere in Belize or Southeastern Peten.

There are also at least three occurrences on an unusual *Huk* (T544.501-**ni**) *Bolon* T544.501-**ni** title that seems to identify individuals associated with two groups, "Seven (T544.501-**ni**) [and] Nine T544.501-**ni**." All three examples have a connection to Calakmul. One mention comes from the stairway block at Calakmul (Figure 60i) and its context is unknown (Martin 1998). The other example is found in the caption to a captive on the stucco relief of Structure 5D–57 at Tikal (Figure 60j). The other title of the captive, who was taken in the fateful battle against Calakmul and its allies in AD 695, seems to be **AJ-sa**— possibly an abbreviated *aj-sa'aal* "he of Sa'aal"—which would identify him as a person from Naranjo; its ruler at the time was a vassal of Calakmul *Kanu'l* lords (Martin 1996a; Martin and Grube 2008:46, 76). The third example appears in the titles of the Cancuen dynast *K'iib Ajaw* (Figure 60k), who acceded to kingship at Calakmul on the orders of its ruler and in the presence of its gods before he traveled to Cancuen (Guenter 2002).

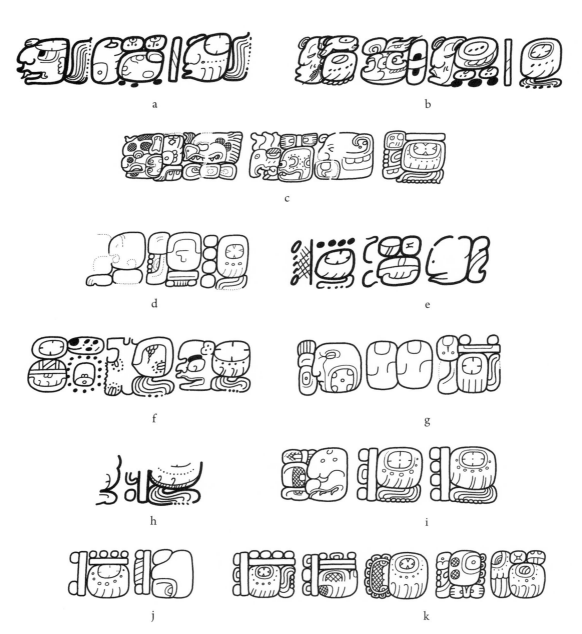

Figure 60 T544.501-**ni** titles in Classic Maya inscriptions: a) detail of the inscription on a Late Classic vessel (K2914); b) detail of the inscription on a Late Classic vessel (K1383); c) detail of a Late Classic panel or stela (E1–E3), Western Maya Lowlands (after Miller and Martin 2004:fig. 51); d) detail of Stela 4, Motul de San Jose (after photograph by the author); e) detail of Drawing 15, Room 2, Structure 1, Bonampak (after drawing by John Montgomery); f) detail of Drawing 82 (E1–E2), Naj Tunich (after Stone 1995:figs. 7–29); g) detail of Stela 19, Aguateca (after drawing by Markus Eberl); h) detail of the inscription on a Late Classic vessel (Q4–P5), Cuychen Cave (after Helmke n.d.:fig. 10); i) detail of Fragment 401-6, Calakmul (after drawing by David Stuart); j) detail of stucco facade, Structure 5D–57, Tikal (after Schele and Mathews 1998:fig. 2.29a); and k) detail of Panel 1 (F3–F5), Cancuen (after drawing by Yuriy Polyukhovych).

TWENTY-EIGHT LORDS

Another important group of lords in Classic Maya inscriptions are the "Twenty-eight" (Figure 53d). This geopolitical collectivity seems to unite rulers of the Southern Peten and Belize, although its full extent might have been greater. Inscriptions at Dos Pilas mention that "Twenty-eight lords witnessed" the burial of *Itzamnaah K'awiil* (Figure 61a)[56] and later were present at one of the childhood rituals of *K'awiil Chan K'inich* (Figure 61b). The text on later Seibal Stela 6 (Graham 1996:23) describes what the Seibal ruler—allied or subordinated to *Mutal* kings at Aguateca—did to T856-**la** lord(s), "Twenty-eight lord(s)," and someone "of *Mutal*" (Tikal?) "with his flint and shield" (Figure 61c) before celebrating the period ending in AD 771. Although the verb is gone, the means by which that action was achieved suggests that it was some kind of warfare. The inscription also makes clear that T856-**la** lords are not part of the "Twenty-eight." The text on Ixtutz Stela 4 (Figure 61d), dedicated ten years later, states that period-ending rituals undertaken by a local ruler were witnessed by "holy *Mutal* lord" and "Twenty-eight lords."[57] Although the references can be interpreted literally, this insistence on the number twenty-eight seems rather unusual. Moreover, the lists make clear that this group does not include *Mutal* and T856-**la** dynasts. Therefore, either there is a traveling band of twenty-eight lords, or this is a designation for a group of dynasties and references to "Twenty-eight lords" mean that members of this group are involved.

The function of the "Twenty-eight" as a group designation becomes clear once we consider cases in which it is used as a title. Like *Huxlajuun Tzuk* and *Huk Tzuk*, *Waxak Winik* appears in personal names (usually at the end) and does not need any additional nouns. Individual rulers at Machaquila (St 2, 5, 6, 8; Figure 61e), Ixtutz (Pn 2; Figure 61f), *Baax Tuun* (NTN Dr 25, 28, 29, 66; Figure 61g), and Nim Li Punit (NMP St 14, 21; Figure 61h) call themselves "Twenty-eight [people]" (*waxak winik*). The term is used to designate an undifferentiated political other: the inscriptions at Ixtutz, Dos Pilas, and Seibal do not specify which Twenty-eight lords are involved, although there are several dynasties associated with the title.

Another case of the Twenty-eight in personal names comes from the inscriptions at Naranjo. As mentioned above, the conquest of Ucanal likely created opportunities to expand Naranjo's sphere of influence into the Petexbatun and the Southern Peten in general. This historical context coincides with the incorporation of the "eastern Twenty-eight" (*elk'in waxak winik*)—a local version of the Twenty-eight title—in the name phrases of *K'ahk' Tiliw Chan Chahk* (NAR St 21; Figure 21i) and subsequent Naranjo rulers, including *K'ahk' Ukalaw Chan Chahk* (NAR St 13, K635, K5723, Baking Pot vase) and *Itzamnaah K'awiil* (NAR St 14). While Nim Li Punit is located much farther east than Naranjo, its lords are just Twenty-eight. Therefore, the Naranjo version of the title likely reflects a deliberate positioning with respect to the rest of the Twenty-eight collectivity. It is also significant that Naranjo inscriptions emphasize the eastern Twenty-eight title and subvert *Huk Tzuk*, their second group identity. It is precisely the opposite when it comes to outside mentions of Naranjo rulers.

The significance of the Twenty-eight title is unclear. It does not appear in colonial sources. The number can be interpreted as four times seven, so it may have something to

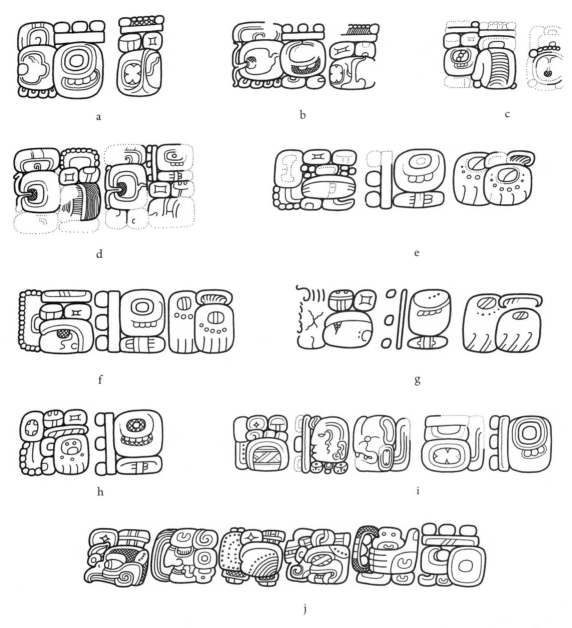

Figure 61 Twenty-eight lords in Classic Maya inscriptions: a) detail of Stela 8 (H16–I16), Dos Pilas (after Houston 1993:fig. 4-14); b) detail of Panel 19 (F1–G1), Dos Pilas (after Houston 1993:fig. 4-19); c) detail of Stela 6 (A5–B5), Seibal (after Graham 1996:23); d) detail of Stela 4 (A5–B5), Ixtutz (after Graham 1980:181); e) detail of Stela 2 (C2–4), Machaquila (after Graham 1967:fig. 44); f) detail of Fragment 6 (2–4), Panel 2, Ixtutz (after photograph by the author); g) detail of Drawing 66 (G1–I1), Naj Tunich (after Stone 1995:figs. 7-5, 7-12); h) detail of Stela 21 (D3–C4), Nim Li Punit (after Wanyerka 2004:fig. 34); i) detail of Stela 21 (A12–B12), Naranjo (after Graham 1975:53); and j) detail of Stela 31 (E10–F12), Tikal (after Jones and Satterthwaite 1982:fig. 52).

do with the quadripartite organization and Seven Divisions. The only reference that may shed some light on the Twenty-eight is a rather cryptic passage on Early Classic Stela 31 at Tikal (Estrada Belli et al. 2009; Stuart 2011b). Its narrative describes the accession of *Yax Nuun Ahiin* in a distant place of *Wite' Naah* possibly associated with Teotihuacan. The text seems to present this event retrospectively as a kind of mandate to rule at a time when the Tikal dynasty was at the peak of its power during the reign of *Sihyaj Chan K'awiil*, one generation after *Sihyaj K'ahk'*'s arrival. As part of the accession rituals, *Yax Nuun Ahiin* reportedly "takes twenty-eight *pet*" (Figure 61j).[58] The word *pet* or *pet[en]* may be translated as "province." Therefore, the term "Twenty-eight" may reflect another concept of the geopolitical organization of Peten dating back to the Early Classic period. While I have been initially skeptical about the connection between the Twenty-eight and the Tikal Stela 31 inscription (Tokovinine 2008), the same hypothesis has been independently proposed by Stuart in a recent overview of the inscription on Stela 31 (Stuart 2011b).

The link to the passage of Tikal Stela 31, which deals with the establishment of the new political order after the possible Teotihuacan intrusion (Estrada Belli et al. 2009; Stuart 2011b), suggests that the Twenty-eight might have been part of that new order. Three of five known dynasties that belong to the Twenty-eight are somehow related to *Wite' Naah* or Early Classic Tikal rulers. Machaquila kings call themselves "*Wite' Naah* ball players" (MQL St 3) and "western *kaloomte'*" (see above). Early Classic links between the Machaquila dynasty and *Wite' Naah* are revealed in the inscriptions at Tres Islas (St 2). Depictions of War Serpents on Ixtutz Panels 1 and 2 (Laporte and Torres 1994:figs. 8–9) also demonstrate a fascination with Teotihuacan-related imagery at that royal court. The Naranjo dynasty was allied to Early Classic Tikal rulers (Tokovinine and Fialko 2007). Recent excavations in the Central Acropolis at Naranjo revealed some evidence of Teotihuacan or Tikal influence in the form of *talud-tablero* platforms of palatial buildings (Vilma Fialko, personal communication 2006). Nim Li Punit and *Baax Tuun* lords do not seem to have any connection to the Early Classic Tikal or Teotihuacan domains. But little is known about either dynasty during the Early Classic period. We do not even know where the residence of *Baax Tuun* lords was located. Therefore, it is tempting to see the Twenty-eight as a group of royal families somehow associated with the Early Classic political landscape as shaped by *Sihyaj K'ahk'* and later Tikal rulers.

CORNFIELDS OF KINGS

Another important set of identities in the Classic Maya landscape is revealed in the "Holmul dancer" scenes: depictions of dancing young lords characterized by elaborate backrack costumes, found on pottery vessels from the eastern part of the Southern Lowlands (Figure 62). Houston, Taube, and Stuart (1992) and Reents-Budet (1991) identified the Holmul dancer as different manifestations of the Classic Maya maize god. Houston et al. also noticed that the elaborate backracks of the dancing maize god—"back dresses" (*paat pi'k*) as they are called on La Corona Panel 1 (Stuart and Martin 2009:31)—were linked to specific place names rather than general representations of the cosmos, as suggested earlier by Reents-Budet (1991:218). Each backrack consisted of a representation of an animal or a

a   b   c

Figure 62 Holmul dancer maize gods on a Late Classic vessel (K633): a) *Wak Hix Nal* maize god; b) toponym in the backrack of *Wak Chan Nal* maize god; and c) toponym in the backrack of *Wak Chuwen Nal* maize god.

fantastic creature seated on top of a mountain surmounted by a sky band. Houston, Taube, and Stuart followed up on an earlier observation by Coe (1978:94–104). Coe noticed that each kind of animal in the backracks corresponded to a different emblem glyph in the captions accompanying the maize gods. Houston and his coauthors proposed that the scenes represented distinct maize gods, possibly four directional forms of the deity, each associated with a different polity and its respective ruling dynasty. They also identified a number of cases in which the kings of the Tikal–Dos Pilas dynasty were represented in the guise of the maize god with the Water Lily Jaguar backrack that was also consistently associated with the Tikal emblem glyph in the Holmul dancer scenes.

Comparing different versions of the captions to the dancing maize god reveals that the message of the backracks centers on the identities of the maize deities. Three maize gods are depicted and labeled in most scenes. They are associated with the places *Wak Hix Nal*, *Wak Chan Nal*, and *Wak Chuwen Nal* (Six Ocelot Corn, Six Sky Corn, and Six Monkey Corn). Fuller versions of these place names likely include the word for mountain, as suggested by the inscription on the Schaffhausen vessel (Prager 2004) that links the Calakmul rulers to *Wak Chan Witziil* (Figure 45). According to the captions on one Holmul dancer vase from the Naranjo area (K633), the maize god with the Water Lily

Jaguar backrack (Figure 62a) is a "Maize *Wak Hix Nal* [person]" who "ascends [to] *Mutal*" (Figure 63a).[59] The maize god with Sky Monster backrack (Figure 62b) is a "Maize *Wak Chan Nal* [person]" who "ascends [to] *Kanu'l*" (Figure 63b).[60] The maize god with a *chuwen* monkey backrack (Figure 62c) is a "Maize *Wak Chuwen Nal* [person]" who "ascends to T174-**su**" (Figure 63c).[61] *Mutal*, *Kanu'l*, and T174-**su** are place names in the emblem glyphs of Tikal, Calakmul, and Machaquila rulers. A caption to a dancing maize god with the Water Lily Jaguar backrack depicted on a plate found in the Late Classic burial at Holmul (Merwin and Vaillant 1932:pls. 29a, c) is accompanied by a simplified caption, "*Wak Hix Nal* [person], holy *Mutal* lord" (Figure 63f), leaving little doubt that these maize gods are identified with specific Classic Maya royal dynasties.

Two captions in the Holmul dancer scene with *Wak Hix Nal* and *Wak Chan Nal* maize gods depicted on a vase found in the photographic archive at Dumbarton Oaks (LC.CB2.412) offer additional clues to the significance of the scenes. The caption to the *Wak Hix Nal* deity states: "[it is] the image of the Maize, *Wak Hix Nal* [person]; [he is in] the west, inside/before the *ch'e'n*, holy *Mutal* lord" (Figure 63d).[62] According to the caption

a b c d e

f

Figure 63 Captions to Holmul dancer maize gods: a) *Wak Hix Nal* maize god (after K633); b) *Wak Chan Nal* maize god (after K633); c) *Wak Chuwen Nal* maize god (after K633); d) *Wak Hix Nal* maize god (after Pre-Columbian Photographs and Fieldwork Archives, Dumbarton Oaks, LC.CB2.412.09); e) *Wak Chan Nal* maize god (after Pre-Columbian Photographs and Fieldwork Archives, Dumbarton Oaks, LC.CB2.412.10); and f) *Wak Hix Nal* maize god (Late Classic plate, Holmul, after photograph by the author).

a   b   c

Figure 64 Maya lords as maize gods: a) Dos Pilas ruler as *Wak Hix Nal* maize god, detail of Stela 17, Dos Pilas (after Schele and Miller 1986:fig.1.4d); b) detail of Panel 1, La Corona (after drawing by David Stuart in Stuart and Martin 2009:31); and c) detail of Lintel 2, Temple 4, Tikal (after Jones and Satterthwaite 1982:fig. 73).

to the *Wak Chan Nal* deity, "[it is] the image of the Maize, *Wak Chan Nal* [person]; [he] tree-opens/makes inside/before the *ch'e'n*, holy *Kanu'l* lord" (Figure 63e).[63] These slightly different captions suggest that there is an association with cardinal directions. Moreover, "ascending" of different maize gods to their *ch'e'n* as kings of various dynasties is referred to as "tree-making" or "tree-opening," potentially implying some agricultural activity like forest-clearing or planting cornfields or orchards. It is potentially significant that the same *kalaaw-te'* expression may occasionally be used in reference to royal accession as in the narrative on the Palace Tablet (Block M7) at Palenque (Robertson 1985:fig. 258).

The association or, properly speaking, embodiment of corresponding maize gods by Classic Maya rulers is revealed in the imagery on carved monuments and other media. For example, *Mutal* lord *Bajlaj Chan K'awiil* of Dos Pilas is depicted on Dos Pilas Stela 17 (Figure 64a) dancing in the backrack costume of the *Wak Hix Nal* maize deity (see also Schele and Miller 1986:pl. 2d). Texts and images on carved bones in *Jasaw Chan K'awiil*'s tomb (TIK MT 38a–d) evoke the descent of the *Wak Hix Nal* maize god into the waters of the underworld "[in] *Mutal*" (Figure 17c; see Moholy-Nagy and Coe 2008:figs. 188–189).

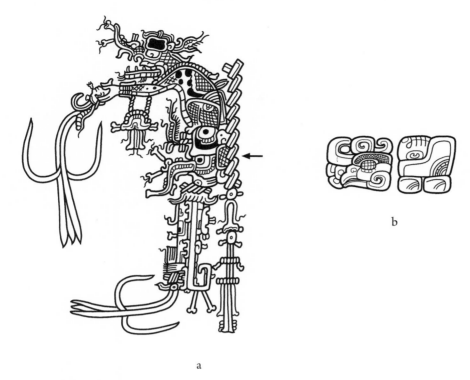

a

b

Figure 65 "Zero-Moon-Bird" place and its maize god: a) detail of a Late Classic vessel, Buenavista del Cayo (K4464); and b) detail of Stela 31 (D6–C7), Tikal (after Jones and Satterthwaite 1982:fig. 52).

The inscription on the third block of Tamarindito Hieroglyphic Stairway 1 (Figure 34a) refers to a *Mutal* lord as "*Wak Hix Nal* person" (*wak hix nal winik*). Calakmul's vassal at La Corona is shown dancing as a *Wak Chan Nal* maize god on La Corona Panel 1 (Figure 64b).

It also seems that maize god identities of Classic Maya rulers were partially overlapping due to the complex histories of royal dynasties. Tikal king *Yik'in Chan K'awiil* is depicted as a *Wak Chan Nal* maize god on Lintel 2 at Temple 4 at Tikal (Figure 64c). Tikal rulers' preoccupation with this maize deity is also evidenced in the scene on an Early Classic lidded vessel (MT 9), which belonged to *Chak Tok Ich'aak* according to the dedicatory statement on the lid (Culbert 1993:fig. 108d). The scene on the body of the vase shows a maize god labeled as "*Wak Chan Nal* person" (Figure 34b).

This overlap of maize god identities can be explained by the fact that the *Mutal* or *Kanu'l* dynasties shared a foundation narrative associated with the place of **chi**-T316. This location, with an undeciphered name known as "Maguey Throne," "Chi Witz," or "Chi-Bent Cauac," is of major importance to the foundation narratives of several Classic Maya polities, as noted in a number of studies (Grube 2004; Schele 1992; Stuart 2004a). The master narrative seems to be about period-ending rituals at **chi**-T316 with a particular emphasis on an event in AD 159. The dynasties of Tikal and Dzibanche/Calakmul equally trace their lines to residents of **chi**-T316, although not specifying their exact relation to the royal line of that place. *Kanu'l* lords are "those of **chi**-T316," (Figure 45) according to the inscription on the Schaffhausen vessel discussed in the previous chapter (Prager 2004). The founding father of *Mutal* lords is referred to as the "*K'awiil* of **chi**-T316" in the inscription on Tikal Stela 22 (Figure 35g). What does it have to do with maize gods? The backrack toponym in the depiction of the *Wak Chan Nal* deity, found on a vase in the burial at Buenavista del Cayo (Figure 65a), links the *Wak Chan Nal* maize god to *Winik ?Mih Witz [Nal]* or "Zero-Moon-Bird" place. According to the inscription on Tikal Stela 31, *Winik ?Mih Witz Nal* and **chi**-T316 are names of the same locale or two related places (Figure 65b), much like double toponyms discussed in Chapter 2. Therefore, the *Wak Chan Nal* maize god is also a **chi**-T316 lord. Tikal and Calakmul rulers share this maize god because they claim common origins at **chi**-T316.[64]

There are indications that the list of different maize gods is not restricted to the three discussed so far. The Cuychen Cave vase (Helmke n.d.) depicts the previously unknown dancing maize god who is a *Wak ?Ook Nal* ("Six Dog [corn] Place") person and who

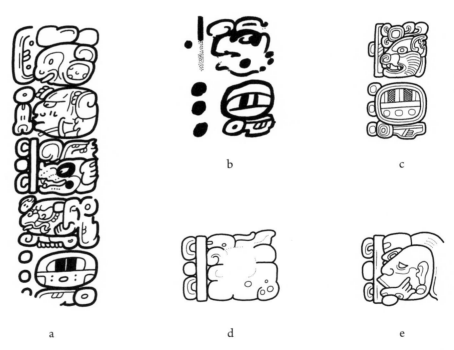

a b c

d e

Figure 66 *Hux Haab Te'* and other maize gods: a) detail of a Late Classic vessel, Cuychen Cave (after Helmke n.d.:fig. 5); b) detail of a Late Classic vessel, Río Azul (after photograph by the author); c) detail of Papagayo Step, Copan (after photograph by the author); d) detail of the "War Panel," Palenque (after Mayer 1991:pl. 239); and e) detail of Miscellaneous Monument 2 (D1), La Corona (after drawing by Nikolai Grube in Stuart and Martin 2009:23).

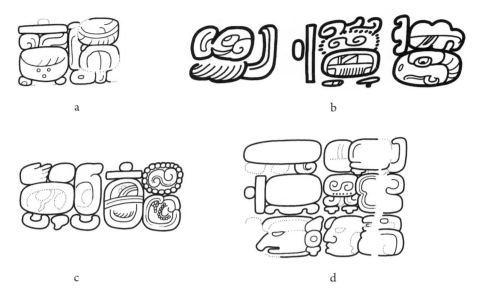

a   b

c   d

Figure 67 Maize god places in the Classic Maya built environment: a) detail of Stela 10 (A2–B2), Caracol (after Houston 1987:fig. 71b); b) detail of East Wall Mural (c–e), Tomb 12, Río Azul (after Stuart 1987:fig. 45); c) detail of Hieroglyphic Panel 10 (A2–B2), Pomona (after drawing by Peter Mathews); and d) detail of Stela 5, El Zapote (after drawing by Ian Graham).

"tree-opens/makes" in *Hux Haab Te'*, the toponym associated with the area of Río Azul (Figure 66a).[65] He is accompanied by more common *Wak Hix Nal* and *Wak Chan Nal* deities. As Helmke (n.d.) pointed out, the same maize god is depicted on a partially preserved vessel found in the looters' discard at Río Azul (Adams 1999:88–89, figs. 3-38). The caption is eroded but may still be read as "*Wak Ook Nal Hux Haab Te'* [person]" (Figure 66b), and a little doglike creature is visible in the backrack.

In addition to this transparent example, the titles of several Classic Maya royal lines follow the pattern of *Wak* [x] *Nal* [person], suggesting that they also embodied local forms of the maize god. Naranjo rulers are often referred to as "*Wak Kab Nal* people" (Tokovinine and Fialko 2007:3; Figure 34c). The same title is claimed by Edzna rulers (EDZ HS 1, St 21, 22). In the inscription on the Early Classic Papagayo Step buried in one of the substructures underneath Temple 26, Copan lord *K'al Tuun Hix* takes the *Wak ?Ook Nal Hux Haab Te'* title (Figure 66c) that likely evokes the same maize god as on the vessels from Río Azul and Cuychen. An obscure logogram appears in the *Wak* [x] *Nal* title of Palenque rulers on the so-called War Panel (Figure 66d). La Corona lords are sometimes called "*Wak Mi[in] Nal* [people]" (Figure 66e).

Place names associated with maize gods are re-created in the Classic Maya built environment. The *Wak Hix Nal* structure is mentioned in Caracol inscriptions (Figure 67a). Funeral shrines at Río Azul (Figure 67b), Pomona (Figure 67c), and a temple or palace at El Zapote (Figure 67d) are called "*Wak Chan* cloudy cornfields/mountains."[66] The choice of name for funeral structures not only reveals the corresponding maize god, but also elaborates on the relationship between the life cycles of the deity and the king as his embodiment: the dying king/maize god returns to the *ch'e'n* in the mountain of his origin, from which he would sprout back to life and sustain the community.

Different maize gods, with their close relationships to specific royal lines, bring us to some important observations about group identities in the Classic Maya landscape. As we have seen in Chapter 2, more than one hundred place names in Classic Maya inscriptions refer to various locales as different kinds of corn or cornfields, as indicated by the *–nal* morpheme. The significance of this pattern may be as literal as it is metaphorical. As pointed out by Fash (2012), it may simply reflect the practice of planting predominantly local races of corn. Such practices are well attested in modern Maya communities (Benz et al. 2007; Perales et al. 2005; Stadelman 1940:111–114) and result in a correspondence between ethnolinguistic boundaries and corn varieties. The connection between maize and human beings, variously perceived as being made of corn, extends to the notions of ethnicity: eating maize "from here" enables one to become part of an ethnic group, speak the language, and perform proper rituals (Christenson 2006:212–213). In light of these observations, the Classic Maya landscape, with its multitude of corn places and maize gods, seems to reflect a similar concept that distinguishes between different groups of people and corn as interrelated entities. The connection of royal families to various maize gods effectively defines these families as sources of group sustenance. For example, as we have seen in the previous chapter, the inscription on Copan Altar A' refers to the anient city as a *nal*, a corn field, of *K'inich Yax K'uk' Mo'*, the founder of the local dynasty. So, later Copan rulers (and perhaps their subjects) were, at least on some symbolic level, the offspring of the maize brought and embodied by the first king. The specific name of that maize god reflects the origins of Copan lords.

This chapter began with an overview of existing approaches to Classic Maya geopolitical collectivities. The key question was whether there were terms denoting or indexing membership in broader groups of royal families. The next step was to relate these contexts to other pieces of evidence suggesting mutual awareness, interactions between dynasties, and references to their roles in a larger political landscape.

As we have seen above, Classic Maya inscriptions reveal some fundamental ideas about the boundaries of the Classic Maya world and geopolitical collectivities held within. There are similarities to notions of geopolitical landscape presented in early colonial sources. One of the key concepts seems to be Thirteen Divisions as thirteen dynasties organized in space-time, like a Postclassic k'atun wheel. But this concept and this group of dynasties are by no means unique. Seven Divisions appear to correspond to another fundamental set of ideas about the world order, and there are some hints of other collectivities of Nine Divisions and Six Divisions. In addition to "divisions," there are two more paradigms and at least four more groups of lords in the list of Classic Maya geopolitical collectivities: the Twenty-eight, Four T544.501-**ni**, Five T544.501-**ni**, and Seven T544.501-**ni**. Specific royal dynasties identified themselves and were identified by others as members of different geopolitical groups. Some group identities overlapped and were used strategically by political actors to highlight certain identities and subvert others.

There is not enough evidence to say that these groups of lords played a major role in Classic Maya politics. Based on the available information, it seems, for example, that Seven Divisions were closely associated with the geopolitical network controlled by Naranjo lords, whereas Tikal was a major political power in the Thirteen Divisions network. Either group saw its origins in the Early Classic geopolitical order. But in practice, a major Classic Maya royal court readily extended its influence beyond the core network. Some royal families, like the Naranjo and the Motul de San José lords, could identify themselves with more than one geopolitical group. Therefore, it seems plausible that the actual political significance and capital associated with one's ascription to any of these geopolitical groups depended on specific historical circumstances. It is significant that references to these group identities peak during the Late Classic period, when belonging to these broader horizontal geopolitical networks could be more advantageous than membership in Tikal or Calakmul hegemonies, which were rapidly losing their relevance. On the other hand, membership in such collectivities seems to affect or at least to be worth mentioning only in the central and eastern part of the studied area. The political landscape of the western kingdoms, where no such categories are attested, appears to be more fractious and unstable.

Can we call these groups communities? Seven Divisions and Thirteen Divisions conform to the definition of the imagined community proposed in Chapter 1. These are groups of people who ascribe themselves to larger social entities. These entities are associated with certain geographical areas and political networks. They can also be experienced on certain occasions, such as massive performances during period-ending ceremonies. It is unlikely that Classic Maya kings and their subordinates would constantly refer to themselves and others in terms of their ascription to certain social, political, or religious groups of no significance. The very fact that these categories of ascription were mentioned on carved monuments implies that they were important and that they affected decisions and actions of Classic Maya lords.

It is difficult to assert whether these identities were shared by subroyal elites and commoners. In the case of Seven Divisions, there are some tentative indications that individuals who did not have the rank of *ajaw* ("lord") indentified themselves with this group. The same observation holds for some members of T544.501-**ni**. On the other hand, the very name of another geopolitical collectivity—"Twenty-eight lords"—implies that it included only members of royal families.

These groups constitute a kind of macroregional landscape, but a landscape of people and not of territories. There is a notion that people are associated with "lands"—this notion is aptly represented on the altar from Altar de los Reyes discussed above. Territories are noticeably absent in contexts when protagonists identify themselves or others as members of certain geopolitical collectivities, however. Instead, local maize god varieties seem to reflect an emic perspective of group identities and classification.

6 | IMAGINING CLASSIC MAYA LANDSCAPES

THE SIMPLEST DEFINITION OF LANDSCAPE IS THINGS IN SPACE AS seen by someone. As we have no direct access to one's mind, this definition, in practice, means things in space as seen and then presented by someone in a certain context. This monograph has explored one of an indefinite number of potential landscapes in the Classic Maya Lowlands, the one revealed to us in indigenous narratives. Two kinds of objects in space have been examined: places as distinct sets of representations of physical locales, and people as members of different levels of political institutions, particularly the royal court.

The corpus of Classic Maya place names reveals that certain features of the surrounding environment—including mountains, pools, and springs—were clearly more important, indexical, than others. The relative abundance of place names ending in the words "house" (*naah*) and "corn" (*nal*) attest to Classic Maya landscape concepts that center on the presence of dwellings and cornfields.

Classic Maya written narratives place *ch'e'n*—the houses of gods and ancestors—at the heart of every community. Some Classic Maya royal families, like Naranjo rulers, still lived by the *ch'e'n* where they thought their gods and ancestors lived thousands of years ago. Other royal dynasties traced their origins to faraway places in deep time. Some dynasties moved or spread and founded new royal courts at various locations, but they retained the association with the places they came from. Consequently, people in Classic Maya landscapes often associated themselves or their ancestors with multiple places of origin, of pilgrimage, of shifting seats of power, and of divine patrons. Different facets or aspects of a person could be linked to different locales and cited strategically depending on the nature of the narrative and its context.

We have also seen that the Classic Maya landscape was divided into Seven Divisions, Thirteen Divisions, Twenty-eight lords, and other groups of royal families and people associated with their courts. These groups appear to grow in importance during the last centuries of the Classic period, possibly because of the increasingly fragmented and populated political landscape in which membership in such regional networks could be more advantageous than traditional liege-vassal hegemonies and alliances. At least one of these geopolitical collectivities, the Thirteen Divisions, has some similarities to ideas about geopolitical order as reported in early colonial documents.

References to local varieties of the Classic Maya maize god reveal a fundamental concept that connects groups of people, their rulers, place, and corn as a source of sustenance and identity. This is probably as close as we can get to the emic notions of place and identity in Classic Maya narratives: the genealogies of the maize gods, places where they came from, and places where they planted themselves as the first kings.

The two big questions inevitable in this review are those of differences through time and space. The issue of differences through time is particularly hard to address because the last two centuries of the Classic period are so much better represented in the surviving written narratives than all the earlier periods put together. Nevertheless, there seems to be a trend for increasingly complex relationships between various royal dynasties and places in their histories. The amount of important places linked to any particular royal dynasty was clearly on the rise in eighth-century texts.

The reasons may have been purely historical—a kind of gradual accumulation of significant places through the lifetime of a dynasty. But the same situation may also have been caused by an erosion of authority and importance attached to such connections. Being a "*Wite' Naah* lord" in the fifth century carried a much more specific meaning than the same title in an eighth-century text. Just as we see a proliferation of *kaloomte'* titles, the number of lords claiming connection to great places of the past also rises, probably because such claims no longer carry the same amount of prestige and potential risk of contestation as before.

The surge in references to geopolitical collectivities is another clear trend. While these entities likely date back at least to the Early Classic period, their increasing prominence marks a shift in political strategies from explicit statements of allegiance to broadly defined membership in these networks. Once again, the implication seems to be that the traditional strategies are no longer efficient, either because direct political loyalties are invalid or because the eighth-century political landscape is just too complex to be reduced to a set of liege-vassal and marriage links.

This brings us to the question of regional variation as such horizontal geopolitical networks are found primarily in the eastern part of the Southern Lowlands. Consequently, there must be something fundamentally different in the way Late Classic regimes operated between the eastern and the western polities. It is not entirely clear, for example, if the presence of geopolitical networks in the east implied less conflict or fragmentation, although there are indeed more eighth-century references to warfare, captives, and nonroyal nobility in the west. It is also potentially significant that most (if not all) western dynasties position themselves as nonlocal or polylocal, whereas there are examples of self-declared indigenous dynasties in the east, such as the Naranjo. This contrast also implies different relationships between the ruling dynasties and the rest of the polities' populations.

The differences in the ways a given royal family is attached to the landscape of its polity are revealed in a curious separation of royal and local deities in the narratives of the nonlocal dynasties. As we have seen above, such dynasties often associate their origins and divine patrons with distant and/or deep-time places. But their *ch'e'n* often belongs to gods like *Hux Bolon Chahk* at Palenque or the four guardians of *Hux Wintik* at Copan. These deities seem to be linked to specific, local landscape features (such as mountains) and possibly represent the religious beliefs of a broader population. The incorporation of these gods into the royal ceremonies and narratives may represent an attempt to control such cults, an acknowledgment of their importance, or both. In any case, it points to a potential tension between different notions of place and identity within Classic Maya polities. On the other hand, self-identified indigenous royal dynasties did not seem to have this problem. This contrast clearly merits further investigation, along with a consideration of other differences between western and eastern polities in the Southern Lowlands.

Finally, the biggest question that was not considered in this monograph is that of collapse. It is highly significant that it affected all Classic Maya royal dynasties alike, although it seemed to have occurred faster in the west. Consequently, the issue of Classic Maya political identities is likely of lesser significance for determining the reasons of the collapse—although some variation of political strategies in one's relation to place may be useful in understanding the tempo and the impact of the crisis that engulfed Lowland Maya polities at the end of the Classic period.

NOTES

1   Calepino de Motul (Ciudad Real 1995) offers the following examples: *ajotochkab/ajotoch-nal* "man (owner) of a house (town resident)" (CMM:25r); *ajch'e'enkab/ajch'e'ennal* "man (owner) of a cacao grove" (CMM:16r); *ajtziminkab/ajtziminnal* "man (owner) of horses" (CMM:30v); *ajatankab/ajatan[n]al* "man of a wife (married man)" (CMM:4v). The term *ajotochnal* is widely attested in colonial Yukatek texts, including the books of Chilam Balam and the Xiu Papers (Miram and Miram 1988; Quezada and Okoshi Harada 2001), and the cognate *ajototnal* appears in the Chontal Maldonado-Paxbolon Papers (Smailus 1975:36).

2   Some readers may be unfamiliar with the recent decipherment of the "Water Serpent" glyph as **WITZ'**, proposed by Stuart based on a convincing set of substitutions in the name of the twelfth ruler of Copan (Stuart 2007b). The **PALAW** decipherment of the "Water Band" sign by Lopes (2004) remains tentative. T856 and T578 are undeciphered, although the **OOM** "foam" reading has been suggested for one or both of them (Sebastian Matteo, personal communication 2012).

3   *Yehmal* may stand for "descent of," "bottom of," or "below." This range of meanings may be found in Ch'orti' (Wisdom 1950:457). Therefore, *yehmal k'uk' lakam witz* can be translated as "at the bottom of the Great Quetzal Mountain," "the Great Mountain of Quetzal's descent," or "the Great Mountain below the Quetzal."

4   The first of the two place names is spelled with the undeciphered "Shell Dragon" logogram (T369) and the **HA'** sign. But its spellings occasionally include the **la** syllable (Figure 7d). Stuart and Houston (1994:20–21) did not clarify the implications of this variation. The likeliest three interpretations are that **la** spells a suffix that derives an adjective from the T369 noun, serves as its phonetic complement, or stands for a place name *–Vl* suffix after *ha'*. I prefer the last option and read the toponym as T369 *ha'al* because **la** usually appears under the **HA'** grapheme, but the first two interpretations are nearly equally plausible.

5   (pA1) 7-[**ETZ'NAB**] (pB1) 1-**UUN-wa** (pA2) **u-CH'AM-wa** (pB2) **xo-t'o-TE'** (pC1) **K'AHK'-HU'N-na** (pD1) **AJ-CHAK-?JU'-TE'** (pC2) **K'UH-ya-?-AHK-AJAW** (pD2) **yi-chi-NAL** (pE1) **K'AWIIL-la-CHAN-na** (pF1) **K'INICH-chi-ni** (pE2) **u-CHAN-na** (pF2) **AHK-lu-AJAW** (pG1) **K'UH-MUT-la-AJAW** (pH1) **u-ti-ya** (pG2) T369-**HA'-la** (pH2) **K'IN-HA'-ni-NAL?** (pI1) **CHAN-na** (pJ1) **CH'E'N** (pI2) **tu-4-la-ta** (pJ2) **i-HUL-li** (pK1) **TAHN-CH'E'N-na** (pL1) **ha** (pK2) **lu-mi**

   [ta] huk etz'nab juun[te'] uuniiw uch'amaw xot' te' k'ahk' hu'n aj-chak ju' te' k'uh[ul] ... ahk ajaw yichnal k'awiil chan k'inich k'uh[ul] mutal ajaw ucha'n ahkul ajaw u[h]tiiy ... ha'al k'hin ha' nal tu-chan-lat i-huli tahn ch'e'n haluum

   " ... [on the day] seven *Etz'nab*, one *Uuniiw*, man of red *ju'* tree, holy ... *Ahk* lord took the *xot' te'* fire headband in front of holy *Mutal* lord *K'awiil Chan K'inich*. It happened [in] ... *Ha'al, K'hin Ha' Nal*, [in] the sky, [in] the *ch'e'n*. In four days then he arrived [here] in the midst of the *ch'e'n*, [at] *Haluum* ... "

6 In 2006, I had an opportunity to examine and photograph the Río Azul type collection at the Instituto de Antropología e Historia (IDAEH) in Guatemala City. Two Juleki Cream Polychrome sherds and one Uacho Polychrome sherd had inscriptions along the rim with name sections of the dedicatory formula which contained *jo' pet hux haab te'* titles.

7 (A2) **OCH HA'** (B2) **SAK BAHLAM** (A3) **to-no AJAW** (B3) **ya-?** (A4) **ya-AJAW-TE'** (B4) **? 3 HAAB TE'** (A5) **3 HAAB-ya** (B5) **K'A'-yi-ya** (A6) **?LEM-AJ** (B6) **?-TUUN-AJ** (A7) **u-BAAH** (B7) **u-CH'AB-AK'AB** (A8) **u-K'UH-li** (B8) **?**

> *och[i] ha' sak bahlam ton ajaw ... yajawte' ... hux haab te' hux haabiiy k'a'ayiiy lema(j) ... tuuna(j) ubaah uch'ab [y]ak'ab uk'uhuul ...*

8 The following three quotes (in the original orthography) illustrate the use of these terms:

> /22/ *Unacahibal auxaual tali cucumil tali uchuci ca*/23/ *bil cabob vij Hoti umole cah tanodzic* (Smailus 1975:26)

> ... It is the first beginning of Auxaual. He came from Cozumel. He came from there; he took the lands and the communities. Here he came; he gathered together the city of Tanodzic ...

> /7/ ... *uyactiobix cab tixchel bixiob tama*/8/*tun acalan yaan ucahil ciachob tayel cha ya cahal a ciua*/9/*tecpanob tuxakhaa hainob upayolel uvincilel ytz*/10/*tapannecatob* (Smailus 1975:29–30)

> ... They left the land of Tixchel. They went to Tamactun Acalan. There was the city of the Cehache, Tayel, and there those of Cihuatecpan were settled in the confluence of the rivers. Those were the jurisdiction and people of the Itztapaneca ...

> /9/*Vi ta cah ukaua Santa María tixchel upayolel ukabal* /10/ *uillayl San francisco canPeche tuprovinciail yucatan* (Smailus 1975:24)

> ... Here in the city named Santa Maria Tixchel, the jurisdiction of what is called the city of San Francisco Campeche in the province of Yucatán ...

9 *Profeciado de Chilam Balam; de zix coyom—Cauichen mani* (Miram 1988:1:115); *U profesia chilam balam tix kayom cabal chen mani* (Miram 1988:2:91).

10 Temple of the Foliated Cross tablet inscription (Stuart 2006b:146–147):

> (F6) **T'AB-yi** (E7) **K'INICH** (F7) **K'UK' na** (E8) **ta OTOOT-ti** (F8) **ch'a-ho-ma** (E9) **K'INICH KAN BAHLAM-ma** (F9) **K'UH MAT AJAW-wa** (E10) **u-3-TAL-la** (F10) **u-TZAK K'UH** (E11) **nu ya-AJAW CHAN** (F11) **?-ta** (E12) **tu-u-CH'AB-AK'AB** (F12) **u-K'AL-HU'N-AJ** (E13) **u-K'UH-li** (F13) **K'INICH KAN BAHLAM-ma** (E14) **K'UH MAT AJAW** (F14) **u-ti-ya LAKAM HA'** (E15) **CHAN-na CH'E'N-na** (F15) **tu-CH'E'N-na** (E16) **6 CHAN CHAK** (F16) **3 9 CHAHK** (E17) **K'UH ? NAL AJAW**

> *t'abaay k'inich k'uk' na[ah] ta otoot ch'ajoom k'inich kan bahlam k'uh[ul] mat[wiil] ajaw uhuxtal utzakk'uh nu[k] yajaw chan ... t-uch'ab [y]ak'ab uk'alhu'na j uk'uhuul k'inich kan bahlam k'uh[ul] mat[wiil] ajaw u[h]tiiy lakam ha' chan ch'e'n t-uch'e'n wak chan chak hux bolon chahk k'uh[ul] ... nal ajaw*

> "Holy *Matwiil* lord, he who censes, *K'inich Kan Bahlam* ascended to *K'inich K'uk' Naah*, the dwelling. It was the third conjuration of gods by *Nuk Yajaw Chan* ... It was in the penance/creation, in the darkness of the headband-binding person of the god(s) of holy *Matwiil* lord *K'inich Kan Bahlam*. It happened at *Lakam Ha'*, in the sky, in the *ch'e'n*, in the *ch'e'n* of *Wak Chan* red *Hux Bolon Chahk*, holy ... *Nal* lord."

Temple of the Sun tablet inscription (Stuart 2006b:167):

(F8) **T'AB-yi** (E9) **K'IN-chi-ni** (F9) **K'UK' NAAH** (E10) **ta OTOOT-ti** (F10) **ch'a-ho-ma** (E11) **BAAK-le** (F11) **WAYWAL** (E12) **K'INICH KAN BAHLAM-ma** (F12) **K'UH MAT AJAW** (E13) **u-3-TAL-la** (F13) **TZAK-wa K'UH** (E14) **PAT-la-ja** (F14) **LAKAM HA'** (E15) **CHAN-na CH'E'N-na** (F15) **ye-la-ma** (E16) **K'UK' LAKAM wi-tzi**

t'abaay k'inich k'uk' naah ta otoot ch'ajoom baakel waywal k'inich kan bahlam k'uh[ul] mat[wiil] ajaw uhuxtal tzakaw-k'uh patlaj lakam ha' chan ch'e'n ye[h]mal k'uk' lakam witz

"Holy *Matwiil* lord, he who censes, bone sorcerer, *K'inich Kan Bahlam* ascended to *K'inich K'uk' Naah*, the dwelling. It was his third conjuration of gods. It happened (took shape) at *Lakam Ha'*, in the sky, at *Yehmal K'uk' Lakam Witz*."

11 Dumbarton Oaks Carved Panel inscription (Houston and Taube 2012:42):

(A5) **OCH yo-OTOOT NAAH** (B5) **tu-<u>WAHY-bi</u>-li** (C1) **3 9 CHAHK** (D1) **u-KAB-ji-ya** (C2) **K'INICH <u>JANAHB PAKAL</u>-la** (D2) **K'UH BAAK-la AJAW** (C3) **te-k'a-ja** (D3) **yo-OOK** (C4) **tu-WITZ-li** (D4) **u-K'UH-li** (C5) **ha-i** (D5) **u-TZ'AK-bu-ji** (E1) **3 ?-la** (F1) **MAT** (G1) **K'INICH** (H1) **K'AN-na <u>JOY-CHITAM</u>-ma** (I1) **K'UH BAAK-la AJAW** (J1) **9 "Manik"** (K1) **5 MUWAAN-ni** (L1) **OCH K'AWIIL ta-ti-tzi** (M1) **3 9 CHAHK**

och[i] yotoot naah t-uwahybil hux bolon chahk ukabjiiy k'inich janahb pakal k'uh[ul] baakal ajaw te[h]k'aj yook t-uwitzil uk'uhuul haa' utz'akbuji hux ... mat k'inich k'an joy chitam k'uh[ul] baakal ajaw [ta] bolon "manik" jo[te'] muwaan och[i] k'awiil ta titz hux bolon chahk

"He entered the dwelling house of, the dreaming place of *Hux Bolon Chahk*. It was on the orders of holy *Baakal* lord *K'inich Janahb Pakal*. The foot of his god was placed upon his mountain. As for him, holy *Baakal* lord *Hux ... K'inich K'an Joy Chitam* succeeded him. On [the day] nine "Manik," five *Muwaan*, *K'awiil* entered on the summit [of] *Hux Bolon Chahk*."

12 The new drawing of the Dumbarton Oaks Carved Panel, which was based on its 3D scanning undertaken as part of the Maya Catalog project (Houston and Taube 2012:fig. 20), suggests that the likely spelling in Block L1 is **ta-tzi-ti**. The first syllable probably stands for the *ta* locative preposition. Given that the lower part of the full form of the **tzi** sign is often covered by superimposed graphemes, a combination of the upper part of **tzi** on top of **ti** may be read as **tzi-ti** or **ti-tzi** (on how superimposition affects reading order, see Stuart 2005c:35–36). The only gloss that fits the context is *titz* for "rocky outcrop" or "mountain top" found in some colonial Yukatek dictionaries (Barrera Vásquez et al. 1995:798).

13 Victims of such attacks are described as *ehtej/e'tej* (common form) or a variant spelled **ya-?TE'-AJ/a** in the inscriptions at Dzibanche—a poorly understood gloss that probably means "work"—of the victorious ruler (Martin 2004:109–114; Stuart 2005b:76–77).

14 (F4) **OCH-CH'E'N-na-ja** (E5) **T756d-pi CHAN CH'E'N** (F5) **u-BAAH-ji [u]-CH'AB** (E6) **YAX K'UH** (F6) **YAX AJAW**

och-ch'e'naj ... chan ch'e'n ubaah uch'ab yax k'uh yax ajaw

"It *ch'e'n*-entered ... [in] the sky, [in] the *ch'e'n*. It is the penance/creation of the first god, the first lord"

15 **OCH u-CH'E'N-na IHK' ? NAL ye-EHT "G1"**

och[i] uch'e'n ihk' ... nal yeht[ej] "G1"

he/they entered the *ch'e'n* of *Ihk' ... Nal*. It is the work of G1.

16 (C6) <u>OCH CH'E'N</u> (D6) ? (C7) **CHAN-na AJAW** (D7) **K'UH** (C8) **OCH-K'IN** (D8) **18-na u-BAAH KAN**

   och[i] ch'e'n . . . chan ajaw k'uh ochk'in waxaklajuun ubaah kan

17 (E9) <u>PUL-yi</u> (F9) **u-CH'E'N** (E10) **ma <u>CH'AB AK'AB</u>-li** (F10) <u>JOY-ja-ya</u> **CHAHK** (E11) **YAX-a AJAW**

   puluuy uch'e'n ma' ch'ab[il] [ma'] ak'abil joyaj chahk yaxa' ajaw

18 (B5) **u-CHOK K'AHK'** (A6) **NIK <u>AHK MO'</u> pe TUUN AJAW** (B6) **tu-CH'E'N-na <u>k'a-ba</u> CHAN TE'** (A7) **SAK <u>TZ'I' AJAW</u> BAAH ka-ba**

   uchok[ow] k'ahk' nik ahk mo' pe' tuun ajaw t-uch'e'n k'ab chan te' sak tz'i' ajaw baah kab

19 **u²-KAB-CH'E'N 3 11 pi/PIK AJAW ni-<u>TZ'AK-bu</u>-ji**

   ukab uch'e'n hux buluk pik ajaw nitz'akbuji

20 Only the last two blocks of the inscription on that side of Copan Stela 48 remain (Schele 1989:fig. 19c), so the context of the statement is unclear. The inscription states **u-pa-ta-<u>bu</u>-ji wi-ki CHAN CH'E'N**—*upatbuji wi[nt]ik chan ch'e'n*, "he/she shaped *Wi[nt]ik*, the sky, the *ch'e'n*." It is possible that **wi-ki** stands for a version of the Copan *Hux Wintik* place name, but this is by no means certain.

21 The only clear exception to this pattern is the passage on Tamarindito Hieroglyphic Stairway 2 (Figure 21b) stating that "T856-**la**, his *chan ch'e'n*, was chopped" (*ch'ahkaj* T856-**la** *uchan ch'e'n*), which contains the only known possessed form of *chan ch'e'n* and the only case when *chan ch'e'n* is without doubt the object of the action of the transitive verb. It is unclear to what extent this unique example can be used to understand the rest of the cases.

22 In this particular example, the statement appears to be **WA'-OOK-ji-ya K'AWIIL NAL-la nu-NOH-la CHAN-na CH'E'N-na**, *wa'-ookjiiy k'awiil nal nu[k] nohol chan ch'e'n*, "*K'awiil Nal* placed foot [in] the south, [in] the sky, [in] the *ch'e'n*."

23 **PAT-la-ja u-WE' 7-CHAPAHT-tu TZ'IKIIN-na K'IN-ni AJAW-wa EL-K'IN-ni CHAN-na CH'E'N-na**

   patlaj uwe' huk chapaht tz'ikiin k'in[ich] ajaw elk'in chan ch'e'n

24 **MIH OHL-la CHAN-na-NAL K'UH MIH-OHL-la KAB-la K'UH**

   mih-ohl chanal k'uh mih-ohl kabal k'uh

25 (F1) **u-MIH yo-OHL u-CHAN <u>KAB CH'E'N</u>** (G1) **5 WINIK.HAAB u-to-ma** (H1) **7 AJAW 18 CHAK AT-ta**

   umih yohl uchan [u]kab [u]ch'e'n jo' winikhaab u[h]toom huk ajaw waxaklajuun chak at

   "the heart(s) of the skies, the earth, the *ch'e'n* of five k'atuns are made content [until] it shall happen, 7 Ajaw 18 'Zip'"

26 In Ara's original orthography, *mihigh* "abundar" and *mihightez* "acrecentar algo."

27 (F24) **TAHN-LAM-ja** (E25) **1 pi/PIK** (F25) <u>CHAN K'UH</u> (E26) <u>K'AB K'UH</u> (F26) **UH-ti-ya** (E27) **²ku-la CHAN KAB** (F27) **CH'E'N-na**

   tahn-lamaj juun pik chan[al] k'uh kab[al] k'uh uhtiiy kukuul chan kab ch'e'n

28 As in the following terms: *actun cabal* "place with lots of caves" (CMM:3r); *ah col cab* (lit. "he of cornfield place") "peasant" (CMM:10v); *ah ch'en cab* (lit. "he of sinkhole place") "cacao sinkhole owner" (CMM:16r); *ah otoch cab* "resident of the town or province" (CMM:25r).

29 As in *cacab kax, cacab luum* "good land for planting" (CMM:60r) and *chuhlen cab* "land that was burned to prepare it for planting" (CMM:148v).

30 For example, *cabil* "nation" (CMM:59v), *v yanal cab* "other world/region/kingdom" (CMM:59r); *cuch cab, v cuch cab* "community assets or public treasure" (CMM:85v); *cuch cabal* "land, region, precinct; family and people under one's responsibility" (CMM: 86r); *hula cab* "guest, visitor, foreigner" (CMM: 209r); *v nen cab, v nen cah* "mirror of the land, mirror of the town" (a priest or a governor) (CMM:326r); *paa cah, paacabal* "depopulate or vacate town/land" (CMM 354r); *yukba cab* (lit. "land shaking") "disturbance and rioting as in times of hunger" (CMM: 220v).

31 The decipherment of the **KAAJ** logogram (also found in one of the two emblem glyph titles of Yaxchilan and El Zotz rulers) was proposed by Martin (1996b) in his analysis of the inscription on Lintel 2 in Temple IV at Tikal. The sign frequently takes the final **–ji** phonetic complement, but its reading as **KAAJ** remains speculative (Houston 2008). An inscription on a sherd from the special deposit at Buenavista del Cayo (Houston et al. 1992:fig. 12) features a sequence of **i-ka ?KAAJ-ji** graphemes where **ka** may be interpreted as an initial phonetic complement to **KAAJ**. The caveats are lack of semantic context and placement of **i-ka** in a separate glyph block.

32 The block may also be read as *ni-pakal [ni-]took' [ni-]kab* "my shield, my flint, my land," but this phrase would not make much sense in the context of the preceding sentences. The "flint-shield" couplet is not in its usual order (*took' pakal*). In fact, it would be the only example of such reversal in this common couplet. But shield and flint may be an otherwise unique example of a compound **TZ'AK** allograph. These "paired variants" usually show pairs of objects in complementary relationship to each other (Stuart 2003), precisely like the flint and shield couplet that means something like "weapons" or "army." The sudden break of a third-person narrative into a first-person speech is usual, but there are similar examples including the texts on the tablets of Temple of the Inscriptions at Palenque and Copan monuments (St 49, Str 22 Stp).

33 This interpretation is not certain, because **KAB** in **u-KAB-AJ** spelling on the monument may be a variant of **TUUN** or a conflation of **TUUN** and **KAB**.

34 The style of the text leaves open the possibility of **TUN** or **ku** reading for the sign **KAB**.

35 The term *ikaatz* or *ikitz* (**i-ka-tzi** or **i-ki-tzi**) is associated with precious objects in elite transactions (Stuart 1998:409–417, 2006a:128–137). Its primary meaning seems to be restricted to fine jewelry and not jade as raw material because it appears in labels on finished jade artifacts (Stuart 2006a:figs. 4–5).

36 If the mural follows the indigenous cartographic conventions known from early colonial documents such as the map in *Memoria de la distribución de los montes* of the Xiu Papers (Quezada and Okoshi Harada 2001:32, 53), it should be oriented with east on the top and west on the bottom (see also Marcus 1992:153–189, for a broader overview of Mesoamerican cartographic conventions). Therefore, all features on the mural are arranged along the east–west or west–east direction of movement.

37 The decipherment of the *y-ook k'in* title ("foot/support of the sun") is not certain. In the case of Naranjo inscriptions, **yo** is not always present. This may suggest that it functions as a phonetic complement, but it may also be a case of an underspelled third-person ergative pronoun. Some examples of the title, such as those on Naranjo Altar 2, Stelae 1, 13, and 14, look like a conflation of **OOK/tz'i** "dog" and **K'IN**, sometimes with a final **ni** phonetic complement. Other spellings (NAR St 20, 21, 27, 30) feature a **SUUTZ'/tz'i**-like "bat" sign in place of **OOK** in the same context and with the same phonetic complements. This substitution in occurrences of the title was identified by Grube, who suggested that either variant included **tz'i** (Grube 1986:fig. 6c, 226). If so, the title could be read as **yo-tz'i K'IN-ni** for *y-ootz' k'in*, "the *ootz'* of the sun," where *ootz'* could mean "crust, wrinkle" as in Yukatek (Bricker et al. 1998:14). But an occasional absence of **yo** suggests that we are dealing with logograms and

not syllabic signs in the main compound. It is also possible that one or both of these conflations are distinct graphemes with **yo** and **ni** as phonetic complements. There are no examples of "dog"/"bat" and **K'IN** written separately. Nevertheless, the location of the **K'IN** element inside "dog" and "bat" graphemes is not consistent (although the lower-right corner and eye are most frequent choices) and that is more typical of a conflation.

38 Nearly all spellings of this toponym are **3 wi-ti-ki**. But the inscription on Copan Stela 10 (Figure 36e) adds another sign to the spelling—**3 wi-ni-ti-ki**. The absence of **ni** in other examples may be explained by a calligraphic conflation of **ni** and **wi** (these signs are similar and sometimes even identical) or by the elision of *n* in front of *t* in *wintik*. In the latter case, the spelling on Stela 10 would reflect a deliberately archaic pronunciation of the place name.

39 (D8) <u>yi-ta</u>-ji 8 PET AJ-T856 (D9) u-ti-ya (D10) K'INICH <u>PA' WITZ</u> ti T856-la

yitaaj waxak pet aj-. . . u[h]tiiy k'inich pa' witz ti . . . -l

40 The spelling of the place name in this case (Figure 37d) is a highly complex conflation of **NAL** inscribed into the upper part of **CH'E'N**, with T856 inscribed into the left half of **NAL** and **CHAN** infixed into the right half of **NAL**. The **YAX** grapheme is placed to the left of the conflation. The **NAL** grapheme is so heavily modified that it is almost invisible. Fortunately, the inscriptions on Tamarindito Stela 4 and Arroyo de Piedra Stela 6 (Figure 37e) contain a more straightforward **YAX** T856 **NAL-la** spelling with no conflations.

41 Many examples of *Hux Witza'* (Figure 39b–c, e) omit the final *–a'*, but full spellings are also known (Figure 39d). The toponymic registers feature a conflation of a full-figure or head variant of number three (a young wind deity) and the **WITZ** grapheme. These conflations are very elaborate, as in the example illustrated in Figure 39e: the presence of the number three logogram is given away only by the headband of the wind god tied across the forehead of the **WITZ** creature.

42 According to Martin (1998), a Hieroglyphic Stairway block (Fragment 401-6) at Calakmul (Figure 60i) contains the statement **tu-CH'E'N-na KAN** that he reads as *t-uch'e'n kanu'l* and translates as "in the *ch'e'n* of *Kanu'l*—a possible reference to *Kanu'l* as a historical place. But the possible **KAN** logogram has unusual elements in its upper section. It also lacks its initial **ka** phonetic complement and final **la**. The sentence before *t-uch'e'n* is missing and it may as well have dealt with deep-time events.

43 An Early Classic form of the **KAAJ** logogram found in this inscription and texts like El Zotz wooden lintel looks different from its Late Classic version.

44 **K'AWIIL-la MAM 6 CHAN-na WITZ-la AJ-chi-**T316 **AJ-?WITE' NAAH ba-ka-ba**

k'awiil mam wak chan witziil [winik] aj-. . . aj-wite' naah ba[ah] kab

45 The decipherment proposed by Beliaev and Davletshin is based on the aforementioned occasional *–ja* final phonetic complement of the logogram and on a new example of the "foundation" glyph in the inscription of the Early Classic Coba ballcourt panel. It includes an initial phonetic complement **ka-** in the context **ka-**"foundation.glyph" *–yi* **ko-ba-a**, where the second word likely spells *Koba'*, the ancient name of the Coba archaeological site. David Stuart (personal communication 2011) reads that initial **ka** glyph as **u**, however.

46 (G2) **HUL-li** (H2) **k'i-ba-AJAW** (G3)**?KAJ-yi** (H3) **?WAL-AKAN** (G4) **?WAL-tz'e-ka** (H4) **?WAL-NAHB** (G5) **3-AHK** (H5) **PET-ne** (G6) **?WAL-yo-OHL** (H6) **a-ku** (G7) **yu-lu** (H7) **CHAN-na-HA'** (G8) **ha** (H8) **lu-mi**

huli k'iib ajaw ?kajaay wal akan wal tz'eek wal nahb hux ahk peten wal yohl ahk yul chan ha' haluum

The decipherment of **WAL** was proposed by Lacadena García-Gallo in the analysis of inscriptions on Ek Balam painted capstones (2003). It remains tentative because contexts like Yaxchilan Lintel 10 (B2, C1; Graham and Von Euw 1977:31) have not been explained with this reading. As suggested by Albert Davletshin (personal communication 2011), the spelling in Block F4 involves Stuart's **tz'e** syllable (Stuart 2002) so that **tz'e-ka** would correspond to *tz'eek*. Albert Davletshin (personal communication 2012) argues that *tz'eek* in this context may be related to *tz'ek* for a paved area in front of one's home in Yukatek (Barrera Vásquez et al. 1995:881) or *tz'ek* for an edge of a cliff or canyon in Itzaj (Hofling and Tesucún 1997:636).

47 (G1) **?KAJ-yi TAHN-na CH'E'N-na** (H1) **pe-e TUUN-ni** (G2) **yo-?o-NAL a-ku**

   ?kajaay tahn ch'e'n pe' tuun yo'nal ahk

   "*Yo'nal Ahk* settled in the *ch'e'n* [in] *Pe' Tuun*"

48 (A33) **CH'AK-ka-ja** (A34) **ka-ba** (A35) **ta no-NOH** (A36) **a/AJ-AJAW-wa-TAAK** (A37) **ta LAK-K'IN-ni** (A38) **a/AJ-AJAW-wa-TAAK** (A39) **ta ?XAMAN** (A40) **a/AJ-AJAW-?TAAK** (A41) **ta OCH-K'IN-ni** (A42) **a/AJ-AJAW-?TAAK**

   ch'a[h]kaj kab ta noh[ol] ajawtaak ta lak'in ajawtaak ta xaman ajawtaak ta ochk'in ajawtaak

49 The still undeciphered title of Edzna rulers was originally identified as a kind of local emblem glyph by David Stuart (see Grube 2008:182).

50 In colonial Yukatek dictionaries and texts (like the books of Chilam Balam), the term *tz'ul* means "foreigner" and is often used when referring to Spaniards (Barrera Vásquez et al. 1995:892). The Chontal Maldonado-Paxbolon Papers (Smailus 1975:30–31) feature *tz'ulob* in contexts where it could mean "foreigners" (Dmitri D. Beliaev, personal communication 2012). Wisdom's Ch'orti' dictionary (Wisdom 1950:731–732) includes an entry *tzur*—"false, foreign, non-Ch'orti'"—where *tz* likely stands for *tz'* (e.g., Wisdom's *tzurumuy* vs. *tz'urumuy* for "cherimoya" in Pérez Martínez and Quizar's dictionary [1996:234]).

51 The differences between internal and external references and between texts on carved monuments and portable media raise an important question about whether some of these portable objects were made at Naranjo. The presence of titles like *Huk Tzuk* might reflect an exterior perception of the owner's identity. Most of these objects have been looted and have no known provenience. Vessels made for the Middle Classic Naranjo lord "Aj Wosaj," which can be attributed to Naranjo based on the recently discovered special deposits at the site (Fialko 2008), never refer to the king as *Huk Tzuk*. The only eighth-century text on a painted vase designated for a Naranjo lord and signed by a Naranjo scribe (K635) does not refer to the vessel owner or his father as Seven Divisions and only mentions western *Huk Tzuk* in the name of his mother, who is from Yaxha.

52 (C2) **WITZ-ja u-JOL-li** (D2) **13 tzu-ku** (E1) **MUT-la** T1006a-**li**

   witzaj ujolil huxlajuun tzuk mutal

53 The toponym in the title of Xultun lords has recently been deciphered as *Baax Witz* (Prager et al. 2010), thanks to a possible **ba-xi wi-tzi** phonetic spelling on a Late Classic vase (K4996).

54 (D12) **a-AK'-ta-ja** (C13) **ti** T700 **NAL** (D13) **yi-ta-ji** (C14) **7 tzu-ku** (D14) **13 tzu-ku** (C15) **5** T544.501-**ni** (D15) **?-a-AJAW**

   ak'taj ti . . . nal yitaaj huk tzuk huxlajuun tzuk jo' . . . ajaw

55 *Can ahau u kaba k'atun uchci u sihilob pauah aencuh u yahauoob*

   Oxhun te ti k'atun lic u tepalob lay u kabaob   tamuk u tepalob lae

   Can ahau u kaba k'atun emciob noh hemal: dze emal u kabaob lae

   Oxlahun te ti k'atun lic u tepalob lic u kabaticob: tii ualac u cutob

   oxlahun cuthi u cutob lae (Miram 1988:1:98–99)

56 (H16) **yi-IL-ji 8-20** (I16) **a/AJ-AJAW-TAAK**

    yilaaj waxak winik ajawtaak

57 (A5) **yi-IL-? K'UH MUT AJAW-?** (B5) **yi-IL-? 8-20-ki AJAW-TAAK**

    yilaaj k'uh[ul] mut[al] ajaw yilaaj waxak winik ajawtaak

58 (E10) **ti AJAW** (F10) **MAM** (E11) **K'UH ²ku-la AJAW** (F11) **YAX NUUN AHIIN** (E12) **u-CH'AM-wa** (F12) **8-20 PET**

    ti ajaw mam k'uh[ul] kukuul ajaw yax nuun ahiin uch'amaw waxak winik pet

59 **u-BAAH ?1 IXIIM 6 HIX NAL <u>T'AB-yi</u> MUT**

    ubaah juun ixiim wak hix nal [winik] t'abaay mut[al]

60 **u-BAAH ?1 IXIIM 6 CHAN NAL <u>T'AB-yi</u> ka-KAN**

    ubaah juun ixiim wak chan nal [winik] t'abaay kan[u'l]

61 **u-BAAH ?1 IXIIM 6 CHUWEN NAL <u>T'AB-yi</u> T174-su**

    ubaah juun ixiim wak chuwen nal [winik] t'abaay T174-su

62 **u-BAAH IXIIM 6 HIX NAL OCH-K'IN-ni TAHN-na CH'E'N-na K'UH MUT AJAW**

    ubaah ixiim wak hix nal ochk'in tahn ch'e'n k'uh[ul] mut[al] ajaw

63 **u-BAAH IXIIM 6 CNAH NAL KAL-? TAHN-na CH'E'N-na K'UH KAN AJAW**

    ubaah ixiim wak chan nal kal[aaw-te'] tahn ch'e'n k'uh[ul] kan[u'l] ajaw

A more transparent **KAL-wi-TE'** spelling for *kalaaw-te'* is found in the inscription on the vessel from the Cuychen Cave (Helmke n.d.; Figure 66a). The *kal* gloss usually appears in the *kaloomte'* title of Classic Maya rulers. But here it is used as a verb in a noun-incorporating antipassive form (see Lacadena García-Gallo 2000). *Kale'* means "to make" in colonial Ch'olti' (Morán 1695). It can be used in expressions such as "making a cornfield" (*kalbel chol*) and "making a house" (*kalbel otot*) in Moran's manuscript (Robertson et al. 2010:line 479). *Kal* in Ch'ol (Aulie and Aulie 1978:38) and *kere'* in Ch'orti' (Wisdom 1950:491) mean "to open, to divide." Therefore, *kalaaw-te'* may be translated as "tree-make" or "tree-open/divide."

64 As pointed out by Simon Martin (personal communication 2012), it is also possible that *Yik'in Chan K'awiil* was dressed as a *Kanu'l* maize god to highlight his recent victories against Calakmul rulers, which may have resulted in the capture of related palanquins and back-dress costumes.

65 **u-BAAH-hi IXIIM 6 ?OOK NAL KAL-wi TE' 3 HAAB TE'**

    ubaah ixiim wak ?ook nal [winik] kalaaw-te' hux haab te'

66 The Río Azul inscription clearly identifies *Wak Chan Muyal Nal* as a place where the individual was "buried" (*muhkaj*). The narrative at Pomona refers to *Wak Chan Muyal Witz* as a location of an "earth-opening" event (*paskabjiiy*) that probably meant a tomb reentering. The El Zapote example mentions *Wak Chan Muyal Witz* in the context of one's "seating" (*chumlaj*), so that location was probably a dwelling of some kind.

APPENDIX I

TRANSCRIPTION AND TRANSLITERATION CONVENTIONS

...	missing/omitted sign(s)/word(s)
?	unknown sign(s)
[**ba**]	reconstructed sign(s)
?ba	problematic/preliminary/questionable decipherment
T609	sign identified by its number in Thompson's catalogue (1962)
"star.war"	sign identified by its nickname
BAAK	logogram/word sign
ba	syllabogram/syllabic sign
ba-BAAK	spelling in one glyphic block
<u>**ba-BAAK**</u>	spelling with a conflation
baak	word in Classic Ch'olti'an/Hieroglyphic Mayan
?	unknown word(s) spelled with unknown sign(s)
[baak]	reconstructed word(s)
?baak	problematic/preliminary/questionable decipherment

SITE CODES

AGT	Aguateca		NMP	Nim Li Punit
ALS	Altar de Sacrificios		NTN	Naj Tunich
ARP	Arroyo de Piedra		PAL	Palenque
BPK	Bonampak		PMT	Pomona
CLK	Calakmul		PNG	Piedras Negras
CNC	Cancuen		PRU	El Peru
CPN	Copan		PUS	Pusilha
CRC	Caracol		QRG	Quirigua
DCB	Dos Caobas		RAZ	Río Azul
DPL	Dos Pilas		SBL	Seibal
EDZ	Edzna/Etzna		TAM	Tamarindito
ITN	Itzan		TIK	Tikal
IXK	Ixkun		TNA	Tonina
LAC	Lacanha		TRS	Tres Islas
MAR	La Mar		TRT	Tortuguero
MQL	Machaquila		TZD	Tzendales
MTL	Motul de San Jose		YAX	Yaxchilan
NAR	Naranjo		YXH	Yaxha

APPENDIX 3

ABBREVIATIONS

Alt	Altar
CHU	The Book of Chilam Balam of Chumayel (Miram 1988:1)
CMHI	Corpus of Maya Hieroglyphic Inscriptions (Graham et al. 1975)
CMM	Calepino Maya de Motul (Ciudad Real 1995)
Dr	Drawing
HP	Hieroglyphic Panel
HS	Hieroglyphic Stairway
IDAEH	Instituto de Arqueología e Historia
K-number	File number in the Maya Vase Database (Kerr n.d.)
Ln	Lintel
Mn	Monument
MSC	Miscellaneous
MT	Miscellaneous Text
Pn	Panel
SCS	Sculptured Stone
St	Stela
Stp	Step
Str	Structure
T	Temple
Tb	Tablet
TC	Temple of the Cross, Palenque
Thr	Throne
TI	Temple of the Inscriptions, Palenque
TIZ	The Book of Chilam Balam of Tizimin (Miram 1988:2)
TS	Temple of the Sun, Palenque

CLASSIC MAYA PLACE NAME DATABASE

The database of Classic Maya place names is a collection of approximately 2,400 references to toponyms in Classic Maya inscriptions and approximately 600 search queries saved as a Microsoft Access 2007 file. The core of the database is a master table that contains information about each place name occurrence: its spelling (transcription) and transliteration; the transliteration of a sentence where it occurs; its associated site; and its source information, including monument and provenience, context description, date, and image references (if available). A typical entry in the master table looks like this:

			PLACE NAMES MAIN TABLE		
DB #	TRANSCRIPTION	TRANSLITERATION	FULL CONTEXT	ASSOCIATED SITE	CONTEXT INFORMATION
1	LAKAM-HA'	lakam ha'	kajaay lakam ha' b'utz'aj sak chi'k	Palenque	settling, accession, war

OBJECT	PROVENIENCE	DATE (GREGORIAN)	LONG COUNT DATE	REFERENCE	CONTEXT TYPE
Panel	Temple 17, Palenque	9/12/687	9.12.15.7.11	Schele Drawing Archive	direct

In addition to the master table, the database includes a number of derived tables including counts of context types, distinct place names, and source groups. There are approximately 600 queries for specific place names and contexts. A typical place name query simply identifies all occurrences of a given toponym. Context queries search the master table by broader context categories (such as "context type" or "context info") or by specific syntax patterns from the "full context." For example, a search for a combination of the *jubuuy* verb, a toponym, and the term *ch'e'n* may return, among other entries, the following line (with irrelevant fields not included):

02 VERBS *JUBUUY & CH'E'N*				
FULL CONTEXT	PROVENIENCE	OBJECT	REFERENCE	DB #
jub'uuy sa'aal uch'e'n k'uhxaj sak chwen [...]	Naranjo	Step 6, Hieroglyphic Stairway 1	CMHI 2:109	938

The advantage of including the database—rather than printouts of the master table and queries—as an online appendix to the monograph is that readers would be able to modify existing queries and create new ones. Consequently, the database may become a useful research tool.

Although each DB # was originally accompanied by an image (a drawing or a photograph) of the corresponding section of the hieroglyphic inscription, the images are not included in the appendix to avoid problems with copyright. (I obtained many drawings and photographs for research purposes only and not for publication.) At one point, I considered making new drawings, but the time required to complete 2,400 drawings would have been too long. Therefore, the image files, along with handwritten preliminary notes, remain in my possession, and will be available should the need arise to discuss or to correct any entries in the database.

The database can be downloaded at:

www.doaks.org/publications/books-in-print/place-and-identity-in-classic-maya-narratives

REFERENCES CITED

Adams, Richard E. W. (editor)

1989　*Proyecto Rio Azul: Informe cuatro; 1986.* University of Texas at San Antonio, San Antonio.

1999　*Río Azul: An Ancient Maya City.* University of Oklahoma Press, Norman.

Anaya Hernández, Armando, Stanley Guenter, and Peter Mathews

2002　An Inscribed Wooden Box from Tabasco, Mexico. Electronic document, www.mesoweb.com/reports/box/index.html, accessed June 27, 2012.

Anaya Hernández, Armando, Stanley Guenter, and Marc Zender

2003　Sak Tz'i', a Classic Maya Center: A Locational Model Based on GIS and Epigraphy. *Latin American Antiquity* 14(2):179–191.

Anderson, Benedict R.

1991　*Imagined Communities: Reflections on the Origin and Spread of Nationalism.* Rev. ed. Verso, London and New York.

Anschuetz, Kurt F., Richard H. Wilshusen, and Cherie L. Scheick

2001　An Archaeology of Landscapes: Perspectives and Directions. *Journal of Archaeological Research* 9(2):157–211.

Ara, Domingo de

1986　*Vocabulario de lengua tzeldal según el orden de*
[1571]　*Copanabastla.* Universidad Nacional Autónoma de México, Mexico City.

Aulie, H. Wilbur, and Evelyn W. de Aulie

1978　*Diccionario ch'ol: Ch'ol-español, español-ch'ol.* Instituto Lingüístico de Verano, Mexico City.

Barrera Vásquez, Alfredo, Juan Ramón Bastarrachea Manzano, William Brito Sansores, Refugio Vermont Salas, David Dzul Góngora, and Domingo Dzul Poot

1995　*Diccionario maya: Maya-español, español-maya.* 3rd ed. Editorial Porrúa, Mexico City.

Barthel, Thomas

1968　El complejo emblema. *Estudios de cultura maya* 7:159–193.

Bassie-Sweet, Karen

1996　*At the Edge of the World: Caves and Late Classic Maya World View.* University of Oklahoma Press, Norman.

Basso, Keith

1984　"Stalking with Stories": Names, Places, and Moral Narratives among the Western Apache. In *Text, Play, and Story: The Construction and Reconstruction of Self and Society*, edited by Edward M. Bruner, pp. 19–55. Waveland Press, Prospect Heights, Ill.

Baudez, Claude F.

1994　*Maya Sculpture of Copán: The Iconography.* University of Oklahoma Press, Norman.

1996　La Casa de los Cuatro Reyes de Balamkú. *Arqueología mexicana* 3(18):36–41.

Becerra, Marcos E.

1985　*Nombres geográficos indígenas del estado de Chiapas.* 3rd ed. Instituto Nacional Indigenista, Mexico City.

Beetz, Carl P., and Linton Satterthwaite

1981　*The Monuments and Inscriptions of Caracol, Belize.* University Museum, University of Pennsylvania, Philadelphia.

Beliaev, Dmitri D.

2000　Wuk Tsuk and Oxlahun Tsuk: Naranjo and Tikal in the Late Classic. In *The Sacred and the Profane: Architecture and Identity in the Maya Lowlands*, edited by Pierre Robert Colas, pp. 63–81. A. Saurwein, Markt Schwaben.

2004　Wayaab' Title in Maya Hieroglyphic Inscriptions: On the Problem of Religious Specialization in Classic Maya Society. In *Continuity and Change: Maya Religious Practices in Temporal Perspective*, edited by Daniel Graña Behrens, Nikolai Grube, Christian Prager,

Frauke Sachse, Stefanie Teufel, and Elisabeth Wagner, pp. 121–130. Acta Mesoamericana 14. A. Saurwein, Markt Schwaben.

2006   "Verbs of Motion" and Ideal Landscape in the Maya Hieroglyphic Inscriptions. Paper Presented at the 11th European Maya Conference, Malmö, Sweden.

Beliaev, Dmitri D., and Albert Davletshin

2007   Los sujetos novelísticos y las palabras obscenas: Los mitos, los cuentos y las anécdotas en los textos mayas sobre la cerámica del periodo clásico. In *Sacred Books, Sacred Languages: Two Thousand Years of Ritual and Religious Maya Literature*, edited by Rogelio Valencia Rivera and Geneviève Le Fort, pp. 21–44. A. Saurwein, Markt Schwaben.

Beliaev, Dmitri D., and Alexandr Safronov

2004   Ak'e i Shukal'nakh: Istoriia i politicheskaia geografiia gosudarstv maiia Verkhnei Usumasinty. In *Drevnii Vostok i antichnyi mir: Trudy kafedry istorii drevnego mira*, vol. 6, pp. 119–142. Istoricheskiĭ fakul'tet MGU, Moscow.

Bell, Ellen E.

2007   Early Classic Ritual Deposits within the Copan Acropolis: The Material Foundations of Political Power at a Classic Period Maya Center. PhD dissertation, Department of Anthropology, University of Pennsylvania, Philadelphia.

Bender, Barbara

1992   Theorising Landscapes, and the Prehistoric Landscapes of Stonehenge. *Man* 27(4):735–755.

Benz, Bruce, Hugo Perales, and Stephen Brush

2007   Tzeltal and Tzotzil Farmer Knowledge and Maize Diversity in Chiapas, Mexico. *Current Anthropology* 48(2):289–300.

Berlin, Heinrich

1958   El glifo "emblema" en las inscripciones maya. *Journal de la Société des Américanistes* 47:111–119.

Bernal Romero, Guillermo

2002   Analisis epigráfico del tablero de K'an Tok, Palenque, Chiapas. In *La organización social entre los mayas prehispánicos, coloniales, y modernos: Memoria de la tercera Mesa Redonda de Palenque*, vol. 1, edited by Vera Tiesler Blos, Rafael Cobos, and Merle Greene Robertson, pp. 401–424. Instituto Nacional de Antropología e Historia, Mexico City.

Biró, Péter

2005   Sak Tz'i' in the Classic Period Hieroglyphic Inscriptions. Electronic document, www.mesoweb.com/articles/biro/SakTzi.pdf, accessed June 27, 2012.

Boot, Erik

2008   At the Court of Itzam Nah Yax Kokaj Mut: Preliminary Iconographic and Epigraphic Analysis of a Late Classic Vessel. Electronic document, www.mayavase.com/God-D-Court-Vessel.pdf, accessed June 27, 2012.

Braakhuis, H. E. M.

2001   Way of All Flesh: Sexual Implications of the Mayan Hunt. *Anthropos* 96(2):391–409.

Brady, James E., and Pierre Robert Colas

2005   Nikte Mo' Scattered Fire in the Cave of K'ab Chante: Epigraphic and Archaeological Evidence for Cave Desecration in Ancient Maya Warfare. In *Stone Houses and Earth Lords: Maya Religion in the Cave Context*, edited by Keith M. Prufer and James E. Brady, pp. 149–166. University Press of Colorado, Boulder.

Bricker, Victoria Reifler, Eleuterio Po'ot Yah, and Ofelia Dzul de Po'ot

1998   *A Dictionary of the Maya Language: As Spoken in Hocabá, Yucatán*. University of Utah Press, Salt Lake City.

Brubaker, Rogers, and Frederick Cooper

2000   Beyond "Identity." *Theory and Society* 29:1–47.

Canuto, Marcello A.

2002   Tale of Two Communities: Social and Political Transformation in the Hinterlands of the Maya Polity of Copan. PhD dissertation, Department of Anthropology, University of Pennsylvania, Philadelphia.

Canuto, Marcello A., and William L. Fash

2004   The Blind Spot: Where the Elite and Non-Elite Meet. In *Continuities and Changes in Maya Archaeology: Perspectives at the Millennium*, edited by Charles W. Golden and Greg Borgstede, pp. 51–75. Routledge, New York.

Carlsen, Robert S., and Martin Prechtel

1991   The Flowering of the Dead: An Interpretation of Highland Maya Culture. *Man* 26(1):23–42.

Carlson, John B.

1982   Double-Headed Dragon and the Sky: A Pervasive Cosmological Symbol. In *Ethnoastronomy and Archaeoastronomy in the American Tropics*, edited by

Anthony F. Aveni and Gary Urton, pp. 135–163. New York Academy of Sciences, New York.

1988 Skyband Representations in Classic Maya Vase Painting. In *Maya Iconography*, edited by Elizabeth P. Benson and Gillett G. Griffin, pp. 277–293. Princeton University Press, Princeton.

Carlson, John B., and Linda C. Landis

1985 Bands, Bicephalic Dragons, and Other Beasts: The Skyband in Maya Art and Iconography. In *Fourth Palenque Round Table, 1980*, edited by Elizabeth P. Benson, pp. 115–140. Pre-Columbian Art Research Institute, San Francisco.

Carrasco Vargas, Ramón, and Marinés Colón González

2005 El reino de Kaan y la antigua ciudad maya de Calakmul. *Arqueología mexicana* 13(75):40–47.

Castañeda, Quetzil E.

1996 *In the Museum of Maya Culture: Touring Chichen Itzá*. University of Minnesota Press, Minneapolis.

Chase, Arlen F., Nikolai Grube, and Diane Z. Chase

1991 *Three Terminal Classic Monuments from Caracol, Belize*. Research Reports on Ancient Maya Writing 36–37. Center for Maya Research, Washington, D.C.

Chinchilla Mazariegos, Oswaldo

2006 *A Reading for the "Earth-Star" Verb in Ancient Maya Writing*. Research Reports on Ancient Maya Writing 56. Center for Maya Research, Washington, D.C.

Chinchilla Mazariegos, Oswaldo, and Stephen D. Houston

1993 Historia política de la zona de Piedras Negras: Las inscripciones de El Cayo. In *VI Simposio de Investigaciones Arqueológicas, 1992*, edited by Juan Pedro Laporte, Héctor L. Escobedo, and Sandra Villagrán de Brady, pp. 63–70. Ministerio de Cultura y Deportes, Instituto de Antropología e Historia, and Asociación Tikal, Guatemala.

Christenson, Allen J.

2000 *Popol Vuh: The Mythic Sections, Tales of First Beginnings from the Ancient K'iche'-Maya*. Foundation for Ancient Research and Mormon Studies at Brigham Young University, Provo, Utah.

2004 *Popol Vuh: Literal Poetic Version*. O Books, Winchester, United Kingdom, and New York.

2006 You Are What You Speak: Maya as the Language of Maize. In *Maya Ethnicity: The Construction of Ethnic Identity from Preclassic to Modern Times*, edited by Frauke Sachse, pp. 209–216. A. Saurwein, Markt Schwaben.

Ciudad Real, Antonio de (editor)

1995 *Calepino de Motul: Diccionario maya-español*. Universidad Nacional Autónoma de México, Dirección General de Asuntos del Personal Académico, Instituto de Investigaciones Antropológicas, Mexico City.

Ciudad Ruiz, Andrés, and Alfonso Lacadena García-Gallo

2001 Tamactún-Acalán: Interpretación de una hegemonía política maya de los siglos XIV–XVI. *Journal de la Société des Américanistes* 87:9–38.

Closs, Michael P.

1988 *The Hieroglyphic Text of Stela 9, Lamanai, Belize*. Research Reports on Ancient Maya Writing 21. Center for Maya Research, Washington, D.C.

Coe, Michael D.

1965 A Model of Ancient Community Structure in the Maya Lowlands. *Southwestern Journal of Anthropology* 21(2):97–114.

1978 *Lords of the Underworld: Masterpieces of Classic Maya Ceramics*. Art Museum, Princeton University, Princeton.

Connerton, Paul

1989 *How Societies Remember*. Cambridge University Press, Cambridge and New York.

Cosgrove, Denis

1985 Prospect, Perspective, and the Evolution of the Landscape Idea. *Transactions of the Institute of British Geographers* 10:45–62.

Culbert, T. Patrick

1993 *The Ceramics of Tikal: Vessels from the Burials, Caches, and Problematical Deposits*. University Museum, University of Pennsylvania, Philadelphia.

Emmerich, André

1984 *Masterpieces of Pre-Columbian Art from the Collection of Mr. & Mrs. Peter G. Wray*. André Emmerich Gallery, Perls Galleries, New York.

Erikson, Erik H.

1950 *Childhood and Society*. Norton, New York.

1959 *Identity and the Life Cycle: Selected Papers*. International Universities Press, New York.

1968 *Identity, Youth, and Crisis*. Norton, New York.

Escobedo, Héctor L.

1997a Arroyo de piedra: Sociopolitical Dynamics of a Secondary Center in the Petexbatun Region. *Ancient Mesoamerica* 8(2):307–320.

1997b Operaciones de rescate e interpretaciones de la arquitectura mayor de Punta de Chimino, Sayaxche, Petén. In *X Simposio de Investigaciones Arqueológicas en Guatemala, 1996*, edited by Juan Pedro Laporte and Héctor L. Escobedo, pp. 402–416. Ministerio de Cultura y Deportes, Instituto de Antropología e Historia, and Asociación Tikal, Guatemala.

Estrada Belli, Francisco

2007 Investigaciones arqueológicas en la región de Holmul, Peten: Holmul, Cival, La Sufricaya y K'o. Electronic document, www.famsi.org/ reports/07028es/index.html, accessed June 27, 2012.

2011 *The First Maya Civilization: Ritual and Power before the Classic Period*. Routledge, London and New York.

Estrada Belli, Francisco, Alexandre Tokovinine, Jennifer M. Foley, Heather Hurst, Gene A. Ware, David Stuart, and Nikolai Grube

2009 A Maya Palace at Holmul, Peten, Guatemala, and the Teotihuacan "Entrada": Evidence from Murals 7 and 9. *Latin American Antiquity* 20(1):228–259.

Fash, Barbara W.

2012 Personified Maize Head. In *Ancient Maya Art at Dumbarton Oaks*, edited by Joanne Pillsbury, Miriam Doutriaux, Reiko Ishihara-Brito, and Alexandre Tokovinine, pp. 76–83. Dumbarton Oaks Research Library and Collection, Washington, D.C.

Fash, William L., and Barbara W. Fash

2000 Teotihuacan and the Maya: A Classic Heritage. In *Mesoamerica's Classic Heritage: Teotihuacan to the Aztecs*, edited by Davíd Carrasco, Lindsay Jones, and Scott Sessions, pp. 465–513. University Press of Colorado, Boulder.

Fash, William L., Alexandre Tokovinine, and Barbara W. Fash

2009 The House of New Fire at Teotihuacan and Its Legacy in Mesoamerica. In *The Art of Urbanism: How Mesoamerican Kingdoms Represented Themselves in Architecture and Imagery*, edited by William L. Fash and Leonardo López Luján, pp. 201–229. Dumbarton Oaks Research Library and Collection, Washington, D.C.

Fialko, Vilma

2008 Proyecto de investigación arqueológica y rescate en Naranjo: Documentación emergente en el palacio de la realeza de Naranjo, Petén, Guatemala. Electronic document, www.famsi. org/reports/05005es/05005esFialko01.pdf, accessed June 27, 2012.

Fitzsimmons, James L.

2009 *Death and the Classic Maya Kings*. University of Texas Press, Austin.

Foote, Nelson N.

1951 Identification as the Basis for a Theory of Motivation. *American Sociological Review* 16:14–21.

Freidel, David, Linda Schele, and Joy Parker

1993 *Maya Cosmos: Three Thousand Years on the Shaman's Path*. W. Morrow, New York.

Garcia Barrios, Ana

2005 Algunos fragmentos cerámicos de estilo códice procedentes de Calakmul. In *Proyecto Arqueológico Calakmul*. Project report on file, Centro INAH Campeche, Campeche.

2006 Confrontation Scenes on Codex-Style Pottery: An Iconographic Review. *Latin American Indian Literatures Journal* 22(2):129–152.

Garcia Barrios, Ana, and Ramón Carrasco Vargas

2006 Algunos fragmentos cerámicos de estilo códice procedentes de Calakmul. *Los investigadores de la cultura maya* 14(1):126–136.

Garrido López, Jose Luis, Stephen D. Houston, Edwin Román, and Thomas Garrison (editors)

2011 *Proyecto arqueológico El Zotz, Informe no. 6, Temporada 2011*. Electronic document, www.mesoweb.com/zotz/resources/ El-Zotz-2011.html, accessed October 31, 2012.

Giddens, Anthony

1986 *The Constitution of Society: Outline of the Theory of Structuration*. University of California Press, Berkeley.

Gleason, Philip

1983 Identifying Identity: A Semantic History. *The Journal of American History* 69(4):910–931.

Gossen, Gary H.

1972 Temporal and Spatial Equivalents in Chamula Ritual Symbolism. In *Reader in Comparative Religion: An Anthropological Approach*, edited by William A. Lessa and Evon Z. Vogt, pp. 135–149. Harper and Row, New York.

1974 *Chamulas in the World of the Sun: Time and Space in a Maya Oral Tradition.* Harvard University Press, Cambridge, Mass.

Graham, Ian

1967 *Archaeological Explorations in El Peten, Guatemala.* Middle American Research Institute, Tulane University, New Orleans.

1975 *Corpus of Maya Hieroglyphic Inscriptions,* vol. 2, pt. 1, *Naranjo.* Peabody Museum of Archaeology and Ethnology, Harvard University, Cambridge, Mass.

1978 *Corpus of Maya Hieroglyphic Inscriptions,* vol. 2, pt. 2, *Naranjo, Chunhuitz, Xunantunich.* Peabody Museum of Archaeology and Ethnology, Harvard University, Cambridge, Mass.

1979 *Corpus of Maya Hieroglyphic Inscriptions,* vol. 3, pt. 2, *Yaxchilan.* Peabody Museum of Archaeology and Ethnology, Harvard University, Cambridge, Mass.

1980 *Corpus of Maya Hieroglyphic Inscriptions,* vol. 2, pt. 3, *Ixkun, Ucanal, Ixtutz, Naranjo.* Peabody Museum of Archaeology and Ethnology, Harvard University, Cambridge, Mass.

1982 *Corpus of Maya Hieroglyphic Inscriptions,* vol. 3, pt. 3, *Yaxchilan.* Peabody Museum of Archaeology and Ethnology, Harvard University, Cambridge, Mass.

1996 *Corpus of Maya Hieroglyphic Inscriptions,* vol. 7, pt. 1, *Seibal.* Peabody Museum of Archaeology and Ethnology, Harvard University, Cambridge, Mass.

1997 Discovery of a Maya Ritual Cave in Peten, Guatemala. *Symbols* (Spring):28–31.

Graham, Ian, Lucia R. Henderson, Peter Mathews, and David Stuart

2006 *Corpus of Maya Hieroglyphic Inscriptions,* vol. 9, pt. 2, *Tonina.* Peabody Museum of Archaeology and Ethnology, Harvard University, Cambridge, Mass.

Graham, Ian, and Peter Mathews

1996 *Corpus of Maya Hieroglyphic Inscriptions,* vol. 6, pt. 2, *Tonina.* Peabody Museum of Archaeology and Ethnology, Harvard University, Cambridge, Mass.

1999 *Corpus of Maya Hieroglyphic Inscriptions,* vol. 6, pt. 3, *Tonina.* Peabody Museum of Archaeology and Ethnology, Harvard University, Cambridge, Mass.

Graham, Ian, and Eric Von Euw

1977 *Corpus of Maya Hieroglyphic Inscriptions,* vol. 3, pt. 1, *Yaxchilan.* Peabody Museum of Archaeology and Ethnology, Harvard University, Cambridge, Mass.

Graham, Ian, Eric Von Euw, Peter Mathews, and David Stuart

1975 *Corpus of Maya Hieroglyphic Inscriptions.* Peabody Museum of Archaeology and Ethnology, Harvard University, Cambridge, Mass.

Gronemeyer, Sven

2006 *The Maya Site of Tortuguero, Tabasco, Mexico: Its History and Inscriptions.* A. Saurwein, Markt Schwaben.

Grube, Nikolai

1986 An Investigation of the Primary Standard Sequence on Classic Maya Ceramics. In *Sixth Palenque Round Table, 1986,* edited by Virginia M. Fields, pp. 223–232. Pre-Columbian Art Research Institute, San Francisco.

1990 A Reference to Water-Lily Jaguar on Caracol Stela 16. Copan Notes 68. Copan Mosaics Project, Copan, Honduras.

1994 Epigraphic Research at Caracol, Belize. In *Studies in the Archaeology of Caracol,* edited Diane Z. Chase and Arlen F. Chase, pp. 83–122. Pre-Columbian Art Research Institute, San Francisco.

2000a The City-States of the Maya. In *A Comparative Study of Thirty City-State Cultures: An Investigation,* edited by Morgens Herman Hansen, pp. 547–565. Kongelige Danske Videnskabernes Selskab, Copenhagen.

2000b Monumentos esculpidos e inscripciones jero-glíficas en el triángulo Yaxhá-Nakum-Naranjo. In *El Sitio maya de Topoxté: Investigaciones en una isla del Lago Yaxhá, Petén, Guatemala,* edited by Wolfgang W. Wurster, pp. 249–267. P. von Zabern, Mainz am Rhein.

2003 Monumentos jeroglíficos de Holmul, Petén, Guatemala. In *XVI Simposio de Investigaciones Arqueológicas en Guatemala, 2002,* edited by Juan Pedro Laporte, Bárbara Arroyo, Héctor L. Escobedo, and Hector Mejía, pp. 693–702. Ministerio de Cultura y Deportes, Instituto de Antropología e Historia, and Asociación Tikal, Guatemala.

2004 El origen de la dinastía Kaan. In *Los cautivos de Dzibanché,* edited by Enrique Nalda, pp. 117–131. Instituto Nacional de Antropología e Historia, Mexico City.

2005 Toponyms, Emblem Glyphs, and the Political Geography of Southern Campeche. *Anthropological Notebooks* 11(1):87–100.

2008   Monumentos esculpidos: Epigrafía e icono-
grafía. In *Reconocimiento arqueológico en
el sureste del estado de Campeche, México:
1996–2005*, edited by Ivan Šprajc, pp. 177–231.
Archaeopress, Oxford.

Grube, Nikolai, and Simon Martin

2001a The Coming of Kings: Writing and Dynastic
Kingship in the Maya Area between the Late
Preclassic and Early Classic. In *Notebook for
the XXVth Maya Hieroglyphic Forum at Texas*,
pp. II-1–II-53. University of Texas, Austin.

2001b The Coming of Kings: Writing and Dynastic
Kingship in the Maya Area between the
Late Preclassic and the Early Classic. In *The
Proceedings of the Maya Hieroglyphic Workshop:
The Coming of Kings; Epi-Olmec Writing, March
10–11, 2001*, edited by Phil Wanyerka, pp. 1–92.
University of Texas, Department of Art, Austin.

Grube, Nikolai, Simon Martin, and Marc Zender

2002   Palenque and Its Neighbors. In *Notebook for the
XXVIth Maya Hieroglyphic Forum at Texas*, pt. 2,
pp. II-1–II-66. University of Texas, Austin.

Grube, Nikolai, and Werner Nahm

1994   A Census of Xibalba: A Complete Inventory
of Way Characters on Maya Ceramics. In
*The Maya Vase Book: A Corpus of Rollout
Photographs of Maya Vases*, vol. 4, edited by
Barbara Kerr and Justin Kerr, pp. 686–715.
Kerr Associates, New York.

**Grube, Nikolai, Carlos Pallán Gayol, and Antonio
Benavides Castillo**

2011   The Hieroglyphic Stairway of Sabana Piletas,
Campeche. In *The Long Silence: Sabana Piletas
and Its Neighbours; An Architectural Survey of
Maya Puuc Ruins in Northeastern Campeche,
Mexico*, edited by Stephan Merk and Antonio
Benavides Castillo, pp. 251–261. A. Saurwein,
Markt Schwaben.

Guenter, Stanley

2002   A Reading of the Cancuén Looted Panel.
Electronic document, www.mesoweb.com/
features/cancuen/Panel.pdf, accessed June 27,
2012.

2003   The Inscriptions of Dos Pilas Associated
with B'ajlaj Chan K'awiil. Electronic document, www.mesoweb.com/features/guenter/
DosPilas.pdf, accessed June 27, 2012.

2007   On the Emblem Glyph of El Peru. *The PARI
Journal* 8(2):20–23.

Hanks, William F.

1990   *Referential Practice: Language and Lived
Space among the Maya*. University of Chicago
Press, Chicago.

2010   *Converting Words: Maya in the Age of the Cross*.
University of California Press, Berkeley.

Hellmuth, Nicholas M.

1987a *Monster und Menschen in der Maya-Kunst:
Eine Ikonographie der Alten Religionen Mexikos
und Guatemalas*. Akademische Druck- u.
Verlagsanstalt, Graz.

1987b *The Surface of the Underwaterworld: Iconography
of the Gods of Early Classic Maya Art in Peten,
Guatemala*. Foundation for Latin American
Anthropological Research, Culver City, Calif.

Helmke, Christophe

n.d.   An Analysis of the Imagery and Text of the
Cuychen Vase. In *Maya Archaeology* 3, in press.

Hermes Cifuentes, Bernard A.

2000   Entierro 49. In *El sitio maya de Topoxté:
Investigaciones en una isla del Lago Yaxhá, Petén,
Guatemala*, edited by Wolfgang W. Wurster,
pp. 127–143. P. von Zabern, Mainz am Rhein.

Hofling, Charles Andrew, and Félix Fernando Tesucún

1997   *Itzaj Maya-Spanish-English Dictionary/
Diccionario maya itzaj-español-inglés*.
University of Utah Press, Salt Lake City.

Houston, Stephen D.

1983   Warfare between Naranjo and Ucanal.
Contributions to Maya Hieroglyphic Decipherment
1:31–39.

1986   *Problematic Emblem Glyphs: Examples from Altar
de Sacrificios, El Chorro, Río Azul, and Xultun*.
Center for Maya Research, Washington, D.C.

1987   Appendix II: Notes on Caracol Epigraphy and
Its Significance. In *Investigations at the Classic
Maya City of Caracol, Belize, 1985–1987*, edited by
Arlen F. Chase and Diane Z. Chase, pp. 85–100.
Pre-Columbian Art Research Institute, San
Francisco.

1993   *Hieroglyphs and History at Dos Pilas: Dynastic
Politics of the Classic Maya*. University of Texas
Press, Austin.

2000   Into the Minds of Ancients: Advances in Glyph
Studies. *Journal of World Prehistory* 14:121–201.

2008   The Epigraphy of El Zotz. Electronic document, www.mesoweb.com/zotz/articles/
ZotzEpigraphy.pdf, accessed June 27, 2012.

2009 A Splendid Predicament: Young Men in Classic Maya Society. *Cambridge Archaeological Journal* 19(2):149–178.

2012 The Good Prince: Transition, Texting, and Moral Narrative in the Murals of Bonampak, Chiapas, Mexico. *Cambridge Archaeological Journal* 22(2):153–175.

Houston, Stephen D., Claudia Brittenham, Cassandra Mesick, Alexandre Tokovinine, and Christina Warinner

2009 *Veiled Brightness: A History of Ancient Maya Color.* University of Texas Press, Austin.

Houston, Stephen D., and Peter Mathews

1985 *The Dynastic Sequence of Dos Pilas, Guatemala.* Pre-Columbian Art Research Institute, San Francisco.

Houston, Stephen D., and Patricia A. McAnany

2003 Bodies and Blood: Critiquing Social Construction in Maya Archaeology. *Journal of Anthropological Archaeology* 22(1):26–41.

Houston, Stephen D., and David Stuart

1989 The Way Glyph: Evidence for "Co-Essences" among the Classic Maya. Research Reports on Ancient Maya Writing 30. Center for Maya Research, Washington, D.C.

1999 Classic Mayan Language and Classic Maya Gods. In *Notebook for the XXIIIrd Maya Hieroglyphic Forum at Texas*, pt. 2, pp. 1–96. University of Texas, Austin.

Houston, Stephen D., David Stuart, and John Robertson

1998 Disharmony in Maya Hieroglyphic Writing: Linguistic Change and Continuity in Classic Society. In *Anatomía de una civilización: Aproximaciones interdisciplinarias a la cultura maya*, edited by Andrés Ciudad Ruíz, pp. 275–296. Sociedad Española de Estudios Mayas, Madrid.

Houston, Stephen D., David Stuart, and Karl A. Taube

2006 *The Memory of Bones: Body, Being, and Experience among the Classic Maya.* University of Texas Press, Austin.

Houston, Stephen D., and Karl A. Taube

2012 Carved Panel. In *Ancient Maya Art at Dumbarton Oaks*, edited by Joanne Pillsbury, Miriam Doutriaux, Reiko Ishihara-Brito, and Alexandre Tokovinine, pp. 38–47. Dumbarton Oaks Research Library and Collection, Washington, D.C.

Houston, Stephen D., Karl A. Taube, and David Stuart

1992 Image and Text on the "Jauncy Vase." In *The Maya Vase Book: A Corpus of Rollout Photographs of Maya Vases*, vol. 3, edited by Justin Kerr, pp. 498–512. Kerr Associates, New York.

Hull, Kerry M.

2002 A Comparative Analysis of Ch'orti' Verbal Art and the Poetic Discourse Structures of Maya Hieroglyphic Writing. Electronic document, www.famsi.org/reports/00048/index.html, accessed June 27, 2012.

2005 A Dictionary of Ch'orti' Maya, Guatemala. Electronic document, www.famsi.org/reports/03031/index.html, accessed July 27, 2012.

Hurst, Heather

2009 Murals and the Ancient Maya Artist: A Study of Art Production in the Guatemalan Lowlands. PhD dissertation, Yale University, New Haven.

Inomata, Takeshi

2001 The Power and Ideology of Artistic Creation: Elite Craft Specialists in Classic Maya Society. *Current Anthropology* 42(3):321–349.

Inomata, Takeshi, and Laura Stiver

1998 Floor Assemblages from Burned Structures at Aguateca, Guatemala: A Study of Classic Maya Households. *Journal of Field Archaeology* 25(4):431–452.

Isbell, William H.

2000 What We Should Be Studying: The "Imagined Community" and the "Natural Community." In *The Archaeology of Communities: A New World Perspective*, edited by Marcello A. Canuto and Jason Yaeger, pp. 243–266. Routledge, London and New York.

Jackson, Sarah

2004 Interpreting Copan's Structure 21a and Hieroglyphic Bench. *Symbols* (Spring):7–9.

Johnston, Kevin J.

1985 Maya Dynastic Territorial Expansion: Glyphic Evidence from Classic Centers of the Pasion River, Guatemala. In *Fifth Palenque Round Table, 1983*, edited by Virginia M. Fields, pp. 49–56. Pre-Columbian Art Research Institute, San Francisco.

Jones, Christopher, and Linton Satterthwaite

1982　*The Monuments and Inscriptions of Tikal: The Carved Monuments.* University Museum, University of Pennsylvania, Philadelphia.

Joyce, Rosemary A.

2000　High Culture, Mesoamerican Civilization, and the Classic Maya Tradition. In *Order, Legitimacy, and Wealth in Ancient States*, edited by Janet Richards and Mary Van Buren, pp. 64–76. Cambridge University Press, Cambridge and New York.

2001　Planificación urbana y escala social: Reflexiones sobre datos de comunidades clásicas en Honduras. In *Reconstruyendo la ciudad maya: El urbanismo en las sociedades antiguas*, edited by Andrés Ciudad Ruiz, María Josefa Iglesias Ponce de León, and María del Carmen Martínez Martínez, pp. 123–136. Sociedad Española de Estudios Mayas, Madrid.

Joyce, Rosemary A., and Julia A. Hendon

2000　Heterarchy, History, and Material Reality: "Communities" in Late Classic Honduras. In *The Archaeology of Communities: A New World Perspective*, edited by Marcello A. Canuto and Jason Yaeger, pp. 143–160. Routledge, London and New York.

Kaufman, Terrence S.

2002　Introduction to "A Preliminary Mayan Etymological Dictionary." Electronic document, www.famsi.org/reports/01051/index.html, accessed June 27, 2012.

Kaufman, Terrence S., and William M. Norman

1984　An Outline of Proto-Cholan Phonology, Morphology, and Vocabulary. In *Phoneticism in Mayan Hieroglyphic Writing*, edited by John S. Justeson and Lyle Campbell, pp. 77–166. Institute for Mesoamerican Studies, State University of New York, Albany.

Keller, Kathryn C., and G. Plácido Luciano

1997　*Diccionario chontal de Tabasco.* Instituto Lingüístico de Verano, Tucson, Ariz.

Kerr, Justin

n.d.　Maya Vase Database: An Archive of Rollout Photographs. Electronic document, www.mayavase.com, accessed June 27, 2012.

Kistler, S. Ashley

2004　The Search for Five-Flower Mountain: Re-Evaluating the Cancuen Panel. Electronic document, www.mesoweb.com/features/kistler/Cancuen.pdf, accessed June 27, 2012.

Lacadena García-Gallo, Alfonso

2000　Antipassive Constructions in the Maya Glyphic Texts. *Written Language and Literacy* 3(1):155–180.

2002　Apuntes para un estudio sobre literatura maya antigua. Manuscript in the posession of the author.

2003　The Glyphic Corpus from Ek' Balam, Yucatán, México. Electronic document, www.famsi.org/reports/01057/index.html, accessed June 27, 2012.

2007　El origen prehispánico de las profecías katúnicas mayas coloniales: Antecedentes clásicos de las profecías de 12 Ajaw y 10 Ajaw. In *Sacred Books, Sacred Languages: Two Thousand Years of Ritual and Religious Maya Literature*, edited by Rogelio Valencia Rivera and Geneviève Le Fort, pp. 201–225. A. Saurwein, Markt Schwaben.

2009　Apuntes para un estudio sobre literatura maya antigua. In *Text and Context: Yucatec Maya Literature in a Diachronic Perspective*, edited by Antije Gunsenheimer, Tsubasa Okoshi Harada, and John F. Chuchiak, pp. 31–52. Shaker, Aachen.

Lacadena García-Gallo, Alfonso, and Søren Wichmann

2004　On the Representation of the Glottal Stop in Maya Writing. In *The Linguistics of Maya Writing*, edited by Søren Wichmann, pp. 100–164. University of Utah Press, Salt Lake City.

2005　Harmony Rules and the Suffix Domain: A Study of Maya Scribal Conventions. Electronic document, email.eva.mpg.de/~wichmann/harm-rul-suf-dom7.pdf, accessed June 27, 2012.

Laporte, Juan Pedro, and Carlos Rolando Torres

1994　Los señoríos del sureste de Petén. In *I Simposio de Investigaciones Arqueológicas en Guatemala, 1987*, edited by Juan Pedro Laporte and Héctor L. Escobedo, pp. 112–134. Museo Nacional de Arqueología y Etnología, Instituto de Antropología e Historia, and Asociación Tikal, Guatemala.

Laughlin, Robert M., and John Beard Haviland

1988　*The Great Tzotzil Dictionary of Santo Domingo Zinacantán.* Smithsonian Institution Press, Washington, D.C.

Liendo Stuardo, Rodrigo

1995　El descubrimiento de un tablero con inscripciones. In *Memorias del Segundo Congreso Internacional de Mayistas*, pp. 382–387. Universidad Nacional Autónoma de México, Instituto de Investigaciones Filologicas, Centro de Estudios Mayas, Mexico City.

Linton, Ralph

1936 *The Study of Man: An Introduction*. D. Appleton-Century, New York.

Looper, Matthew G.

2003 *Lightning Warrior: Maya Art and Kingship at Quirigua*. University of Texas Press, Austin.

Lopes, Luís

2004 The Water-Band Glyph. Electronic document, www.mesoweb.com/features/lopes/Waterband.pdf, accessed June 27, 2012.

López Austin, Alfredo, and Leonardo López Luján

1999 *Mito y realidad de Zuyuá: Serpiente emplumada y las transformaciones mesoamericanas del clásico al posclásico*. Colegio de México, Fideicomiso Historia de las Américas, Fondo de Cultura Económica, Mexico City.

Luin, Camilo, and Sebastian Matteo

2010 Notas sobre algunas textos jeroglíficos en colecciones privadas. In *XXIII Simposio de Investigaciones Arqueológicas en Guatemala, 2009*, edited by Bárbara Arroyo, Adriana Linares Palma, and Lorena Paiz Aragón, pp. 1235–1250. Ministerio de Cultura y Deportes, Instituto de Antropología e Historia, and Asociación Tikal, Guatemala.

Marcus, Joyce

1973 Territorial Organization of the Lowland Classic Maya. *Science* 180:911–916.

1976 *Emblem and State in the Classic Maya Lowlands: An Epigraphic Approach to Territorial Organization*. Dumbarton Oaks, Trustees for Harvard University, Washington, D.C.

1992 *Mesoamerican Writing Systems: Propaganda, Myth, and History in Four Ancient Civilizations*. Princeton University Press, Princeton.

Martin, Simon

1996a Calakmul en el registro epigráfico. In *Proyecto arqueológico de la biosfera de Calakmul, temporada 1993–94*, edited by Ramón Carrasco Vargas. Unpublished report, Instituto Nacional de Antropología e Historia, Mexico City.

1996b Tikal's "Star War" against Naranjo. In *Eighth Palenque Round Table, 1993*, edited by Martha J. Macri and Jan McHargue, pp. 223–236. Pre-Columbian Art Research Institute, San Francisco.

1997 Painted King List: A Commentary on Codex-Style Dynastic Vases. In *Maya Vase Book: A Corpus of Rollout Photographs of Maya Vases*, vol. 5, edited by Barbara Kerr and Justin Kerr, pp. 847–867. Kerr Associates, New York.

1998 Report on Epigraphic Fieldwork at Calakmul: 1995–1998. In *Proyecto arqueológico de la biosfera de Calakmul, temporada 1995–*, edited by Ramón Carrasco Vargas. Unpublished report, Instituto Nacional de Antropología e Historia, Mexico City.

2000 Nuevos datos epigraficos sobre la guerra maya del clasico. In *La guerra entre los antiguos mayas: Memorias de la Primera Mesa Redondo de Palenque*, edited by Silvia Trejo, pp. 105–124. Instituto Nacional de Antropologia e Historia, Consejo Nacional para la Cultura y las Artes, Mexico City.

2001 Court and Realm: Architectural Signatures in the Classic Maya Southern Lowlands. In *Royal Courts of the Ancient Maya*, vol. 1, *Theory, Comparison, and Synthesis*, edited by Takeshi Inomata and Stephen D. Houston, pp. 168–194. Westview Press, Boulder, Colo.

2003 Moral-Reforma y la contienda por el oriente de Tabasco. *Arqueología mexicana* 11(61):44–47.

2004 Preguntas epigráficas acerca de los escalones de Dzibanché. In *Los cautivos de Dzibanché*, edited by Enrique Nalda, pp. 105–115. Instituto Nacional de Antropología e Historia, Mexico City.

2005 Of Snakes and Bats: Shifting Identities at Calakmul. *The PARI Journal* 6(2):5–15.

Martin, Simon, and Nikolai Grube

1995 Maya Superstates: How a Few Powerful Kingdoms Vied for Control of the Maya Lowlands during the Classic Period (AD 300–900). *Archaeology* 48(6):41–46.

2000 *Chronicle of the Maya Kings and Queens: Deciphering the Dynasties of the Ancient Maya*. Thames and Hudson, London.

2008 *Chronicle of the Maya Kings and Queens: Deciphering the Dynasties of the Ancient Maya*. 2nd ed. Thames and Hudson, London.

Mathews, Peter

1979 The Glyphs on the Ear Ornaments from Tomb A-1/1. In *Excavations at Altun Ha, 1964–1970*, vol. 1, edited by David M. Pendergast, pp. 79–80. Royal Ontario Museum, Toronto.

1988 The Sculpture of Yaxchilán. PhD dissertation, Department of Anthropology, Yale University, New Haven.

1991 Classic Maya Emblem Glyphs. In *Classic Maya Political History: Hieroglyphic and Archaeological Evidence*, edited by T. Patrick Culbert, pp. 19–29. Cambridge University Press, Cambridge and New York.

1998 Una lectura de un nuevo monumento de El Cayo, Chiapas, y sus implicaciones politicas. In *Modelos de entidades politicas mayas: Primer seminario de las Mesas Redondas de Palenque*, edited by Silvia Trejo, pp. 113–139. CONACULTA-INAH, Mexico City.

2001 Dates of Tonina and a Dark Horse in Its History. *The PARI Journal* 2(1):1–6.

Mathews, Peter, and John S. Justeson

1984 Patterns of Sign Substitution in Mayan Hieroglyphic Writing: The Affix Cluster. In *Phoneticism in Mayan Hieroglyphic Writing*, edited by John S. Justeson and Lyle Campbell, pp. 185–231. Institute for Mesoamerican Studies, State University of New York at Albany, Albany.

Maudslay, Alfred Percival

1889– *Biologia Centrali-Americana, or, Contributions to*
1902 *the Knowledge of the Fauna and Flora of Mexico and Central America. Archaeology.* R. H. Porter and Dulau, London.

Mayer, Karl Herbert

1989 *Maya Monuments: Sculptures of Unknown Provenance*, Supplement 2. Verlag von Flemming, Berlin.

1991 *Maya Monuments: Sculptures of Unknown Provenance*, Supplement 3. Verlag Von Flemming, Berlin.

1995 *Maya Monuments: Sculptures of Unknown Provenance*, Supplement 4. Academic Publishers, Graz.

Means, Philip Ainsworth

1917 *History of the Spanish Conquest of Yucatan and of the Itzas.* Papers of the Peabody Museum of American Archaeology and Ethnology 7. The Museum, Cambridge, Mass.

Meltzer, Bernard N., John W. Petras, and Larry T. Reynolds

1975 *Symbolic Interactionism: Genesis, Varieties, and Criticism.* Routledge and K. Paul, London and Boston.

Merton, Robert King

1957 *Social Theory and Social Structure.* Free Press, Glencoe, Ill.

Merwin, Raymond Edwin, and George Clapp Vaillant

1932 *The Ruins of Holmul, Guatemala.* Memoirs of the Peabody Museum of American Archaeology and Ethnology 3, no. 2. Peabody Museum of American Archaeology and Ethnology, Harvard University, Cambridge, Mass.

Miller, Mary Ellen

1986 *The Murals of Bonampak.* Princeton University Press, Princeton.

Miller, Mary Ellen, and Simon Martin

2004 *Courtly Art of the Ancient Maya.* Fine Arts Museums of San Francisco, San Francisco, and Thames and Hudson, New York.

Miram, Helga-Maria

1988 *Transkriptionen der Chilam Balames/ Transcriptions of the Chilam Balames/ Transcripciones de los Chilam Balames.* 2 vols. Toro-Verlag, Hamburg.

Miram, Helga-Maria, and Wolfgang Miram

1988 *Konkordanz der Chilam Balames/Concordance of the Chilam Balames.* Toro-Verlag, Hamburg.

Moholy-Nagy, Hattula, and William R. Coe

2008 *The Artifacts of Tikal: Ornamental and Ceremonial Artifacts and Unworked Material.* Tikal Report 27, pt. A. University of Pennsylvania Museum of Archaeology and Anthropology, Philadelphia.

Morales, Alfonso

2002 Recording New Inscriptions of Palenque. Electronic document, www.famsi.org/ reports/94025/94025Morales01.pdf, accessed June 27, 2012.

Morales, Paulino I.

1993 Reconocimiento en el Chal, Dolores. In *Reporte 7, Atlas arqueológico de Guatemala*, edited by Juan Pedro Laporte, pp. 14–35. Instituto de Antropología e Historia, Guatemala.

Morán, Francisco

1695 *Arte y vocabulario en la lengua cholti.* Mss. 497.4.M79. American Philosophical Society, Philadelphia.

Nalda, Enrique (editor)

2004 *Los cautivos de Dzibanché.* Instituto Nacional de Antropología e Historia, Mexico City.

O'Neil, Megan E., and Alexandre Tokovinine

2012 Carved Panel. In *Ancient Maya Art at Dumbarton Oaks*, edited by Joanne Pillsbury, Miriam Doutriaux, Reiko Ishihara-Brito, and Alexandre Tokovinine, pp. 59–67. Dumbarton Oaks Research Library and Collection, Washington, D.C.

Palka, Joel W.

1996 Sociopolitical Implications of a New Emblem Glyph and Place Name in Classic

Maya Inscriptions. *Latin American Antiquity* 7(3):211–227.

Patterson, Leonardo (editor)
1992 *The Magic of Middle American Culture before 1492.* n.p.

Pendergast, David M.
1982 *Excavations at Altun Ha, Belize, 1964–1970,* vol. 2. Royal Ontario Museum, Toronto.

Perales, Hugo, Bruce Benz, and Stephen Brush
2005 Maize Diversity and Ethnolinguistic Diversity in Chiapas, Mexico. *Proceedings of the National Academy of Science* 102(3):949–954.

Pérez Martínez, Vitalino, and Robin Ormes Quizar
1996 *Diccionario del idioma ch'orti'.* Proyecto Lingüístico Francisco Marroquín, Antigua, Guatemala.

Pincemín, Sophia
1994 *Entierro en el palacio: La tumba de la Estructura III, Calakmul, Campeche.* Universidad Autónoma de Campeche, Campeche.

Prager, Christian M.
2004 A Classic Maya Ceramic Vessel from the Calakmul Region in the Museum Zu Allerheiligen, Schaffhausen, Switzerland. *Human Mosaic* 35(1):31–40.

Prager, Christian M., Elisabeth Wagner, Sebastian Matteo, and Guido Krempel
2010 A Reading for the Xultun Toponymic Title as B'aax (Tuun) Witz 'Ajaw "Lord of the B'aax-(Stone) Hill." *Mexicon* 32(4):74–77.

Pred, Allen
1984 Place as Historically Contingent Process: Structuration and the Time-Geography of Becoming Places. *Annals of the Association of American Geographers* 74(2):279–297.

Quezada, Sergio, and Tsubasa Okoshi Harada
2001 *Papeles de los Xiu de Yaxá, Yucatán.* Universidad Nacional Autónoma de México, Plaza y Valdés, Mexico City.

Rapoport, Amos
2002 Spatial Organization and the Built Environment. In *Companion Encyclopedia of Anthropology,* edited by Tim Ingold, pp. 460–502. Routledge, New York and London.

Reents-Budet, Dorie
1991 The Holmul Dancer Theme in Maya Art. In *Sixth Palenque Round Table, 1986,* edited by Virginia M. Fields, pp. 217–222. University of Oklahoma Press, Norman.
1994 *Painting the Maya Universe: Royal Ceramics of the Classic Period.* Duke University Press, Durham, N.C.

Reese-Taylor, Kathryn, and Rex Koontz
2001 The Cultural Poetics of Power and Space in Ancient Mesoamerica. In *Landscape and Power in Ancient Mesoamerica,* edited by Rex Koontz, Kathryn Reese-Taylor, and Annabeth Headrick, pp. 1–27. Westview Press, Boulder, Colo.

Rice, Prudence M.
2004 *Maya Political Science: Time, Astronomy, and the Cosmos.* University of Texas Press, Austin.

Robelo, Cecilio Agustín
1902 *Toponimia maya-hispano-nahoa.* Imprenta de J. D. Rojas, Cuernavaca, Mexico.

Robertson, John, Danny Law, and Robbie Haertel
2010 *Colonial Ch'olti': The Seventeenth-Century Morán Manuscript.* University of Oklahoma Press, Norman.

Robertson, Merle Greene
1983 *The Sculpture of Palenque,* vol. 1, *Temple of the Inscriptions.* Princeton University Press, Princeton.
1985 *The Sculpture of Palenque,* vol. 3, *The Late Buildings of the Palace.* Princeton University Press, Princeton.
1991 *The Sculpture of Palenque,* vol. 4, *The Cross Group, the North Group, the Olvidado, and Other Pieces.* Princeton University Press, Princeton.

Robichaux, Hubert R., and Brett A. Houk
2005 A Hieroglyphic Plate Fragment from Dos Hombres, Belize: Epigraphic and Archaeological Evidence Relating to Political Organization in the Three Rivers Region of Northwestern Belize and Northeastern Guatemala. *Mono y Conejo* 3:4–12.

Robicsek, Francis, and Donald M. Hales
1981 *The Maya Book of the Dead: The Ceramic Codex; The Corpus of Codex Style Ceramics of the Late Classic Period.* University of Virginia Art Museum, Charlottesville, and University of Oklahoma Press, Norman.

Roys, Ralph L.
1954 *The Maya Katun Prophecies of the Books of Chilam Balam, Series I.* Carnegie Institution of Washington, Washington, D.C.

1973 *The Book of Chilam Balam of Chumayel*. 2nd ed. University of Oklahoma Press, Norman.

Sachse, Frauke, and Allen J. Christenson
2005 Tulan and the Other Side of the Sea: Unraveling a Metaphorical Concept from Colonial Guatemalan Highland Sources. Electronic document, www.mesoweb.com/articles/tulan/Tulan.pdf, accessed June 27, 2012.

Safronov, Alexandr
2006 Gosudarstva Maya Zapadnogo Regiona V Klassicheskiy Period (Maya States of Western Region in the Classic Period). PhD dissertation, Department of Ancient History, Faculty of History, Moscow State University, Moscow.

Saturno, William A., Karl A. Taube, David Stuart, and Heather Hurst
2005 *The Murals of San Bartolo, El Petén, Guatemala*, pt. 1, *The North Wall*. Center for Ancient American Studies, Barnardsville, N.C.

Sauer, Carl Ortwin
1963 *Land and Life: A Selection from the Writings of Carl Ortwin Sauer*. Edited by John Leighly. University of California Press, Berkeley.

Schele, Linda
1987 *The Reviewing Stand of Temple 11*. Copan Mosaics Project, Copan, Honduras.
1988 Xibalba Shuffle: A Dance after Death. In *Maya Iconography*, edited by Elizabeth P. Benson and Gillett G. Griffin, pp. 294–317. Princeton University Press, Princeton.
1989 The Early Classic Dynastic History of Copan: An Interim Report. Copan Notes 70. Copan Mosaics Project, Copan, Honduras.
1992 Founders of Lineages at Copán and Other Maya Sites. *Ancient Mesoamerica* 3:135–144.
1998 Iconography of Maya Architectural Facades during the Late Classic Period. In *Function and Meaning in Classic Maya Architecture*, edited by Stephen D. Houston, pp. 479–517. Dumbarton Oaks Research Library and Collection, Washington, D.C.

Schele, Linda, and Nikolai Grube
1990 A Preliminary Inventory of Place Names in the Copan Inscriptions. Copan Notes 93. Copan Mosaics Project, Copan, Honduras.

Schele, Linda, and Mathew Looper
1996 Inscriptions of Quirigua and Copan. In *Notebook for the XXth Maya Hieroglyphic Forum at Texas*, edited by Linda Schele and Mathew Looper, pp. 90–226. University of Texas, Austin.

Schele, Linda, and Peter Mathews
1998 *The Code of Kings: The Language of Seven Sacred Maya Temples and Tombs*. Scribner, New York.

Schele, Linda, and Mary Ellen Miller
1986 *The Blood of Kings: Dynasty and Ritual in Maya Art*. Kimbell Art Museum, Fort Worth.

Schele, Linda, David Stuart, and Nikolai Grube
1984 A Commentary on the Restoration and Reading of the Glyphic Panels from Temple 11. Copan Notes 64. Copan Mosaics Project, Copan, Honduras.

Schmidt, Peter, Mercedes de la Garza, and Enrique Nalda
1998 *Maya*. Bompiani, Milan.

Shapiro, Meyer
1953 Style. In *Anthropology Today: An Encyclopedic Inventory*, edited by A. L. Kroeber, pp. 287–312. University of Chicago Press, Chicago.

Sharer, Robert J.
1990 *Quirigua: A Classic Maya Center and Its Sculptures*. Carolina Academic Press, Durham, N.C.

Sheseña, Alejandro
2007 Los textos jeroglíficos mayas de la cueva de Jolja, Chiapas. Electronic document, www.mesoweb.com/es/articulos/jolja/Jolja.pdf, accessed June 27, 2012.

Skidmore, Joel
2002 New Piece or Precolumbian New Box. Electronic document, www.mesoweb.com/reports/box/piece.html, accessed June 27, 2012.
2007 An Updated Listing of Early Naranjo Rulers. *The PARI Journal* 7(4):23–24.

Smailus, Ortwin
1975 *El maya-chontal de Acalán: Análisis lingüístico de un documento de los años 1610–12*. Universidad Nacional Autónoma de México, Coordinación de Humanidades, Mexico City.

Smith, Adam T.
2003 *The Political Landscape: Constellations of Authority in Early Complex Polities*. University of California Press, Berkeley.

Šprajc, Ivan, and Nikolai Grube
2003 Archaeological Reconnaissance in Southeastern Campeche, Mexico: 2002 Field Season Report. Electronic document, www.famsi.org/reports/01014/01014Sprajc01.pdf, accessed October 5, 2012.

Stadelman, Raymond

1940   *Maize Cultivation in Northwestern Guatemala.* Carnegie Institute of Washington, Washington, D.C.

Stone, Andrea

1995   *Images from the Underworld: Naj Tunich and the Tradition of Maya Cave Painting.* University of Texas Press, Austin.

Stone, Andrea, and Marc Zender

2011   *Reading Maya Art: A Hieroglyphic Guide to Ancient Maya Painting and Sculpture.* Thames and Hudson, New York.

Stuart, David

1985   *The Yaxha Emblem Glyph as Yax-Ha.* Research Reports on Ancient Maya Writing 1–2. Center for Maya Research, Washington, D.C.

1987   Paintings of Tomb 12, Río Azul. In *The Río Azul Archaeological Project*, edited by Richard E. W. Adams, pp. 161–167. Center for Archaeological Research, San Antonio.

1997   The Hills Are Alive: Sacred Mountains in the Maya Cosmos. *Symbols* (Spring):13–17.

1998   "The Fire Enters This House": Architecture and Ritual in Classic Maya Texts. In *Function and Meaning in Classic Maya Architecture*, edited by Stephen D. Houston, pp. 373–425. Dumbarton Oaks Research Library and Collection, Washington, D.C.

2000   The Arrival of Strangers: Teotihuacan and Tollan in Classic Maya History. In *Mesoamerica's Classic Heritage: Teotihuacan to the Aztecs*, edited by Davíd S. Carrasco, Lindsay Jones, and Scott Sessions, pp. 465–513. University Press of Colorado, Boulder.

2002   Glyphs for "Right" and "Left"? Electronic document, www.mesoweb.com/stuart/notes/RightLeft.pdf, accessed June 27, 2012.

2003   On the Paired Variants of Tz'ak. Electronic document, www.mesoweb.com/stuart/notes/tzak.pdf, accessed June 27, 2012.

2004a   The Beginnings of the Copan Dynasty: A Review of the Hieroglyphic and Historical Evidence. In *Understanding Early Classic Copan*, edited by Ellen E. Bell, Marcello A. Canuto, and Robert J. Sharer, pp. 215–248. University of Pennsylvania Museum of Archaeology and Anthropology, Philadelphia.

2004b   The Paw Stone: The Place Name of Piedras Negras, Guatemala. *The PARI Journal* 4(3):1–6.

2004c   A Possible Logogram for Tz'ap. Electronic document, www.mesoweb.com/stuart/notes/tzap.pdf, accessed October 5, 2012.

2005a   A Foreign Past: The Writing and Representation of History on a Royal Ancestral Shrine at Copan. In *Copan: The History of an Ancient Maya Kingdom*, edited by E. Wyllys Andrews and William L. Fash, pp. 373–394. School of American Research Press, Santa Fe, N.Mex.

2005b   *The Inscriptions from Temple XIX at Palenque: A Commentary.* Pre-Columbian Art Research Institute, San Francisco.

2005c   *Sourcebook for the 29th Maya Hieroglyphic Forum, March 11–16, 2005.* Department of Art and Art History, University of Texas, Austin.

2006a   Jade and Chocolate: Bundles of Wealth in Classic Maya Economics and Ritual. In *Sacred Bundles: Ritual Acts of Wrapping and Binding in Mesoamerica*, edited by Julia Guernsey and F. Kent Reilly, pp. 127–144. Ancient America Special Publication 1. Boundary End Archaeology Research Center, Barnardsville, N.C.

2006b   The Palenque Mythology: Inscriptions and Interpretations of the Cross Group. In *Sourcebook for the 30th Maya Meeting, March 14–19, 2006.* University of Texas, Austin.

2007a   The Origin of Copan's Founder. Electronic document, decipherment.wordpress.com/2007/06/25/the-origin-of-copans-founder, accessed June 27, 2012.

2007b   Reading the Water Serpent as Witz'. Electronic document, decipherment.wordpress.com/2007/04/13/reading-the-water-serpent, accessed June 27, 2012.

2007c   *Sourcebook for the XXXI Maya Meetings, March 9–14, 2007; Inscriptions of the River Cities: Yaxchilan, Pomona, Piedras Negras.* University of Texas, Austin.

2008   Bonampak's Place Name. Electronic document, decipherment.wordpress.com/2008/03/16/bonampaks-place-name, accessed June 27, 2012.

2010   Notes on an Inscription Fragment from the Southern Peten. Electronic document, decipherment.wordpress.com/2010/10/03/notes-on-an-inscription-fragment-from-the-southern-peten, accessed June 27, 2012.

2011a   *The Order of Days: The Maya World and the Truth about 2012.* Harmony, New York.

2011b   Some Working Notes on the Text of Tikal Stela 31. Electronic document, www.mesoweb.com/stuart/notes/Tikal.pdf, accessed June 27, 2012.

2012 Notes on a New Text from La Corona. Electronic document, decipherment.wordpress.com/2012/06/30/notes-on-a-new-text-from-la-corona/, accessed June 27, 2012.

n.d. Cave References in Maya Inscriptions. Unpublished manuscript in possession of the author.

Stuart, David, and Ian Graham

2003 *Corpus of Maya Hieroglyphic Inscriptions,* vol. 9, pt. 1, *Piedras Negras.* Peabody Museum of Archaeology and Ethnology, Harvard University, Cambridge, Mass.

Stuart, David, and Stephen D. Houston

1994 *Classic Maya Place Names.* Dumbarton Oaks Research Library and Collection, Washington, D.C.

Stuart, David, Stephen D. Houston, and John Robertson

1999 Recovering the Past: Classic Maya Language and Classic Maya Gods. In *Notebook for the XXIIIrd Maya Hieroglyphic Forum at Texas,* pt. 2, pp. 1–96. University of Texas Press, Austin.

Stuart, David, and Simon Martin

2009 *Snake Kingdom: History and Politics at Calakmul and Related Royal Courts; Sourcebook for the 2009 Maya Meetings and Symposium.* University of Texas, Austin.

Taube, Karl A.

1985 Classic Maya Maize God: A Reappraisal. In *Fifth Palenque Round Table, 1983,* edited by Virginia M. Fields, pp. 171–181. Pre-Columbian Art Research Institute, San Francisco.

1988 Prehispanic Maya Katun Wheel. *Journal of Anthropological Research* 44(2):183–203.

1998 The Jade Hearth: Centrality, Rulership, and the Classic Maya Temple. In *Function and Meaning in Classic Maya Architecture,* edited by Stephen D. Houston, pp. 427–478. Dumbarton Oaks Research Library and Collection, Washington, D.C.

2000 The Turquoise Hearth: Fire, Self Sacrifice, and the Central Mexican Cult of War. In *Mesoamerica's Classic Heritage: Teotihuacan to the Aztecs,* edited by Davíd Carrasco, Lindsay Jones, and Scott Sessions, pp. 269–340. University Press of Colorado, Boulder.

2003 Ancient and Contemporary Maya Conceptions About Field and Forest. In *The Lowland Maya Area: Three Millennia at the Human-Wildland Interface,* edited by Arturo Gómez-Pompa,

Michael F. Allen, Scott L. Fedick, and Juan J. Jiménez-Osorino, pp. 461–492. Haworth Press Press, Binghamton, N.Y.

2004a Flower Mountain: Concepts of Life, Beauty, and Paradise among the Classic Maya. *Res: Anthropology and Aesthetics* 45:69–98.

2004b Structure 10L-16 and Its Early Classic Antecedants: Fire and the Evocation and Resurrection of K'inich Yax K'uk' Mo'. In *Understanding Early Classic Copan,* edited by Ellen E. Bell, Marcello A. Canuto, and Robert J. Sharer, pp. 265–296. University of Pennsylvania Museum of Archaeology and Anthropology, Philadelphia.

Teufel, Stefanie

2000 Interpretación de artefactos del Entierro 49. In *El sitio maya de Topoxté: Investigaciones en una isla del Lago Yaxhá, Petén, Guatemala,* edited by Wolfgang W. Wurster, pp. 149–158. P. von Zabern, Mainz.

Thompson, J. Eric S.

1962 *A Catalog of Maya Hieroglyphs.* University of Oklahoma Press, Norman.

Tilley, Christopher Y.

1994 *A Phenomenology of Landscape: Places, Paths, and Monuments.* Berg, Providence, R.I.

Tokovinine, Alexandre

2006 Reporte epigrafico de la temporada de 2005. In *Investigaciones arqueológicas en la region de Holmul, Petén, Guatemala: Informe preliminar de la Temporada 2005,* edited by Francisco Estrada Belli. Electronic document, www.vanderbilt.edu/estrada-belli/holmul/reports/, accessed June 27, 2012.

2007a Classic Maya Place Name Database Project. Electronic document, www.famsi.org/reports/06054/06054Tokovinine01.pdf, accessed June 27, 2012.

2007b Of Snake Kings and Cannibals: A Fresh Look at the Naranjo Hieroglyphic Stairway. *The PARI Journal* 7(4):15–22.

2008 The Power of Place: Political Landscape and Identity in Classic Maya Inscriptions, Imagery, and Architecture. PhD dissertation, Department of Anthropology, Harvard University, Cambridge, Mass.

2011 People from a Place: Re-Interpreting Classic Maya Emblem Glyphs. In *Ecology, Power, and Religion in Maya Landscapes,* edited by Christian Isendahl and Bodil Liljefors-Persson, pp. 81–96. A. Saurwein, Möckmuhl.

Tokovinine, Alexandre, and Vilma Fialko

2007 Stela 45 of Naranjo and the Early Classic Lords of Sa'aal. *The PARI Journal* 7(4):1–14.

Tokovinine, Alexandre, and Marc Zender

2012 Lords of Windy Water: The Royal Court of Motul de San José in Classic Maya Inscriptions. In *Politics, History, and Economy at the Classic Maya Center of Motul de San José, Guatemala*, edited by Antonia Foias and Kitty Emery, pp. 30–66. University Press of Florida, Gainesville.

Tozzer, Alfred M.

1941 *Landa's* Relación de las cosas de Yucatán*: A Translation*. Peabody Museum of Archaeology and Ethnology, Harvard University, Cambridge, Mass.

Tunesi, Raphael

2007 A New Monument Mentioning Wamaaw K'awiil of Calakmul. *The PARI Journal* 8(2):13–19.

Velásquez García, Erik

2004 Los escalones jeroglíficos de Dzibanché. In *Los cautivos de Dzibanché*, edited by Enrique Nalda, pp. 78–103. Instituto Nacional de Antropología y Historia, Mexico City.

2005 The Captives of Dzibanche. *The PARI Journal* 6(2):1–4.

Vogt, Evon Z.

1964 Some Aspects of Zinacantan Settlement Patterns and Ceremonial Organization. In *Actas y memorias del XXXV Congreso Internacional de Americanistas, México, [19–25 agosto] 1962*, vol. 1, pp. 307–319. Instituto Nacional de Antropología e Historia, Mexico City.

1965 Structural and Conceptual Replication in Zinacantan Culture. *American Anthropologist* 67(2):342–353.

1969 *Zinacantan: A Maya Community in the Highlands of Chiapas*. Harvard University Press, Cambridge, Mass.

1981 Some Aspects of the Sacred Geography of Highland Chiapas. In *Mesoamerican Sites and World-Views*, edited by Elizabeth P. Benson, pp. 119–142. Dumbarton Oaks Research Library and Collection, Washington, D.C.

Vogt, Evon Z., and David Stuart

2005 Some Notes on Ritual Caves among the Ancient and Modern Maya. In *In the Maw of the Earth Monster: Mesoamerican Ritual Cave Use*,

edited by James E. Brady and Keith M. Prufer, pp. 155–185. University of Texas Press, Austin.

Von Euw, Eric

1978 *Corpus of Maya Hieroglyphic Inscriptions*, vol. 5, pt. 1, *Xultun*. Peabody Museum of Archaeology and Ethnology, Harvard University, Cambridge, Mass.

Von Euw, Eric, and Ian Graham

1984 *Corpus of Maya Hieroglyphic Inscriptions*, vol. 5, pt. 2, *Xultun, La Honradez, Uaxactún*. Peabody Museum of Archaeology and Ethnology, Harvard University, Cambridge, Mass.

Wagner, Elisabeth

2006 Ranked Spaces, Ranked Identities: Local Hierarchies, Community Boundaries, and an Emic Notion of the Maya Cultural Sphere at Late Classic Copan. In *Maya Ethnicity: The Construction of Ethnic Identity from Preclassic to Modern Times*, edited by Frauke Sachse, pp. 143–164. A. Saurwein, Markt Schwaben.

Wagner, Elisabeth, and Christian Prager

2006 Early Ruler List on CPN 3033. Manuscript in possession of the author.

Wanyerka, Phillip J.

2004 The Southern Belize Epigraphic Project: The Hieroglyphic Inscriptions of Southern Belize. Electronic document, www.famsi.org/reports/00077/, accessed June 27, 2012.

Warkentin, Viola, and Ruby Scott

1978 *Gramática chol*. Instituto Lingüístico de Verano, Mexico City.

Watanabe, John M.

1984 "We Who Are Here": The Cultural Conventions of Ethnic Identity in a Guatemalan Indian Village, 1937–1980. PhD dissertation, Department of Anthropology, Harvard University, Cambridge, Mass.

1990 From Saints to Shibboleths: Image, Structure, and Identity in Maya Religious Syncretism. *American Ethnologist* 17(1):131–150.

1995 Unimagining Maya: Anthropologists, Others, and the Inescapable Hubris of Authorship. *Bulletin of Latin American Research* 14(1):25–45.

Wisdom, Charles

1950 *Materials on the Chorti Language*. Microfilm Collection of Manuscripts of Cultural Anthropology 28. University of Chicago Library, Chicago.

Yaeger, Jason, and Marcello A. Canuto

2000   Introducing an Archaeology to Communities. In *The Archaeology of Communities: A New World Perspective*, edited by Marcello A. Canuto and Jason Yaeger, pp. 1–15. Routledge, London and New York.

Zender, Marc

2001   The Conquest of Comalcalco: Warfare and Political Expansion in the Northwestern Periphery of the Maya Area. Paper presented at the 19th Annual Maya Weekend, University of Pennsylvania Museum, Philadelphia.

2004   A Study of Classic Maya Priesthood. PhD dissertation, Department of Anthropology, University of Calgary, Calgary.

2005   The Raccoon Glyph in Classic Maya Writing. *The PARI Journal* 5(4):6–16.

INDEX

D

dancing maize gods and group identities, *59, 115–22, 116–21*

dancing ritual in Naranjo Stela 30 inscription, 104–6, *105*

database of Classic Maya place names, *140*, 140–41, *141*

Davletshin, Albert, 80, 81

deep-time places, place names in emblem glyphs pointing to, 71–79, *73–76, 78, 79*

deities. *See* sacred or ritual landscapes; *specific deities*

demons (*wahy*), 18, 69, 96, 109

Denver Museum panel, 34, *35*

distance, spatial scale, and hierarchy in place names, 13–18, *14, 15, 17*

division (*tzuk*), 91, 92, 98–99

Dos Caobas: Stela 1 at, *73, 75, 93*

Dos Pilas: Calakmul, paired place names for, 17; El Duende group, 14; emblem glyphs, 66–67, *67, 77*, 81–82; Hieroglyphic Stairway 2 at, 16, 102, *103*; Hieroglyphic Stairway 4 at, 102, *103*; *K'ihn Ha' Nal* or *K'in Nal Ha'* and T369 *Ha'al* place names, 14–16, *15*; Main Plaza, 14, 16; maize gods, 116–18, *118*; *Mutal* lords, 67, 77, 81–82; Panel 19 at, *15, 16*, 113, *114*; Stela 1 at, 14, *15*; Stela 2 at, 14, *15*; Stela 8 at, 14, *15, 16*, 20, 113, *114*; Stela 9 at, 102; Stela 11 at, 14, *15, 16*; Stela 14 at, 14, *15, 16*, 48; Stela 15 at, 14, *15, 16*, 22, 48–49, *49*, 66; Stela 17 at, *118*; Water Lily Jaguar backrack, 116

Dumbarton Oaks carved panels: PC.B.145, 82, 84; PC.B.528, 29, *30*, 131nn11–12

Dumbarton Oaks, Pre-Columbian Photographs and Fieldwork Archives, LC.CB2.412, 117

dynastic origins: competing dynasties and diasporas, 81–85, *83*; foundation and settlement events, 79–81, *80*; place names in emblem glyphs pointing to, 71–79, *73–76, 78, 79*, 125; variations over time and space in expressing, 126–27

Dzibanche: **chi**-T316 and, 120; *ehtej/e'tej* at, 131n13; Hieroglyphic Stairway 1 at, 32, *33*; *Kanu'l* kings and, 33, 71, 72, 79, 96, 106

E

earflares, Tomb A-1/1, Altun Ha, 106, *107*

earth/land. *See kab* (earth/land)

Edzna lords, 97, 106, 121, 135n49

ehtej/e'tej, 131n13

Ek Balam: inscriptions, 94; painted capstones, 134n46

El Cayo: Altar 4 at, 8, *9, 20*; Panel 1 at, 26, *31*

El Cedro or Nuevo Jalisco: knot.hair toponyms on panels from, 84

El Chal: Stela 4 at, 49

El Peru: emblem glyphs, 67–69, *68*; Stela 33 at, 67, *68. See also Waka'*

El Zapote: Stela 5 at, *121*

El Zotz: Stela 4 at, 69; wooden lintel, 134n43. *See also Pa' Chan* lords

emblem glyphs, 57–85; archaeological site areas and place names in, 61–66, *65*; backracks of dancing maize gods and, 116; cardinal directions and quadripartite geopolitical division, 87–89, *88*; competing dynasties and diasporas, 81–85, *83*; dynastic origins/deep-time places, place names pointing to, 71–79, *73–76, 78, 79*, 125; identity and context, importance of considering, 85–86; interpretations of place names in, 57; larger-than-site spatial entities, place names for, 66–69, *67, 68*; multiple glyphs or place name references, 69–71, *70*; as place-related titles, 58; polity name theory, 57, 61–71, 90; sites with at least seven references, place names in emblem glyphs at, 61, *62–63*

epigraphic study of place and identity. *See* place and identity in Classic Maya narratives

Erikson, Erik H., 3

F

Feathered Serpent, 54

Five (*Jo'*) T544.501-**ni** groups, 104, *105*, 106, 110–11, *112*, 122

Flores: Stela 1 at, 106, *107. See also Ik'a'* and *Ik'a'* lords

foreigners/others (*tz'ul*), concept of, 97, *98*

foundation and settlement events, 79–81, *80*

four cardinal directions. *See* cardinal directions

Four (*Chan*) T544.501-**ni** titles, 111, 122

frames as landscape conventions, 52–53

G

geopolitical order in Classic Maya society. *See* group identities

God L, 76

gods. *See* sacred or ritual landscapes; *specific deities*

Gossen, Gary, 6

great capitals model, 89–90

group identities, 87–123, 125–26; *Bolon Tzuk* (Nine Divisions), 100, 109–10, *110*, 122; communities and community identity, 3–4, 123; *Huk Tzuk* (Seven Divisions), 98–102, *100, 101*, 104–6, *105*, 108–9, 113, 115, 122, 123, 125, 135n51; *Huxlajuun Tzuk* (Thirteen Divisions), 98–99, *100*, 102–8, *103, 105*, 109, 122, 123, 125, 126; maize gods and, *59*, 115–22, *116–21*, 126; quadripartite geopolitical schemes, 87–89, *88*, 91–97, *93, 95, 96, 98*, 115 (*See also* cardinal directions); research historiography, 87–91, *88*; T544.501-**ni** groups, 104, *105*, 106, 110–11, *112*, 122, 123; *tz'ul* (foreigners/others), concept of, 97, *98*; variations over time and space in expressing, 126–27; *Wak Tzuk* (Six Divisions), 100, 109, *110*, 122; *Waxak Winik* (Twenty-Eight Lords), 16, 100, 113–15, *114*, 122, 123, 125

Grube, Nikolai, 57, 90

Guenter, Stanley, 69

Nik Ahk Mo' (*Pe' Tuun* lord), 34

Nim Li Punit: Stela 2 at, 109, *110*; Stela 15 at, 44, *45*; Stela 21 at, 113, *114*; T679 lords, 94, 106

Nine Divisions (*Bolon Tzuk*), *100*, 109–10, *110*, 122

"Nine Mountains," 92

Nuevo Jalisco or El Cedro: knot.hair toponyms on panels from, 84

Nuun Bahlam (lord of *Wak* T510 *Nal*), 102

Nuun Ujol Chahk (Tikal ruler), 102–4

O

ochi ch'e'n events, 33, 34, 38

ohl (nonmaterial heart), 39

Ojo de Agua: Stela 1 at, 84

origin, titles of, 58

origins of dynasties. *See* dynastic origins

others/foreigners (*tz'ul*), concept of, 97, *98*

otoot/naah (houses/buildings), 11, *11–12, 12*, 29–31, *30, 31*, 125

Oxkutzcab, 10

Oxpemul: Stelae 7, 12, and 14 at, 16

P

Pa' Chan, 11, *12*, 28, 33. *See also* Yaxchilan

Pa' Chan lords, 46, 69–70, 73, 84. *See also* El Zotz; Yaxchilan

Pakbuul lords, *75*, 76. *See also* Pomona

Palenque: cave (*ch'e'n*) and *naah/otoot* (buildings/houses) at, 29; Dumbarton Oaks carved panel (PC.B.528), 29, *30*, 131nn11–12; East Court, Palace, 44, *45*; emblem glyphs, 70, *70–71*, 82; four cardinal directions, association with, 87, 89; Hieroglyphic Stairway 1 at, 7, *8*, 59; *Lakam Ha'* and *Yehmal K'uk'* (*Lakam*) *Witz* place names, 7, 13, *14*, 70, 71; maize gods, 121; *Matwiil* and *Matwiil* lords, 70, 72–73, 130–31n10; Palace Tablet, 118; place names as direct and indirect references at, 7, *8*; royal family in quadripartite schemes, 97; Tablet of the Slaves, 10, *12*; Temple 14 at, 33, *34*, *50*; Temple 16 at, 9, 10; Temple 17 at, 33, 61, 70, 79, *80, 81*; Temple 18 at, 13, *14*; Temple XVII, 77; Temple XIX, 51; Temple of the Cross, 39, *40*, 51–52, 70; temples of the Cross Group, 25, 29; Temple of the Foliated Cross, 7, *8*, 20, 29, *30*, *50*, 75, 130n10; Temple of the Inscriptions, 31, 32, 39, 47, 70, 92–93, *93*; Temple of the Inscriptions Sarcophagus, 48; Temple of the Sun, 13, *14*, 29, *30*, *49*, 130–31n10; War Panel, *120*; "Water dog" place name at, 64; West Court, Palace, 60, *61*; *Yax Han* mountain at, 52

people and places, 57–86, 125; foundation and settlement events, 79–81, *80*; identity and context, importance of considering, 85–86; royal titles, place names in, 13;

titles incorporating place names, *58–60*, 58–61. *See also* emblem glyphs; group identities

Petexbatun *Mutal* rulers, 81–82

Pe' Tuun and *Pe' Tuun* lords, 10, 34, 132n18, 135n47. *See also* La Mar

pictorial conventions in landscapes, 48–55, *49–51*, *53*, *54*

Piedras Negras: Altar 1 at, 74–75, *75*; emblem glyph of *Yokib* lords, 74, *74–76, 75*; Panel 2 at, 84; Panel 4 at, *80*, 81; Panel 7 at, 46; Panel 12 at, 75; Stela 3 at, 44, *45*; Stela 5 at, 52; Stela 6 at, 53; Stela 11 at, 53; Stela 12 at, 76; Stela 25 at, 53; Stela 26 at, 11, *12*; Stela 40 at, 10, *12*; Structure O-13 at, 75; Throne 1 at, 79, *80, 81*

Pipa' lords, *75*, 76. *See also* Pomona

place and identity in Classic Maya narratives, 1–6, 125–27; cartographic and epigraphic studies, 5–6; database of Classic Maya place names, *140*, 140–41, *141*; definitions pertinent to, 1–4; eighth-century inscriptions, dominance of, 5; group identities, 87–123 (*See also* group identities); landscapes, 1–2, 19–55 (*See also* landscapes); map of principal sites, *4, 5*; methodological issues, *4*, 4–5, *5*; names of places, 7–18 (*See also* place names); people and places, 57–86 (*See also* people and places); in postmodern scholarship, 4; relationship of written narratives to other forms of experience of, 5; representations of objects and landscapes, narratives as, 2; scholarly tradition of, 6; society and landscape, relationship between, 2–3; variations over time and space in, 126–27

place, defined as objects or features in landscape, 2

place names, 7–18, 125; basic and derived terms, *8, 9*; database of Classic Maya place names, *140*, 140–41, *141*; direct and indirect references, 7, *8*; frequency of certain locale categories, 10–13, *11, 12*; lexical nature of, 18; *–nal* morpheme and **NAL** logogram, 8–10, *9*, 122, 125; paired citations of, 13–17, *14*; placement of, 48; spatial scale, distance, and hierarchy, 13–18, *14, 15, 17*; *ta, ti',* and *tahn*, 10; titles incorporating, *58–60*, 58–61

plant species, terms in place names associated with, *11, 12*

politico-geographical order in Classic Maya society. *See* group identities

polity name theory of emblem glyphs, 57, 61–71, 90

Pomona: emblem glyphs of *Pipa'* lords and *Pakbuul* lords, *75*, 76; Hieroglyphic Panel 5 at, *75*, 76; Hieroglyphic Panel 10 at, 121, 136n66

Popol Vuh, 36, 43, 48, 73

pottery. *See* ceramics

Prager, Christian M., 78

Principal Bird Deity, 52

pul (burning), 33–34

Punta de Chimino: vessel from, 66

Pusilha, 79, 94

STUDIES IN PRE-COLUMBIAN ART AND ARCHAEOLOGY

PUBLISHED BY DUMBARTON OAKS RESEARCH LIBRARY AND COLLECTION, WASHINGTON, D.C.